T. S. Eliot

Twayne's United States Authors Series

Kenneth Eble, Editor

University of Utah

T. S. ELIOT
(1888–1965)
© *George McCullough, 1982.*
Used by permission.

T. S. Eliot

By Philip R. Headings

Twayne Publishers • *Boston*

T. S. Eliot, Revised Edition

Philip R. Headings

Copyright © 1982 by **G. K.** Hall & Company
Published by Twayne Publishers
A Division of **G. K.** Hall & Company
70 Lincoln Street
Boston, Massachusetts 02111

First Paperback Edition, 1985

Book production by Marne B. Sultz
Book design by Barbara Anderson

Printed on permanent/durable
acid-free paper and bound in
The United States of America.

Library of Congress Cataloging in Publication Data

Headings, Philip Ray, 1922-1982
T. S. Eliot.

(Twayne's United States authors series; TUSAS 57)
Bibliography: p. 218
Includes index.
1. Eliot, T. S. (Thomas Stearns), 1888-1965—Criticism and
interpretation. I. Title. II. Series
PS3509.L43Z682   1982   821'.912   81-23525
ISBN 0–8057–7357–6   **AACR2**
ISBN 0–8057–7443–2 (pbk.)

Contents

About the Author

Philip Ray Headings, born in northern Ohio on the day Eliot published *The Waste Land* in the first issue of the *Criterion* (October 15, 1922), is the son of ex-Mennonite carpenter-preacher Aquila John and Maud Miller Headings. Before discovering twentieth-century poetry via *The Love Song of J. Alfred Prufrock* in the late 1940s, he served a four-year apprenticeship at Henry Ford Trade School (River Rouge plant, Dearborn), two years as a journeyman tool and diemaker, and two more years in the United States Naval Reserve, being trained there as an aviation electronics technician and spending five months at MIT in a special radar project. After mustering out, he spent another seven years in and out of toolmaking, taking night and, later, daytime classes and earning the B.S. in Education (Language Arts and Speech, 1950) from Indiana University.

After a year as a training supervisor at a United States Naval Ordnance plant, he returned to Indiana University and earned the Ph.D. in Comparative Literature (English, French, and German; minors in Modern Drama and Philosophy, 1958). Since then he has taught some forty different college courses in literature and writing at Chico State College, California; the University of Illinois at Champaign-Urbana; Indiana University, Bloomington; and Indiana University–Purdue University at Fort Wayne, where he has been an associate professor of English since 1964. He has served as a consultant to the National Endowment for the Humanities and as a visiting professor at the University of Wisconsin, Milwaukee. Since 1963 he has been a contributing member of the American Literature section of the *MLA International Bibliography*. He is a devoted advocate of education in the liberal arts—the Graeco-Roman, Judeo-Christian tradition—as a basis for citizenship in the twentieth century.

His thirty years' study and teaching of T. S. Eliot's writings have been bolstered by visits to the libraries and places associated with and written about by Eliot, both in the United States and abroad. A 1971 sabbatical leave in England (chiefly London, East Coker, Little Gidding, Oxford, and Cambridge) and Europe (especially Paris, Venice, and Florence) and a 1979 visit to Little Gidding, Burnt Norton, Rannoch by Glencoe, and Usk, among other sites, expanded his understanding of the works associated with those places and Eliot's experiences in them. He has published articles and reviews on Eliot in *Revue des Langues Vivantes*, *Contemporary Literature*, and *T. S. Eliot Review* (now renamed *Yeats-Eliot Review*), as well as the first edition of the present volume, parts of which have been reprinted in other works on Eliot.

He has a married son, one granddaughter, and two stepdaughters. He and his wife, Fran, live in Fort Wayne.

Editor's Note: Professor Philip R. Headings, one of the earliest contributors to Twayne's United States Authors Series, died in February, 1982 before he could review the final proofs of this volume, published in June.

Preface

"It was an education beyond anything else I had encountered in academic routines. I had grabbed hold of something, and it moved, and I hung on." So wrote Professor Leonard Unger of the preparation of his graduate thesis on T. S. Eliot's *Ash-Wednesday*.[1] By the time I took Professor Unger's Eliot course in 1957, I already felt the same way about *The Cocktail Party*. By the end of the course I was hopelessly and permanently hooked on Eliot research. The 1964 edition of this book was the direct result. Since then I have abandoned some of the views and ideas expressed there and have found, I hope, better ways of presenting others that I still hold. I should have liked to rewrite entirely every page, but have had to settle for less. The rest must await another revision, which will benefit from additional new materials and insights as well as the ones I was unable to use here.

The advances in Eliot scholarship within the last decade seem to me tremendous, and I expect that trend to continue if not accelerate. If my recent 4:30 A.M. doodling tabulation of the *MLA International Bibliography* is correct, only one American and two English twentieth-century authors were written about more often in 1977 than T. S. Eliot in the periodicals listed. Those three, Joyce, Hardy, and Faulkner, are known primarily for their prose fiction, not their poetry. Besides those three, only five other authors from all centuries of English literature (Shakespeare, Dickens, Milton, Blake, and Chaucer, in that order—with Shakespeare almost quadrupling his nearest competitor's total) were written on oftener than Eliot.

This means that a staggering amount has already been written on Eliot's works, and I hope that this book will be helpful to those readers wanting a brief, manageable synthesis of the current state of Eliot interpretation.

T. S. ELIOT

I hope to show that Eliot's most difficult works are more unified and understandable than has often been thought and that his most accessible ones will reward rereadings with new and deeper insights. My chief aim is to approach the poems and plays on their own terms—to find the core of intent and focus for each major work and to read it from there.

To the personable and admirable Mrs. Valerie Eliot, all Eliot scholars owe a great debt not only for her many contributions to her husband's happiness, writings, and career and for being a capable executrix of his literary estate, but also for her own excellent contributions to Eliot scholarship. To general gratitude for those accomplishments, I wish to add my personal thanks for her very helpful correspondence, for permission to quote from her and her husband's writings, and for her gracious hospitality and stimulating conversation on two memorable occasions.

I wish to thank Indiana University–Purdue University at Fort Wayne for the 1969 Faculty Summer Grant that bears fruit in chapter 8 of this study and for the 1971 Sabbatical Leave and Faculty Summer Grant that enabled me to meet Mrs. Eliot and explore sites and materials in England and on the European continent relevant to T. S. Eliot and his works. The results of those seven months in England and Europe permeate many of the chapters in this revised edition. I am also grateful to Dr. Henry Kozicki, a gentleman and scholar in the best sense, for encouragement and for teaching assignments related to my research, especially two excellent graduate seminars on Eliot that worked me very hard and taught me many things. My indebtedness to several of the students in them is acknowledged in appropriate notes, but I wish here to thank all of them and the many former students who continue to bring to my attention any new Eliot materials they encounter.

Another gracious scholar-gentleman-friend, Dr. Erhardt Essig, is to be thanked for inviting me to give the 1970 Paul F. Bente Memorial lecture at Concordia Senior College in Fort Wayne; that lecture, extensively reworked, appears here as chapter 5. I also thank the Fortnightly Club of Fort Wayne for their 1978 lecture assignment which produced a primitive version of the *Prufrock* analysis in chapter 2.

To my wife, Fran, I am unspeakably indebted for her considerable share in our 1979 explorations of Little Gidding, Rannoch by Glencoe, Burnt Norton, Usk, and other sites in England, Scotland, and Wales and her generous total support at every stage of this revision; also for superb typing and editing (often in long stints and repeated drafts), for valuable insights into *Preludes* and *Conversation Galante*, and for frequently asking the right questions to make me hunt and discover exciting answers and syntheses.

Warm thanks go to her daughters, Marilyn and Barb Derr, and my son Brian and his wife, Luann Traxler Headings, for understanding and support at crucial stages in the revision—especially to Brian for help with the index and notes and for much besides over many years. Frequent aid of many practical kinds from our good friend and neighbor Russell Johnson has enabled me to concentrate more effectively on the revision.

Librarians being some of God's choice creations, I wish to thank heartily all those who have helped me at the libraries of Indiana University–Purdue University at Fort Wayne (especially Louise Hass, Ruth Harrod, and Judith Violette); Indiana University at Bloomington; the University of Michigan; the University of Illinois; the University of Chicago; Columbia University; Washington University in St. Louis; the University of London; King's College, Cambridge (especially Mr. Peter Croft and the late Dr. A. N. L. Munby); as well as at the Houghton Library at Harvard, the Newberry Library in Chicago, the Berg Collection of the New York Public Library (Lola Szladits), the British Museum Reading Room, the Bodleian Library at Oxford, and a number of London area libraries.

For hospitality, conversation, and information at various Eliot-related sites I thank Mr. C. J. Scinnell, Mr. A. E. Page of Lloyds Bank Ltd., Mrs. Gray at Little Gidding, unidentified ladies at the Chipping Campden Post Office and the Usk Museum, Mrs. Humphries at Usk Castle, a cordial gentleman at the Gwent Tourist Bureau in Abergavenny, three children in a donkey cart at a

Welsh castle gate, and at Bettws Newydd the proprietor of the Black Bear, and Rector Mr. Goodrich, and especially Postmistress Mrs. Brooks and her daughter. Special thanks also go to Mr. Andy McGinley at Tulloch Station and Major Rennie at Rannoch Station.

For much help of various kinds, I am grateful to Lois Shepherd Headings, Hope Raymond, Bertrand Davis, John Tolley, Philip Wikelund, Patricia Griest, Suzie Weaver, Harvey Cocks, Sister Barbara Doherty, Margaret Wiggs, Mazelle Van Buskirk, Pierre and Christiane Michel, Keith and Barbara Clarke, Harry and Dorothy Ramsay; Mavis Pindard of Faber and Faber and Rita Vaughan of Harcourt Brace Jovanovich; Professors Francis Fergusson, Leonard Unger, Newton Stallknecht, Richard Ellmann, Roy Battenhouse, Roy Swansen, Horst Frenz, Sylvia Bowman, John Alford, Hubert Heffner, Donald and Barbara Smalley, George McCullough, and especially Norbert Fuerst; and to the many persons involved in my Dante and Eliot seminars at First Presbyterian Church, Fort Wayne, over the past fifteen years and in the First Presbyterian Theater's productions of *The Cocktail Party* and *The Elder Statesman*. The fruits of those productions must await incorporation into a further edition.

I am indebted in numerous ways no longer possible to sort out to all those writers on Eliot cited in the notes and selected bibliography and to many not cited.

Christine Lamb, Emily McKeigue, and Janet Quimby of G. K. Hall & Co., have been very helpful, and Professor Kenneth E. Eble, a first-rate editor, deserves hearty thanks for judicious pruning of some 2,000 lines from this study. I am, nevertheless, responsible for whatever deficiencies or errors may be found here.

Philip R. Headings
Indiana University—Purdue University at Fort Wayne

Acknowledgments

Quotations from the writings of T. S. Eliot are reprinted by permission of his English and American publishers as follows:

Excerpts are reprinted by permission of Mrs. Valerie Eliot and Faber and Faber Ltd from *The Waste Land: A Facsimile and Transcript of the Original Drafts including the Annotations of Ezra Pound* edited by Valerie Eliot.

Excerpts are reprinted by permission of Faber and Faber Ltd from *Collected Poems 1909–1962* by T. S. Eliot, and from the plays, *Selected Essays, The Use of Poetry and the Use of Criticism, Dante, To Criticize the Critic, The Rock,* and other previously published quotations from uncollected writings, all by T. S. Eliot.

Excerpts from the poetry of T. S. Eliot, *Selected Essays, Murder in the Cathedral, The Family Reunion, The Cocktail Party, The Confidential Clerk,* and from *The Waste Land: A Facsimile and Transcript of the Original Drafts* edited by Esme Valerie Eliot are reprinted by permission of Harcourt Brace Jovanovich, Inc.; copyright 1932, 1935, 1936, 1950 by Harcourt Brace Jovanovich, Inc.; copyright 1939, 1943, 1954, 1960, 1963, 1964 by T. S. Eliot; copyright © 1967, 1971, 1978 by Esme Valerie Eliot.

Reprinted by permission of Farrar, Straus and Giroux, Inc.: Excerpts from *On Poetry and Poets* by T. S. Eliot. Copyright © 1943, 1945, 1951, 1954, 1956, 1957 by T. S. Eliot. Excerpts from *The Elder Statesman* by T. S. Eliot. Copyright © 1959 by Thomas Stearns Eliot. Excerpts from *Poems Written in Early Youth* by T. S. Eliot. Noonday edition copyright © 1967 by Valerie Eliot.

Excerpts from *The Sacred Wood: Essays on Poetry and Criticism* are reprinted by permission of Methuen & Co., Ltd.

Other quotations are reprinted by permission of the copyright owners as follows:

Excerpts from *The Divine Comedy* by Dante Alighieri, trans-

Chronology

1660s   Andrew Eliot emigrated from East Coker, Somerset, England, to Beverly, Massachusetts.

1834   The Reverend William Greenleaf Eliot graduated from Harvard; moved to St. Louis.

1888   September 26, Thomas Stearns Eliot born to Henry Ware Eliot and Charlotte Champe Stearns Eliot.

1888–1905   Lived in St. Louis; spent summers in New England; attended Miss Lockwood's Primary School and Smith Academy; wrote "Byronic" first poems.

1905–1906   Attended Milton Academy, Massachusetts.

1906–1910   Harvard undergraduate and then graduate student (class of 1910); *Harvard Advocate* poems; met Emily Hale.

1910–1911   Paris year; studied at Sorbonne; visited Munich August 1911.

1911–1914   Continued graduate studies at Harvard in philosophy and taught as an assistant; president, Harvard Philosophical Society; became student (and friend) of Bertrand Russell.

1914   Traveling fellowship to Germany (especially Marburg) interrupted by World War I; moved to Merton College, Oxford; began close association with Ezra Pound, whose help and sponsorship led to Eliot's early publications and to various reviewing, writing, and editing assignments.

1915   Married Vivien Haigh-Wood.

1915–1916   Taught school at High Wycombe and Highgate;

completed thesis on F. H. Bradley.

1917 *Prufrock and Other Observations*; assistant editor of the *Egoist* (to 1919); worked in Foreign Department of Lloyds Bank (to 1923).

1919 Death of his father, Henry Ware Eliot.

1920 *Poems 1919; Ara Vos Prec; The Sacred Wood.*

1921 Summer visit by his mother and sister Marian; health problems and enforced rest; writing of *The Waste Land* at Marburg and Lausanne.

1922 Founded the *Criterion*, which he edited with distinction until 1939; *The Waste Land* published, won $2,000 *Dial* award; sent early verse and *Waste Land* manuscripts to John Quinn.

1924 *Homage to John Dryden.*

1924–1927 First published attempts at drama: Sweeney fragments.

1925 Joined publishing firm of Faber and Gwyer (after 1929 Faber & Faber), of which he was a director until his death in 1965; *Poems 1909–1925.*

1926 Clark Lecturer, Trinity College, Cambridge.

1927 Became British citizen and member of Anglican Church. *Journey of the Magi; Shakespeare and the Stoicism of Seneca*; "Salutation."

1928 *For Lancelot Andrewes; A Song for Simeon; Perch' io non spero.*

1929 *Animula; Dante; Al som de l'escalina*; death of his mother.

1930 *Ash-Wednesday; Marina*; St.-J. Perse's *Anabase* (translation).

1931 *Triumphal March; Thoughts After Lambeth; Charles Whibley: A Memoir.*

1932   *Sweeney Agonistes: Fragments of an Aristophanic Melodrama; Selected Essays 1917–1932; John Dryden, the Poet the Dramatist the Critic*; separation from Vivien; return to Harvard as Charles Eliot Norton Professor of Poetry, 1932–33.

1933   *The Use of Poetry and the Use of Criticism* (Norton Lectures); Page-Barbour Lecturer, University of Virginia; honorary degree (hereafter h.d.) Columbia University.

1934   *The Rock; After Strange Gods: A Primer of Modern Heresy* (Page-Barbour Lectures); "A Dialogue on Poetic Drama"; *Elizabethan Essays.*

1935   Major dramatic success: *Murder in the Cathedral; Words for Music; Two Poems* (*Cape Ann* and *Usk*).

1936   *Collected Poems 1909–1935* (included *Burnt Norton*); *Essays Ancient and Modern.*

1937   H.d. Edinburgh.

1938   H.d. Cambridge and Bristol.

1939   *The Family Reunion; The Idea of a Christian Society; Old Possum's Book of Practical Cats;* discontinuance of *The Criterion*; h.d. Leeds.

1940   *East Coker.*

1941   *The Dry Salvages; Points of View.*

1942   *Little Gidding; The Music of Poetry; The Classics and the Man of Letters.*

1943   *Four Quartets; Reunion by Destruction.*

1947   Death of Vivien Haigh-Wood Eliot, after years of illness; h.d. Yale, Princeton, Harvard.

1948   Nobel Prize; Order of Merit; French Legion of Honor; resident member of Princeton University

Institute for Advanced Study; *From Poe to Valéry*; h.d. Aix-en-Provence, Oxford.

1949   *Notes Towards the Definition of Culture; The Aims of Poetic Drama; The Undergraduate Poems* (unauthorized); *The Cocktail Party.*

1950   *Poems Written in Early Youth* (private printing); h.d. London.

1951   *Poetry and Drama.*

1954   Hanseatic Goethe Prize; *The Confidential Clerk.*

1956   Lectured to audience of about 14,000 at University of Minnesota.

1957   Married Valerie Fletcher; *On Poetry and Poets.*

1958   Member of Psalter revision commission.

1959   *The Elder Statesman*; Dante Medal (Florence); German Order of Merit; by this time he had received many other honors, including h.d.'s from Washington, St. Andrews, Rome, Munich, Rennes, Paris.

1963   British Museum exhibit in tribute to him.

1964   *Knowledge and Experience in the Philosophy of F. H. Bradley*; United States Medal of Freedom.

1965   January 4, died in London; burial in East Coker; *To Criticize the Critic and Other Writings*; Kent University college named for him.

1967   Westminster Abbey Poet's Corner memorial unveiled; *Poems Written in Early Youth.*

1968   Missing *Waste Land* manuscript "found."

1969   *The Complete Poems and Plays of T. S. Eliot* (London only); Browne's *The Making of T. S. Eliot's Plays* publishes much new material; Gallup's *Bibliography* updated.

1971   Publication of Valerie Eliot's edition of *Waste Land* facsimile and transcript.

1972   Martin's secondary bibliography *A Half-Century of Eliot Criticism.*

1974   Maxwell and Bagchee's *T. S. Eliot Newsletter* (later *T. S. Eliot Review* [1975–77] and then *Yeats Eliot Review* [1978–]) first published.

1977   Gordon's *Eliot's Early Years* publishes important biographical materials; *T. S. Eliot Review* publishes Frank, Frank, and Jochum's supplement to Martin's bibliography.

1978   Gardner's *The Composition of Four Quartets* publishes important draft, letter, and biographical materials.

Chapter One
Significant Soil

"In my beginning is my end" may be read on a modest, yellow-pink stone plaque in St. Michael's Church in East Coker, a sleepy Somerset village in England. At the bottom of the memorial plaque to the poet Thomas Stearns Eliot one reads "In my end is my beginning." These are the first and last lines of *East Coker*, the second of Eliot's *Four Quartets*. It was in East Coker that the poet wished to be buried, for it was there that his paternal ancestors, earlier from Devonshire, had lived for some two centuries until around 1669,[1] when one of them, a cordwainer named Andrew Eliot, emigrated to Beverly, Massachusetts. Andrew Eliot later became town clerk and one of the jurors who tried the Salem witches. The poet's maternal ancestry goes back to "Isaac Stearns, who had come out [from England] with John Winthrop in 1630 as one of the original settlers of the Bay Colony."[2] Both families were influential participants in what Russell Kirk calls the "New England aristocracy of ministers and merchants."[3]

In 1834, the Reverend William Greenleaf Eliot, D.D. (1811–87), the poet's grandfather, graduated from Harvard and moved to St. Louis, where he founded the first Unitarian church in that city. He also helped found Washington University and in 1872 became its chancellor. He firmly opposed slavery and helped keep Missouri in the Union. Of his writings, some of his sermons and *The Story of Archer Alexander* (a slave whose freedom he bought and whose statue may be seen in the Lincoln Memorial in Washington, D.C.) were published and widely read.[4] Emerson called him a preacher of really good sermons.[5]

Though Ezra Pound could write to T. S. Eliot in 1914 "London

I

may not be the Paradiso Terrestre, but it is at least some centuries nearer it than is St. Louis,"[6] the St. Louis of William Greenleaf Eliot's time was "famous across the continent as a forum of philosophy and the arts," according to Herbert Howarth; the St. Louis Idealists "wrapped themselves in enthusiasms, indulged in verbal pirouettes for each other's wonder, loved the aspiring, and loved the abstruse because it seemed to aspire.... In the parlors the men and women were coming and going and talking of Michelangelo.... It produced a culture, a circumambience favorable to the growth of genius."[7]

Henry Ware Eliot (1841–1919), father of the poet, was the second son of William Greenleaf Eliot. Educated at Washington University, he married Charlotte Champe Stearns (1843–1929), a St. Louis schoolteacher whose family still lived in New England. He became successively secretary, treasurer, president, and then chairman of the St. Louis Hydraulic Press Brick Company. He contributed stoutly to the civic welfare of St. Louis and was, Herbert Howarth writes, "responsive to the arts: he had been in his younger days a member of the Philharmonic and Choral Societies; had some talent for painting; filled his home with pictures. But his taste was conservative. In politics he was staunchly Republican, in all matters conservative. It was hard for him to conceive of a life devoted to *experimenting* with words."[8]

The poet's mother, a woman of keen intellectual interests, was also deeply involved in St. Louis social service. She was largely instrumental in reorganizing the juvenile court system of not only the city but also the state. Herbert Howarth's moving description of her includes these comments on her writing: "All her life she wrote poems.... Except for a tiny booklet, *Easter Songs*, she only found acceptance in religious journals...: *The Unitarian, The Christian Register, Our Best Words*. From time to time they published her poems, and occasionally her essays, including a series on *Hymn-Writers of the Liberal Faith*.... she clipped the columns and pasted them in scrapbooks for her children."[9] Her dramatic poem *Savonarola* was published by R. Cobden-Sanderson in 1926, with an introduction by her son, T. S. Eliot. She also experimented with "shapes of stanzas and the management of metrics and rhyme,"[10] with musical form, with the amalgamation of poetry and religion. Her biography of William Greenleaf Eliot, finished when the poet was very young, was dedicated to her children, lest they forget.

Personal Landscape

Thomas Stearns Eliot, youngest of seven children, was born September 26, 1888, in a no-longer-extant house on Locust Street, St. Louis, not far from the Eads Bridge across the Mississippi. As a boy he, like Tom Sawyer and Huck Finn, could go down in flood time to watch the river with its cargo of drowned cows and chicken coops, learning to know the Mississippi as "a strong brown god— sullen, untamed and intractable" (*The Dry Salvages*). Both he and his father were deeply impressed by the untamed river's rampages: before achieving prosperity in the 1870s, his father had twice seen the river flood the chemical factory he and a partner had started unsuccessfully.[11]

Thanks to his New England-bred paternal grandfather, growing up in the poet's family was a rigorous process. He told a 1953 St. Louis audience:

I never knew my grandfather: he died a year before my birth. But I was brought up to be very much aware of him: so much so, that as a child I thought of him as still the head of the family—a ruler for whom *in absentia* my grandmother stood as vicegerent. The standard of conduct was that which my grandfather had set; our moral judgments, our decisions between duty and self-indulgence, were taken as if, like Moses, he had brought down the tables of the Law, any deviation from which would be sinful. Not the least of these laws, which included injunctions still more than prohibitions, was the law of Public Service . . . [which] operated especially in three areas: the Church, the City, and the University. The Church meant, for us, the Unitarian Church of the Messiah, then situated in Locust Street, a few blocks west of my father's house and my grandmother's house; the City was St. Louis—the utmost outskirts of which touched on Forest Park, terminus of the Olive Street streetcars, and to me, as a child, the beginning of the Wild West; the University was Washington University, then housed in a modest building in lower Washington Avenue. These were the symbols of Religion, the Community and Education: and I think it is a very good beginning for any child, to be brought up to reverence such institutions, and to be taught that personal and selfish aims should be subordinated to the general good which they represent.[12]

Tom Eliot later found indigestible some of his grandfather's and parents' beliefs: defining Christianity as "a belief in the Incarnation," he wrote to Bertrand Russell in 1927 that he had been "brought up 'outside the Christian Fold' ";[13] as a graduate student he characterized the Unitarian Code in the phrase "onward and upward forever."[14] Perhaps the Unitarian faith of the family was qualified for him to some extent by Annie Dunne, the Catholic nurse who on at least one occasion took the young boy to her church service; Lyndall Gordon writes of "her discussing with him, at the age of six, the existence of God."[15]

In 1953, T. S. Eliot called himself "fortunate to have been born here [St. Louis], rather than in Boston, or New York, or London."[16] Nevertheless, the family's ties with New England were kept strong and they formed, according to the poet, an important part of his early impressions. By 1897, his father had built their summer home at Eastern Point, Gloucester, Massachusetts, bringing from his St. Louis company his best brick to construct what Herbert Howarth calls "the magnificent fireplaces and chimneys."[17] When in 1959 the American Academy of Arts and Sciences presented the Emerson-Thoreau Medal to T. S. Eliot for his achievement in literature, he told the New England assemblage that his childhood summers had been spent on the New England coast and the remaining seasons in drably urban St. Louis, so that his store of recurrent imagery included the Mississippi River and Massachusetts seashore and the St. Louis background modified later by that of London and Paris.[18] In this address Eliot was preparing his listeners for a reading of *The Dry Salvages*, where the river and the seashore are powerful images, but the two chief settings referred to—the city and the New England coast—have been used and imaged in much of his poetry.

Early Schooling

When he was seven or eight, according to T. S. Matthews, Thomas Stearns Eliot was sent to Miss Lockwood's primary school "a little way out beyond Vandeventer Place,"[19] where he proved precocious.

His next school was Smith Academy, a private preparatory school (later discontinued) about which he wrote in 1953:

The earlier part—and I believe, the most important part—of my education is what I received in that preparatory department of [Washington] University which was named Smith Academy. My memories of Smith Academy are on the whole happy ones. . . . It was a good school. There one was taught, as is now increasingly rare everywhere, what I consider the essentials. . . . As I failed to pass my entrance examination in physics, you will not be surprised that I have forgotten the name of the master who taught it. But I remember other names of good teachers, my gratitude to whom I take this opportunity of recording: Mr. Jackson in Latin, Mr. Robinson in Greek, Mr. Rowe— though I was not one of his good pupils—in mathematics, Madame Jouvet-Kauffmann and Miss Chandler in French and German respectively. Mr. Hatch, who taught English, commended warmly my first poem, written as a class exercise, at the same time asking me suspiciously if I had had any help in writing it. Mr. Jeffries I think taught modern history; our ancient history was taught by the Greek and Latin masters. Well! so far as I am educated, I must pay my first tribute to Smith Academy; if I had not been well taught there, I should have been unable to profit elsewhere.[20]

Lyndall Gordon writes that young Eliot "had a congenital double hernia and Charlotte, afraid it would rupture, forbade football and strenuous sports. During summers at Cape Ann, when 'the Skipper' used to give him sailing lessons, Charlotte would go along, fortified by a guard of grown-up sisters, to ensure that he did not get

too wet or too hot or too tired. He accepted his mother's domina-
tion in good humour."[21]

In 1905, his last year at Smith, his first published poem, *A Fable
for Feasters*, appeared in the February issue of the *Smith Academy
Record*. John Hayward, Eliot's longtime friend and housemate,
called the poem a "Byronic exercise."[22] Already this poem shows
a quixotic delight in words, using such rhymes as doin's-ruins,
dollar-hollow, and jiminy-chimney. An arch, light-hearted, oral
poem, it foreshadows *Old Possum's Book of Practical Cats*, written
thirty-four years later. Two other poems appeared in 1905, one,
A Lyric, in the *Smith Academy Record.* When his mother told him
it was better than any of her own verses, he was sufficiently impressed to remember many years later that they were walking
along Beaumont Street when she said it.[23] The other poem, titled
At Graduation, 1905, was, according to John Hayward, "recited
by the poet on Graduation Day."[24]

These were not Eliot's first attempts at poetry. At nine or ten,
Valerie Eliot reveals, he wrote "a few little verses" and at fourteen,
"some very gloomy quatrains in the form of the *Rubáiyát.*"[25]

In addition, Eliot had three pieces of prose in 1905 issues of
the *Smith Academy Record*: "The Birds of Prey," "Tale of a Whale,"
and "The Man Who Was King."[26]

Early Poetic Influences

In *The Use of Poetry and the Use of Criticism* (1933), Eliot
distinguishes three stages in the development of his enjoyment of
poetry: first, the normal childhood attraction to such "martial
and sanguinary poetry" as "*Horatius, The Burial of Sir John Moore,
Bannockburn,* Tennyson's *Revenge,* some of the border ballads...."
He equates this taste with a taste for "lead soldiers and pea-shooters."
From about twelve to fourteen he lost interest in poetry until he
happened to pick up Fitzgerald's *Rubáiyát of Omar Khayyám,*
an "almost overwhelming introduction to a new world of feeling...
like a sudden conversion; the world appeared anew, painted with
bright, delicious and painful colours. Thereupon I took the usual

adolescent course with Byron, Shelley, Keats, Rossetti, Swinburne." This second stage lasted till he was twenty-two, and gave rise to "an outburst of scribbling which we may call imitation." The mature third stage, the development of genuine taste, he says, comes when one reads with his critical faculties open rather than in "a kind of daemonic possession by one poet."[27]

Milton Academy, 1905-1906

At the age of seventeen (1905) Eliot was sent to the sprawling, 115-acre campus of Milton Academy at Milton, Massachusetts, ten miles from the State House in Boston. Chartered in 1798, Milton has long been a proper prep school for Harvard University. Milton, as *Newsweek* reported on its 150th birthday in 1948, numbers among its graduates (besides Eliot) such notables as playwright Robert Sherwood, author Cleveland Amory, editor W. I. Nichols, author Helen Howe, University of Michigan dean Alice Lloyd, and pediatrician Charles Janeway. And graduate rolls "are liberally sprinkled with such solid New England names as Saltonstall, Forbes, Amory, and Wigglesworth."[28] Two of Eliot's classmates there were Howard Morris, later his roommate at Harvard, and Schofield Thayer, later publisher of the *Dial*.[29]

Little has been written on his Milton year, most of it stemming from two later returns to Milton, the first when he gave the commencement address to the class of 1933 and the second in 1948, when he went there to deliver the academy's seventeenth War Memorial Lecture (in a series including earlier speeches by Franklin D. Roosevelt, Sumner Welles, John Buchan, and Sir Richard Livingston). On that occasion, wrote Malcolm Barter in the *Boston Globe*, he "wore the orange and blue Milton school tie and he hadn't forgotten his way about the school grounds." Barter continues, "At ease, friendly, with delightful humor, eager to answer the questions students put to him, T. S. Eliot was a 'hit' at Milton.... He could not speak for a moment... after headmaster Arthur Bliss Perry announced to the students that their distinguished guest had just been awarded the Nobel Prize and led them in a

Milton cheer for him." Earlier in the same article we are told that
"he took no English courses, but concentrated in studying history,
Latin, physics, and chemistry and was, he says, 'always three or
four laboratory experiments behind' and never able 'to get anything to explode.' "[30] Alfred Nobel, munitions manufacturer, had
not had that difficulty.

Harvard University, 1906-10

On his eighteenth birthday, September 26, 1906, Eliot's Harvard
undergraduate studies began. As Herbert Howarth points out:

> It was Harvard's "golden era." At the beginning of this century
> William James was lecturing; Santayana; Royce; Babbitt; Kittredge;
> and others who, if their names have sounded less persistently across
> the world, were almost equally royal. Great teachers, intellectual ath-
> letes with a zest for many branches of knowledge, were training their
> students to their own versatility.[31]

Eliot later spoke with admiration of such teachers as Irving Babbitt, Paul Elmer More, E. K. Rand, Charles Homer Haskins, W. H.
Schofield, and others, and made throughout his writing career
many references to and uses of the works that he studied in those
Harvard courses. He continued his Greek and Latin studies begun
at Smith Academy earlier, taking, Howarth says, seven classical
courses out of his eighteen undergraduate ones. Besides the ancient
classics, Eliot studied Dante and the Middle Ages, French, English,
philosophy, and comparative literature.

In 1937, as Kristian Smidt points out, Eliot called Harvard professors Irving Babbitt and Paul Elmer More "the two *wisest* men that
I have known."[32] Howarth emphasizes Babbitt's classicism and
respect for tradition and says that Eliot

> went to the French to whom Babbitt directed him, immersed himself
> in their neoclassicism, immersed himself so thoroughly that it was
> practically a rebaptism in the doctrine; and then [1914 and after],
> with the excitement of Pound's work to impel him, and his philo-

sophical training to provide the means, decisively systematized the theory of tradition in his essays and decisively demonstrated it in his poetry; through both of which a Harvard taste crystallized into an English literary counterrevolution and, shortly, into a world movement.[33]

Lyndall Gordon's *Eliot's Early Years* places surprisingly little emphasis on Eliot's Harvard teachers and courses, but does throw much new light on Eliot's published and unpublished poems from that period. The seven published poems appeared in the *Harvard Advocate* (of which Eliot became an editor, in 1909) along with two prose pieces: a review of Van Wyck Brook's *The Wine of the Puritans* and an essay titled "Gentlemen and Seamen." Gordon emphasizes that though he had become indifferent to the church by the time he went to Harvard, Eliot's orientation already at this early period was deeply religious—he was already groping toward the religious views that would result in his adoption of Anglican Catholicism in 1927.

The *Advocate* Poems

The first of the *Harvard Advocate* poems (published May 24, 1907) is the song beginning "When we came home across the hill." It seems to me clearly based on wittily altered borrowings from Keats's poem *La Belle Dame Sans Merci*.

A week after this first poem appeared, the June 3, 1907, *Advocate* carried Eliot's slightly altered version of his lyric *If Time and Space*, previously printed in the *Smith Academy Record*. Now titled *Song*, it is a *carpe diem* poem thoroughly traditional in its diction and imagery. The next *Advocate* poems (November 1908) were *Before Morning*, innovative in meter, and *Circe's Palace*, the first of Eliot's poems to deal with Homer's Odysseus.

On a Portrait (January 1909), a Petrarchan sonnet Laforguian in tone, describes Manet's *La Femme au perroquet* [The Lady with the Parrot].[34] A month earlier Eliot had read what proved a most important book for him: Arthur Symons's *The Symbolist Movement in Literature*. He wrote of Symons (in a January 1930

Criterion book review of Peter Quennell's *Baudelaire and the Symbolists*):

> But for having read his book, I should not . . . have heard of Laforgue or Rimbaud; I should probably not have begun to read Verlaine; and but for reading Verlaine, I should not have heard of Corbière. So the Symons book is one of those which have affected the course of my life. . . . (357–59)

The nature of the influences derived from that reading is further clarified in Eliot's "What Dante Means to Me," where he says that he learned from Baudelaire the possibilities for poetry of

> the more sordid aspects of the modern metropolis, of the possibility of fusion between the sordidly realistic and the phantasmagoric, the possibility of the juxtaposition of the matter-of-fact and the fantastic. From him, as from Laforgue, I learned that the sort of material that I had, the sort of experience that an adolescent had had, in an industrial city in America, could be the material for poetry. . . . That, in fact, the business of the poet was to make poetry out of the unexplored resources of the unpoetical. . . .[35]

Another chief mark of Laforgue's influence was the sometimes bitter irony of tone and the rather cynical self-criticism of the personae or masks through whom Eliot's early poems are spoken.

An even more highly Laforguian poem than *On a Portrait* is *Conversation Galante*, the earliest-written of the poems in the Prufrock volume of 1917. According to Lyndall Gordon, it was written in November 1909 into Eliot's notebook; originally it was titled "Short Romance."[36] This poem is the self-consciously witty dialogue of a playful sparring match between a young male protagonist and the young lady with whom he is walking. Its exhausting gaiety has a pathetic quality. The moon imagery of the first stanza reflects Laforgue's whimsical treatment of poetical things, comparing the moon to "Prester John's balloon/Or an old battered lantern hung aloft/To light poor travellers to their distress," suggesting the luring of ships onto rocky coasts by would-be salvagers.

In the same month the Petrarchan sonnet *Nocturne* appeared in the *Advocate*. This, too, is modeled directly on a Laforgue poem. It evokes what Symons calls "his [Laforgue's] own world, lunar and actual, speaking slang and astronomy."[37] The poem is related, says Lyndall Gordon, to the unpublished poem "Opera" in Eliot's notebook in the Berg collection at the New York Public Library.[38] Romeo, courting Juliet, is stabbed by a servant and dies, which Eliot calls "the perfect climax all true lovers seek!"[39]

In January 1910 *Humoresque: After J. Laforgue* was published in the *Advocate*. It is patterned on Laforgue's Marionette poems, and begins "One of my marionettes is dead."[40] The remarks attributed to this marionette echo the current slang of Eliot's fellow students; it is not only the marionette that is described in the final phrase, "what mask *bizarre!*" These poems are something new in English, a far cry from the Victorian convention of the earlier *Advocate* poems. Grover Smith characterizes what Eliot got from Laforgue:

He [Laforgue] had a disposition to jibe clownishly at sentiment. This habit, though it shaded his poems with a subtle pathos, brightened them with a tinsel novelty all the more bizarre because of their slang. Splitting or "doubling" himself into languid sufferer and satiric commentator, he wrote poems deriding in one passage the tenderness of another. Eliot accommodated this idiosyncrasy to his own needs. . . .[41]

In 1908 Eliot had met Conrad Aiken, one year behind him at Harvard, and they became fast friends (Aiken says), sharing meals, funny papers, jokes, vaudeville shows, and dissatisfaction with the artistic climate of the United States.[42] In his *Ushant*, Aiken says they had a

prolonged debate as to whether one could, or should, lay siege to one or another of the European countries, or cultures, and with what prospects of success, and which one. The Tsetse [Eliot], early inoculated by the subtle creative venoms of Laforgue and Vildrac, looked rather to France than to England. . . .[43]

Spleen, the last of the *Advocate* poems except for the class ode, expresses dissatisfaction with the dull conspiracy of Sunday behavior in staid New England. Its final stanza portrays a Prufrockian character hovering "on the doorstep of the Absolute," as Eliot himself was poised on the doorstep of Europe, specifically of Paris.

Portrait of a Lady

In February 1910 Eliot wrote part 2 of what became *Portrait of a Lady*. The title of this poem evokes Henry James's novel and Ezra Pound's poem *Portrait d'une Femme*, a closer source. Despite the title, the poem is equally a portrait of a young man; through his examinations and reexaminations of himself and the lady, we become intimately acquainted with both of them and find the protagonist a somewhat tortured youth who may or may not develop into the middle age of a Prufrock. The lady has been identified in Aiken's *Ushant* as

the oh so precious, the oh so exquisite, Madeleine, the Jamesian lady of ladies, the enchantress of the Beacon Hill drawing-room—who, like another Circe, had made strange shapes of Wild Michael and the Tsetse—[and] was afterwards to be essentialized and ridiculed (and his own pose with it) in the Tsetse's *Portrait d'une Femme*.[44]

Lyndall Gordon also links her to Eliot's poems *Conversation Galante*, *Circe's Palace*, and *Prufrock*, calling her "an emotional older woman...who used to serve tea to Harvard men in a home crowded with bric-a-brac, behind Boston's State House."[45] The poem's references to her April sunsets, her buried life, and Paris in the spring let us see what attracts the young man to her, but we also see the differences in ages and tastes and habits of mind which make him resist the attraction.

Most of the yet-unpublished poems Eliot was writing at this time, says Lyndall Gordon, are "rejections of family and Boston life."[46] The first two *Preludes* are such poems. They were written in Cambridge, Massachusetts, in October 1910 and originally titled "Preludes in Roxbury."[47] Grimy wind-blown trash and dingy shades in furnished rooms characterize them. Eliot's religious concerns, according to Gordon, were documented in two others, "Easter: Sensations of April," written in April 1910, and "Silence," written in June 1910. The first, she says, expresses nostalgia for religious certainties. The second is about what she calls "the defining experience of his life," a timeless, mystical moment in which he saw the Boston streets "suddenly shrink and divide. His everyday preoccupations, his past, all the claims of the future fell away."[48]

Judging by Aiken's remarks in *Ushant*, Eliot must have hoped in the fall of 1910 that he was going to Paris more or less permanently. His mother seems to have opposed that move and he did come back at the end of 1911, but in the meantime *Prufrock*, the two remaining *Preludes*, and some other poems were written.

The Paris Year, 1910-11

Eliot's 1944 response (in French) to the question of "What France Means to You" tells that in 1910 he first set foot in Europe on the docks of Cherbourg by moonlight. He considered it exceptional good fortune to have discovered Paris in 1910 as an adolescent. He explained that he had looked forward to sojourning in Paris for several years, since for him France represented *la poésie*, and opined that but for his discovery of such French poets as Baudelaire, Laforgue, Corbière, Rimbaud, and Mallarmé, he would never have been able to write.[49]

In that brief article he described the excitement of arriving an hour-and-a-quarter early to get a seat at Henri Bergson's lectures, of seeing Anatole France along the docks, and of buying the latest Gide or Claudel book on the day of publication. In his "Commentary" in the *Criterion* for April 1934 he compared the 1910 intellectual aridity of England and America with the vitality and excitement of Paris. Such artists and thinkers as Bergson, Anatole France, Remy de Gourmont, Matisse, Picasso, Barrès, Peguy, Gide, Claudel, Vildrac, Romains, Duhamel, Faguet, Durkheim, Lévy-Bruhl, Janet, and Loisy added to the unsettled but stimulating atmosphere that could help a young man learn to think for himself and make up his own mind.[50]

Montgomery Belgion, who grew up in pre-1914 Paris, credits Irving Babbitt, Eliot's French professor at Harvard, with a key role in developing not only Eliot's respect for tradition and his distrust of romanticism in general and Rousseau in particular, but his idea that Paris was the center of the intellectual world. Belgion engagingly describes the antiromantic and royalist movement, the Roman Catholic revival, the literary and political movements that Eliot encountered through his acquaintance with *Nouvelle Revue française* editor Jacques Rivière, Rivière's brother-in-law Henri-Alban Fournier (who tutored Eliot in French), and others.[51] He read Dostoyevsky and also a book figuring in several of his poems—Charles-Louis Philippe's *Bubu of Montparnasse*. After his study in Paris, he visited Munich, where in 1911 he finished *Prufrock*, begun at Harvard in 1910. He also visited London before returning to the United States, and must have taken at least a brief jaunt or two to Italy, since he told Kristian Smidt of his unsuccessful search there for an old museum piece, *La Figlia che Piange*.[52] Eliot's poem of that title would be finished in 1911 in Cambridge, shortly after his return from the Paris year.

Rhapsody on a Windy Night was copied into Eliot's notebook March 3, 1911. It is set in the Paris streets at midnight and after: a young man walks through the streets at twelve o'clock, half past one, half past two, half past three, and four o'clock in the morning. The various hours, like the streetlamps, punctuate the divisions of the poem. The walker is searching for some essence or experience which comes toward him or looms at him obliquely but never appears—searching for the nature of things, for a philosophic but also lived and felt principle that will organize his sordid and chaotic perceptions, will unify the dissociated sensibility of the philosopher and the lover. The genuine desperation of the search comes through the language convincingly; the scene might come from Dante's *Inferno*. This trip through the streets is echoed in other early poems: In *The "Boston Evening Transcript"* (1915), evening comes "waking the appetites of life in some/And to others bringing the *Boston Evening Transcript*." In the third *Prelude* (1911), the nightwalker contemplates a prostitute modeled on one in *Bubu of Montparnasse*, for which Eliot would later write a preface.[53] She is told, "You had such a vision of the street/As the street hardly understands." In those poems, Eliot seems to be showing that in his nighttime observations he comes to understand Roxbury, Boston, and Paris as Philippe understood Montparnasse, though Philippe's pimp and prostitute characters sense its nature without sensing their own. The poet himself is "The conscience of the blackened street/ Impatient to assume the world" (fourth *Prelude*).

The four sections of *Preludes* present images—sights, sounds, smells, and inner tensions—all of which mirror back the "notion of some infinitely gentle/Infinitely suffering thing," the human soul. That apprehension is as close as Eliot could come to understanding his perceptions of the cities. (Prufrock parallels his experience.) At the end of *Preludes*, the poet looks at himself and his empathy and sardonically adds, "Wipe your hand across your mouth, and laugh;/The worlds revolve like ancient women gathering fuel in vacant lots."

In *Rhapsody*, after a prostitute hesitates toward the walker from a doorway, looking for encouragement, the gas streetlamp mutters, "Regard the moon." We are told that the moon does not hold any grudge. It is compared to a prostitute who has lost her memory, who (like the Thames-daughters in *The Waste Land*) lacks enough moral awareness to resent the vacuity of her life. At poem's end, the protagonist mounts the stairs to his room. "'Memory!/ You have the key,/The little lamp spreads a ring on the stair.'" This echoes the rings of light from the candles in Juliet's tomb cited at the beginning of *Portrait of a Lady*, so here there is tragic import whether or not there is tragic awareness. "Memory!/You have the key" is a "key" idea of Eliot's which we will observe throughout his poetry.

The prosaic details of everyday life are presented ironically in that *Rhapsody* conclusion: "'Mount./The bed is open; the toothbrush hangs on the wall,/ Put your shoes at the door, sleep, prepare for life.'/The last twist of the knife." The protagonist has not found anything that satisfies him, has been as unsuccessful in his quest as the boys in Joyce's *Dubliners* story "An Encounter." The vision of "Silence" comes only once or twice—cannot be compelled—and for the quester desperately seeking it, as in *Burnt Norton* (1936), "Ridiculous [is] the waste sad time/Stretching before and after." As in *Prufrock*, "It is impossible to say just what [he] mean[s]!/But as if a magic lantern threw the nerves in patterns on a screen."

Lyndall Gordon distinguishes between those poems set in the street and the "vigil poems" in which the protagonist abandons the street for an all-night vigil in his rented room, noting that such a vigil was seen in the third and fourth *Preludes*, in the long-unpublished *So through the evening* and *Song* fragments now available in the *Waste Land Manuscripts* facsimile, and in the yet-unpublished "Oh little voices" and in "Prufrock's Pervigilium" (a section excised from *The Love Song of J. Alfred Prufrock*.)[54]

Harvard Graduate Years, 1911-14

In the fall of 1911, at the age of twenty-three, Eliot returned to Harvard and studied, under Professor Josiah Royce, the epistemological systems of Meinong and Bradley. He was also occupied with Sanskrit, Pali, and the metaphysics of Patanjali. Although he wrote several poems during this time, no writing of Eliot's was published between 1910 and 1915. The third and fourth *Preludes*, discussed above, were finished shortly after his return, as was *La Figlia che Piange*.

La Figlia che Piange makes of a described parting of lovers something of a Joycian epiphany—a recreated moment of dawning moral awareness. The protagonist pretends to have been only an observer, but his deep involvement in the scene makes the reader feel that the narrator was a participant. He sees himself as the mind of an artist, and he regards the girl as a body torn and bruised. And the parting is described as resembling the mind's desertion of the body it has used. The poem contains strong echoes of sestina 11 in Dante's *Vita Nuova*, of Rossetti's *Blessed Damozel*, and of the end of Conrad's *Heart of Darkness*. The protagonist tries to use artistic significance as justification for the desertion, but he has not wholly succeeded in convincing himself, let alone the reader.

For the 1912–13 and 1913–14 school years, Eliot was appointed an assistant in philosophy, and indeed philosophy seems during this period to have received most of his attention. While an assistant, he met and studied with Bertrand Russell, then a visiting lecturer and, later, the model for the title character of *Mr. Apollinax.*

Though he had returned to Harvard to complete his graduate studies in philosophy, we may be sure that Eliot's urge to live and write in Europe had been alive and growing for some time. As Kristian Smidt writes:

The notion of settling there [in England] was not strange to him. As early as 1909, recognising "the failure of American life" at that time, he wrote [*Harvard Advocate,* May 7, 1909] in a book review of the class of "Americans retained to their native country by business relations or socialities or by a sense of duty—the last reason implying a real sacrifice—while their hearts are always in Europe." Henry James was a Londoner, and was soon to become a British subject. Pound, J. G. Fletcher, Aiken, H. D. [Hilda Doolittle], and Robert Frost all lived in England in the years preceding and during the Great War. And Mr. Tinckom-Fernandez tells us that while at college he and Eliot discussed the idea of emigrating to a milieu more congenial to a writer, as Ezra Pound had done. When Tinckom-Fernandez did go to Europe, Eliot saw him off.[55]

His Paris year (and whatever family and financial pressures may have existed) had convinced him that he should return to study philosophy at Harvard. A natural finish to such a graduate program would be to spend a year at German universities. His excellent standing in the Harvard Philosophy Department made that option available in 1914.

Chapter Two

Dantean Observations

Eliot's first slim volume of poems, written earlier but not published until 1917, was entitled *Prufrock and Other Observations.* The word *observations,* like the epigraph to the volume, is a Dantean allusion; the poet is paralleling the observer of those poems to Dante the Pilgrim as he observed various shades in his symbolic fiction of a journey through Hell and Purgatory.

We see in most of Eliot's poems, early and late, a persona, a usually male protagonist or organizing consciousness who watches around him the ravages of improperly ordered love (sometimes his own) and who raises questions of justice and injustice, merit or blame, the responsibility of the watchers (including himself and the reader) implied in the scenes and souls depicted. It is important to discern whether, in each poem, the central consciousness or persona is only passing negative judgment on those he observes or being himself rejected by the Dantean poet. That question will be crucial in determining the tone of each poem.

What qualifications for the Dantean role had the relatively unknown poet Eliot in 1911 (when most of *Prufrock* was copied into the still-unpublished notebook that Eliot took with him to Paris in 1910)?[1] He had been writing poems for some years. Further, his study of Charles Grandgent's *Dante* and of medieval history, ancient and modern philosophy, Italian language, Florentine painting, and comparative literature (including the history of allegory), were both general and specific preparation for his assumption of a Dantean role. If those studies were not sufficient, his deep concern with "the absolute"—with martyrs and with the mystical and saintly matters so central to Dante's *Commedia*—is convincingly documented in Lyndall Gordon's *Eliot's Early*

Eliot's motives in writing his Dantean observations no ᵤₒᵤᵦₜ echo those expressed at the beginning of Dante's *Commedia*: "So bitter is it, that scarcely more is death: but to treat of the good that I there found, I will relate the other things that I discerned" (*Inferno* 1. 7–9).[2]

The *Prufrock* volume is dedicated to Jean Verdenal, whom Gordon calls the "one personal friend" that Eliot made during his Paris year.[3] Probably a common interest in poetry, in Dante, and in the Dantean concerns expressed above, plus a sharing of Eliot's plans, were the bases of that friendship. *The Love Song of J. Alfred Prufrock* was finished by the end of Eliot's Paris year, 1910–11. The two friends corresponded during the next four years until Verdenal died in World War I, about a month before the poem was first published in Harriet Monroe's *Poetry* (Chicago). The poem's dedication, "For Jean Verdenal, 1889–1915; mort aux Dardanelles," probably adds only the "For" to an item in a French newspaper list of World War I casualties. Verdenal was no doubt the one referred to in a 1934 "Commentary" by Eliot in the *Criterion*:

> . . . My own retrospect [on Paris] is touched by a sentimental sunset, the memory of a friend coming across the Luxembourg Gardens in the late afternoon, waving a branch of lilac, a friend who was later (so far as I could find out) to be mixed with the mud of Gallipoli.[4]

The Love Song of J. Alfred Prufrock

In 1946 Eliot wrote in the *New English Weekly*:

> I had kept my early poems (including *Prufrock* and others eventually published) in my desk from 1911 to 1915—with the exception of a period when Conrad Aiken endeavored, without success, to peddle them for me in London. In 1915 [actually 1914, as Pound's letters show] (and through Aiken) I met Pound. The result was that *Prufrock* appeared in *Poetry* in the summer of that year; and through Pound's efforts, my first volume was published by the Egoist Press in 1917.[5]

When *Prufrock* was first published, a number of respected critics in both the United States and England greeted it with cries of outrage, labeling it insane and unpoetic and a hoax.[6] A few others immediately saw its merits, as Ezra Pound had earlier when he called it "the best poem I have yet had or seen from an American," adding "PRAY GOD IT BE NOT A SINGLE AND UNIQUE SUCCESS."[7] His prayer was answered, though the first book edition of five hundred copies took four years to sell out, bringing the author royalties of just ten guineas.[8] During the next several decades, half a dozen or more authors were to describe how *Prufrock*, at first reading, had burst onto their consciousness like a bombshell, making them realize how well poetry can be adapted to the twentieth century and what complex subtlety can be embodied in even a brief poem. Two-thirds of a century after its publication, it is easy to assemble dozens of critiques of *Prufrock*, almost all highly laudatory.

Dantean Parallels. Many Dantean echoes are found in the title, dedication, two epigraphs, and frequently throughout the poem. The Verdenal dedication and Dantean first epigraph apply to the whole 1917 volume *Prufrock and Other Observations*. After a second epigraph quoted in Italian from Dante, Eliot's opening lines echo those of *Inferno* 1:

> In the middle of the journey of our life I came
>   to myself in a dark wood where the straight
>   way was lost.
> Ah! how hard a thing it is to tell what a wild,
>   and rough, and stubborn wood this was, which
>   in my thought renews the fear!
> So bitter is it, that scarcely more is death: . . .
> I cannot rightly tell how I entered it, so full of
>   sleep was I about the moment that I left the
>   true way. (11. 1–12)

The sequence in *Prufrock* parallels the first two cantos of *Inferno*, also drawing many details from cantos 3 (the trimmers), 4 (Limbo—the virtuous pagans), 26, and 27 (bolgia 8 of circle 8—

the evil-counselors, including Ulysses and Guido of Montefeltro).

Prufrock, like Dante, is beginning a journey in forbidding terrain whose meaning and significance he cannot fully grasp; his bald spot and thin legs place him "in the middle of the journey of life." He too has "refound" himself (*"mi ritrovai"*), has become aware that he has measured out his life in coffee spoons, and finds it hard to explain his situation ("Oh, do not ask, 'What is it?'"). Just as Dante's "straight way was lost," Prufrock will lead us through half-deserted, tedious, insidious streets that may constitute his Dark Wood.

Dante's looking back toward the dark pass he has escaped parallels Prufrock's thinking back on the women coming and going in the drawing room, where he has measured out his life. Continuing his climb (Prufrock's stairs?), Dante encounters three beasts (leopard, lion, and she-wolf) that frighten him back toward the Dark Wood of error; Prufrock's three beasts are suggested in the fog section of the poem through its animal imagery and symbolic parallels: he watches from the window as fog envelops the house.[9] The sensuous, catlike movements of the fog suggest Dante's leopard, allegorically representing the sins of incontinence and the first major division of Hell.

The streets and fog to be traversed (or, more likely, contemplated) in the first three stanzas of *Prufrock* echo Ulysses' description of Dante's bolgia of the evil-counselors (*Inferno* 26), and are metaphors for Prufrock's state of mind, just as the opening comparison of the evening sky to a patient etherized upon a table shows us not the scene, but his condition, his unrest, mental confusion, and self-induced paralysis. (We shall see him anaesthetize himself and, in a sense, cut out the part of himself that matters most.)

Apprehensive of approaching "the moment of my greatness," Prufrock reassures himself that there will be time for vacillation, for visions and revisions, and for other avoidances of the moment of crisis. His "murder and create" line seems melodramatic, but it refers to the "preparing of a face," the choosing of an identity for himself and to the question whether "to act or not to act, and hence to be or not to be."[10] That *Hamlet* echo is immediately

reinforced: Prufrock goes on to commend himself on his garments
and worry about the impression his appearance makes, as does
Polonius in his famous advice to Laertes. (Eliot's uses of *Hamlet*
parallel his uses of *Inferno*. This will become clearer when Prufrock
shows he is no Hamlet but a Polonius, no Dante but a Guido.)

Like Dante's *Commedia*, Prufrock's journey is an imaginative
fiction. His "do not ask" shows him to be as unable to frame and
face his question now with his friend as he will prove later in the
poem after envisioning the response to it of the lady (ladies?) in
the drawing-room. His musings on the ladies bring out his vanity
(the leopard of incontinence). He remembers the role-playing
habitual in such gatherings (the wolf of fraud) and the murdering
and creating that misrepresent identities and pin one, wriggling,
to the wall (the lion of violence).

The poem is, in fact, Prufrock's account of his reasons for turning
back to Dante's Dark Wood after reaching the same "how should
I presume?" kind of vacillation that Dante reaches in canto 2.
31–42; Eliot's poem may be seen as an expansion of those lines,
which occur at the beginning of Dante's journey when he is lost
in the Dark Wood until he finally overcomes his vacillation and
follows Virgil through Hell Gate, through the knowledge of all
his own evil tendencies.[11]

Prufrock's "Let us go, then..." introduces the quest-journey, in
which physical movement symbolizes psychic and moral movement.
When Virgil tells Dante of the divine Lady (Beatrice) who sent
him, Dante takes heart and begins his quest. Prufrock, unconfident
of divine approval or of the help of a Lady, takes much longer to
decide.

"Let us go, then, you and I" echoes two further points in canto
4 of *Inferno*. First, on the brink of Hell's chasm, Virgil (who,
among other functions, represents human reason) says to Dante,
"Now let us descend into the blind world here below; I will be
first and thou shalt be second" (ll. 13–15).[12] Seven lines later he
repeats, "Let us go," and continues, "for the length of way
impels us."

They are then entering not the circles where the incontinent, violent, and fraudulent are tortured, but the Limbo where virtuous pagans and unbaptized innocents suffer only the affliction of desire without hope. There Dante meets "the master souls of time." Probably the ladies who "come and go, talking of Michelangelo" (a post-Dantean master soul) are also in limbo. Their voices "dying with a dying fall" echo Dante's Francesca's final line, *"como corpo morto cade"* (*Inferno* 5).

Between Two Worlds. Though Prufrock might not label the two worlds "Hell Gate" and "Heaven Gate," his *condition* is that which Eliot later ascribes to the Stranger in *The Rock* (1934):

> I have known two worlds, I have known two worlds of death.
> All that you suffer, I have suffered before,
> And suffer always, even to the end of the world.
>
> . . . .
>
> There shall be always the Church and the World
> And the Heart of Man
> Shivering and fluttering between them, choosing and chosen,
> Valiant, ignoble, dark and full of light
> Swinging between Hell Gate and Heaven Gate.
> And the Gates of Hell shall not prevail.
> Darkness now, then
> Light.
>
> Light.[13]

The two worlds receive repeated emphasis in Eliot's poetry; they are perpetual alternatives confronting all of us: lower loves or higher loves; indecisions or decisions; time or eternity; revisions or visions; "not to be" or "to be"; hell or purgatory.

In *Prufrock*, as in Dante's *Commedia*, Love is the force that motivates all human actions and moves "the sun and other stars" (*Paradiso* 33); a person's Love Song is his expression of his total striving toward the world of eternity, toward a proper relation with not only his earthly Lady but all others, the entire universe, and ultimately God. To relate properly to life and death in their

true significance is to choose the right world and proper loves—
to sing one's Love Song as it should be sung. The "I" of the poem
seems to me to epitomize failure in the singing of a proper Love
Song; the "you" epitomizes at least provisional success, as promised
in the end of the *Rock* quotation.

Prufrock Pronouns: "One," "You," and "I."

"ONE"

The "one" of the poem presents no great problems. She seems
to be a feminine counterpart of either "you" or "I," frequenting the
same Boston teas, expressing on occasion dissatisfactions with the
unfulfilling, conventionalized life of that whole milieu. Her awarenesses may parallel theirs, though "I" is not sure. He probably does
not even have a particular lady in mind; if he had, he would likely
have used "she" instead of "one." This is not to deny the sexual
component in his Love Song; it is rather to say that he is open
to various possibilities in that regard—to whatever lady demonstrates the qualities requisite to become his Lady, his Beatrice.

"YOU" AND "I"

The "you" and "I" of the first line present greater difficulties.
Critics have commonly interpreted them as referring to two parts
of Prufrock, carrying on a conversation with himself. This interpretation now seems to me both too clever and much simpler than
the actual situation in the poem, though a Laforguian doubling of
Prufrock survives in the alternatives between which we see him
"choosing" (as he thinks).

Sometime before 1949 Eliot wrote to Kristian Smidt:

As for THE LOVE SONG OF J. ALFRED PRUFROCK anything
I say now must be somewhat conjectural, as it was written so long ago
that my memory may deceive me; but I am prepared to assert that
the "you" in THE LOVE SONG is merely some friend or companion,
presumably of the male sex, whom *the speaker* is at that moment
addressing . . . [italics mine].[14]

Having finally carefully compared *Prufrock* to Dante's *Inferno* and read dozens of critiques of the poem, I now see no reason to dissent from Eliot's straightforward statement. In fact, I see no other way of interpreting the poem that will fit all its complexities. Old Possum's delightful sense of humor is apparent in that phrase "presumably of the male sex" and in "the speaker"; he knew very well that he himself, allegorically projected to the age of thirty-five, or a persona very like that projection, was the "friend or companion," the Dante-figure of the poem. The "I" who addresses him is an unidentified friend.

"You" and "I" are probably close friends and confidants who have attended such teas together, though perhaps they have only discussed them.

Though the presence of "you" is crucial to Eliot's Dantean intent, *Prufrock* is a dramatic monologue, not a dialogue. It parallels monologues of Shakespeare's Polonius, Dante's Pilgrim, Guido, and Ulysses. The only functions of the "you" are to elicit confidences, set the Dantean tone, indicate Prufrock's equivalence with Guido in the poem's second epigraph, listen to the "I," and write the poem—bring back the story.

The Second Epigraph. Who is addressed in the first line, "Let us go *then*, you and I" [italics mine]? The *then* drives us back to the second epigraph, quoted from Dante's *Inferno* 27. 61–66 (circle 8, bolgia 8), where the shades of Ulysses, Guido of Montefeltro, and many other *counselors of evil* are hidden in tongues of flame which shake when they speak. They defrauded others of their integrity (just as Prufrock tries to convince the "you" that the overwhelming question should not be asked). The appropriateness of the punishment to the sin should be apparent: each shade has been defrauded of both his appearance—in a tongue of flame—and his own volition (and Prufrock talks himself into a state of paralysis). They used their burning speech, their tongues, to persuade others to do sinful things, to their listeners' eternal harm (but Prufrock's advice will be rejected by the Dante-like "you"). Here they cannot speak except in burning, and they roar with pain between speeches (Prufrock's torture is similar, though milder—he lacks their vigor). After Dante's memorable meeting with Ulysses and Diomed, enclosed in a two-pronged flame, Guido approaches in his flame to question Dante about Italy. After answering his questions, Dante asks who he was and what sin has brought him to such torture. His answer constitutes the second *Prufrock* epigraph. It is spoken to Dante and to Virgil, but Virgil is not really there, except in the influence on Dante of his writings; this is emphasized by Dante: "I, one alone [*io sol uno*] was preparing myself to bear the war both of the journey and the pity" (*Inferno* 2. 3–5).

Guido answers Dante, "If I thought you were alive, I would not speak; but since you are dead and cannot repeat my story to the living, I have no fear and I shall answer you."[15]

In Eliot's poem, Prufrock is confessing to the Dante-like poet his own sin of evil-counseling. Both Prufrock and Dante's Guido badly misjudge the persons in whom they confide. Guido's sin was advising the Pope on how to defeat his enemies by fraud; he was reluctant to give such advice, but the Pope promised to absolve his guilt in advance. Guido was impelled by weighty arguments to think silence worse, so he advised the Pope to make large promises to his enemies but not keep them. (Prufrock, just the opposite, finds weighty [?] arguments for thinking silence best. He also has promised much, but asks no question.) After Guido's death, the devil pointed out to him that it is impossible to plan a sin and repent it simultaneously (Prufrock seems to repeat that mistake), and then hauled his soul off to Hell.

The second epigraph and the "then" identify the "I" with Guido. He speaks not to Dante the author, who knows all and will come back to tell us all, but to Dante the Pilgrim, who understands only partially and learns as he goes along. Similarly, Prufrock's "you" is a persona created by the author and closely allied to him, but one subject to the limitations of his context, not yet knowing where his journey will end.

Prufrock and Ulysses. Prufrock's monologue also parallels that of a much more famous evil-counselor, Ulysses' stirring speech in *Inferno* 26. 112–20. (The beginning of that canto is evoked by Eliot's opening lines.)

Ulysses' eloquence in rousing his men to action is less heroically matched by Prufrock's in lulling himself into inaction, and Prufrock's final line parallels the end of Ulysses' moving speech, where he describes his drowning.

Prufrock's remarks include an "I have known" series (a traditional cataloguing device which also appears in Eliot's *The Death of Saint Narcissus*):

> And I have known the eyes already, known them all—
> The eyes that fix you in a formulated phrase,
> And when I am formulated, sprawling on a pin,
> When I am pinned and wriggling on the wall,
> Then how should I begin
> To spit out all the butt-ends of my days and ways?
> And how should I presume?

Prufrock is not the only one here who can "murder and create," but as victim, he is sure he would feel like a grasshopper or butterfly pinned and wriggling on the wall and "spitting tobacco juice" as he tried to formulate his overwhelming question.

The "I have known" series also introduces the theme of love for a lady:

> And I have known the arms already, known them all—
> Arms that are braceleted and white and bare
> (But in the lamplight, downed with light brown hair!)
> Is it perfume from a dress
> That makes me so digress?
> Arms that lie along a table, or wrap about a shawl,
> And should I then presume?
> And how should I begin?

Ian Hamilton cogently observes that, for Eliot,

a superb trinity of culture, sex and religion is humanity's most worthy goal and the sickness of modern civilisation is that the three impulses

operate in isolation. . . . His distaste for casual sexuality is emotionally
based on a conviction that sexuality is sacred, that it is in some way
involved with, or endorsed by, religious feeling.[16]

Balachandra Rajan notes that "the overwhelming question is more
than the proposal of marriage to a lady...the love song must
eventually be sung to Beatrice."[17]

In both *The Waste Land* and *Prufrock*, the Waste-Landers, so
long as they fail to ask their overwhelming questions, are dead
and in Hell, and an air of damnation is appropriate. They cannot
sing their Love Songs; but the Dante-like poet can, and the entire
corpus of his observations is intended to be his own Love Song.
Prufrock's problem is not just his own; his whole society—streets
and drawing room—is a Waste Land out of joint, and it would take
a Hamlet to set it right. He does ponder the possibility, and now,
in terms of Ulysses' monologue, Prufrock has come into the narrow
pass of the Pillars of Hercules (the Straits of Gibraltar) where
he must deliver the stirring oration to defraud his men of their
duty to home and family or turn back. Ulysses so fired his ship-
mates' imaginations that he could not have turned them back if he
had tried, and they sailed off into the unknown to their deaths,
on what only now in Hell does he see as "our foolish flight." Prufrock, on the other hand, hems and haws:

> Shall I say, I have gone at dusk through narrow streets
> And watched the smoke that rises from the pipes
> Of lonely men in shirt-sleeves, leaning out of windows? ...
>
> I should have been a pair of ragged claws
> Scuttling across the floors of silent seas.
> .   .   .   .
> And the afternoon, the evening, sleeps so peacefully!
> Smoothed by long fingers,
> Asleep . . . tired . . . or it malingers,
> Stretched on the floor, here beside you and me.
> Should I, after tea and cakes and ices,
> Have the strength to force the moment to its crisis?

Obviously he has talked himself out of trying. What we are getting here is not his talk, but his confession to the "you," the poet, not at the party but in their confidential conversation. This is his nearest approach to singing his Love Song. He is aware of the Book of Revelation, of the "I John saw these things" that will be an excised line in the *Waste Land* manuscript, and of the martyrdom of another John—the Baptist:

> But though I have wept and fasted, wept and prayed,
> Though I have seen my head (grown slightly bald) brought
>   in upon a platter,
> I am no prophet—and here's no great matter;
> I have seen the moment of my greatness flicker,
> And I have seen the eternal Footman hold my coat,
>   and snicker,
> And in short, I was afraid.

Prufrock, fearing he can cut no heroic figure and might prove only laughable, gives up the attempt. He is convinced that he is not the man to set right times that are out of joint, is no hero, but rather a Polonius:

> No! I am not Prince Hamlet, nor was meant to be;
> Am an attendant lord, one that will do
> To swell a progress, start a scene or two,
> Advise the prince; no doubt, an easy tool,
> Deferential, glad to be of use,
> Politic, cautious, and meticulous;
> Full of high sentence, but a bit obtuse;
> At times, indeed, almost ridiculous—
> Almost, at times, the Fool.

For Prufrock's English tradition, Hamlet, an imperfect but heroic establisher of the conditions for a successful society, can serve the symbolic functions of Aeneas in the Roman tradition of Virgil and Dante. Clearly Prufrock-Polonius is a mere time-server. Hamlet shared also Dante's vacillations as to whether he should

act, but unlike Prufrock, Hamlet and Dante did ask their overwhelming questions, did act. Hamlet's option, "to be or not to be,"
is echoed ironically in Prufrock's phrase "nor was meant to be."
So Prufrock has murdered his Hamlet, Lazarus, Dante, and John
the Baptist and created of himself a Polonius, a Guido, a Ulysses.
He will not again come close to creating. In Hugh Kenner's words,
he cannot modify the mornings, evenings, afternoons any more
"than one of Dante's subjects can desert his circle of Hell.... One
doesn't ... 'disturb the universe.' In Hell you do what you are
doing."[18]

> I grow old . . . I grow old . . .
> I shall wear the bottoms of my trousers rolled.
>
> Shall I part my hair behind? Do I dare to eat a peach?
> I shall wear white flannel trousers, and walk upon the beach.

Here, "heavy accents and long vowels and the repetition emphasize his consciousness of age and exhaustion...."[19] The rolled
trouser bottoms reflect his decision to go along with the latest
style of wearing cuffs on his trousers, a dandyish conformity. As
Professor Rajan writes, "The gesture of comic and yet of cosmic
defiance—'Do I dare/Disturb the universe?'—collapses now into
mere sartorial rebellion."[20] Conrad Aiken's *Ushant* tells what "a
sensation was caused" at Harvard when a fellow student "returned
from Paris ... in exotic Left Bank clothing, and with his hair
parted behind." The hair-style "was regarded as daringly bohemian."
The peach crisis refers not to Prufrock's digestion, but to the inde-
corum of eating a juicy peach ("the sole forbidden fruit he is likely
to pluck") and having to dispose of the seed with messy fingers.[21]
    Yet Prufrock has had his moments, his awarenesses—has read
of Dante's singing maidens in the Earthly Paradise:

> I have heard the mermaids singing, each to each.
> I do not think that they will sing to me.

The sounds of the waves are beautifully captured in the long,
open vowels and the W sounds of the following lines:

> I have seen them riding seaward on the waves
> Combing the white hair of the waves blown back
> When the wind blows the water white and black.

But in Prufrock's concluding lines, the mermaids are linked to Ulysses' sirens, who lure sailors to their deaths:

> We have lingered in the chambers of the sea
> By sea-girls wreathed with seaweed red and brown
> Till human voices wake us, and we drown.

The sea-girls have also been linked by various critics with Gérard de Nerval's sonnet *El Desdichado* (cited by Eliot in *The Waste Land*):

> *J'ai rêvé dans la grotte où nage la sirène.*[22]
> (I dreamed in the cave where the siren swims.)

and with the Salome works (another strong link to John the Baptist) of Laforgue and of Wilde.[23]

The final emphasis of *Prufrock* echoes the dark, damned finale of the evil-counselor, of Guido and especially of drowned, damned Ulysses. Prufrock has at the beginning tried to serve as a Virgil to his poet-friend's Dante, has next assumed Dante's unconfident and vacillating role, and finally has taken on the evil-counselor's role. He and his friend have dreamed of their submarine life and of climbing out into the air, as in Plato's *Phaedo*. But the voices and pressures of the remembered drawing-room setting wake him, and he drowns. He only thinks that "we" drown, just as Guido thinks Dante is dead. But Dante is not dead. He returns to the world and writes his poem, just as Prufrock's poet-friend ("you") does; in singing Prufrock's aborted Love Song, the poet is singing his own unaborted one—showing his rejection of Prufrock's evil counsel and his progress beyond *Inferno*.

Chapter Three

Dante's Logic of the Sensibility: The Simple Soul

"His was the true Dantescan voice—not honoured enough...." So wrote Ezra Pound, mourning Eliot's death.[1] Eliot's interest in Dante predated by at least five years his writing of *Prufrock*. In his 1950 talk on Dante, he indicated that "over forty-five years" earlier, he had been indelibly impressed by the Dantean qualities in Shelley's poetry. He added:

> I read Dante only with a prose translation beside the text. Forty years ago I began to puzzle out the Divine Comedy in this way; and when I thought I had grasped the meaning of a passage which especially delighted me, I committed it to memory; so that, for some years, I was able to recite a large part of one canto or another to myself, lying in bed or on a railway journey. Heaven knows what it would have sounded like, had I recited it aloud; but it was by this means that I steeped myself in Dante's poetry. ... I still, after forty years, regard his poetry as the most persistent and deepest influence upon my own verse. ...[2]

Eliot's increasing immersion in Dante was apparent in *Lune de Miel* (1917), *A Cooking Egg* (1919), *Ara Vos Prec* (1920), his 1920 "Dante" essay, and the 1927 Clark Lectures on mystical attitudes in Dante and Donne, as well as in his *Ash-Wednesday* poems ("Salutation"—1927; "*Perch' io non spero*"—1928; "*Som de l'escalina*"—1929) and *Animula* (1929). In his *Dante* volume (1929), he described what a poet learns from the *Divine Comedy*:

32

One has learned from the *Inferno* that the greatest poetry can be written with the greatest economy of words, and with the greatest austerity in the use of metaphor, simile, verbal beauty, and elegance. . . . From the *Purgatorio* one learns that a straightforward philosophical statement can be great poetry; from the *Paradiso,* that more and more rarefied and remote *states of beatitude* can be the material for great poetry.[3]

Eliot also remarked that Dante's *Divine Comedy* is "in some way a 'moral education' " and that "Dante has to educate our senses as he goes along."[4] Throughout his poetic career, Eliot set those same tasks for himself, and he used in his works "the logic of sensibility" that he took largely from Dante. Hence a number of his remarks on Dante are the most helpful available guides to Eliot's work:

The next step after reading Dante again and again should be to read some of the books that he read, rather than modern books about his work and life and times, however good. . . . With Dante there is just as much need for concentrating on the text [as with Shakespeare], and all the more because Dante's mind is more remote from the ways of thinking and feeling in which we have been brought up. . . . the forms of imagination, phantasmagoria, and sensibility . . . [are] strange to us. We have to learn to accept these forms.[5]

Similarly, the reader of Eliot's poems who senses "the forms of imagination, phantasmagoria, and sensibility" at work in them will find implied the locus from which each poem can be read. And only then will it be profitable to attempt tracing the chronologically developing intentions and assumptions of the author, or even to evaluate any one of the poems in the proper terms. M. L. Rosenthal, discussing Eliot's method of combining shorter segments into new, longer poems, says it quite differently:

The struggle for form is not to write something that will be thought attractive by the general reader but to awaken realization of a felt state, in language adequate to the need. Formal structure, in this exploratory, improvisatory sense, is always open, a venture at risk. The poet needs to convey a subjective condition by composing a music of feeling in language; he does not quite know what he is set to convey until his own phrasing realizes into it. So a certain number of tentative starts is ordinarily required along the way, before he can see the scale he is really working on. Eliot's instinct for this process was probably the keenest of any poet writing in our language in this century.[6]

As we have seen, Eliot's works often echo Dante's forms, techniques, subject matter, or even exact words. Like Dante himself, Eliot was a writer steeped in the Western cultural and literary tradition. Both his creative and critical works echo a wide range of authors. Even in his earliest prose volume, *The Sacred Wood* (1920), he wrote on—besides Dante and other topics—Euripides, Christopher Marlowe, *Hamlet*, Ben Jonson, Philip Massinger, Swinburne, and Blake.

But for reasons already apparent in the 1920 "Dante" essay, no other writer was to assume such a central position in the whole body of Eliot's poetry as the Florentine exile. Dante's *Divine Comedy* familiarizes its reader with the path by which the earliest intimations of immortality and of felicity in a childhood love become transmuted to the boundless felicity of the highest love, "redeeming the time" (*Ash-Wednesday*) that passes between. As of Dante's masterpiece, the experience of that path is the central theme of Eliot's poetry from *The Love Song of J. Alfred Prufrock* to the end of *Four Quartets*. From the beginning, Eliot repeatedly emphasized this relevance of Dante to his poems.

What Dante had in common with Eliot's other chief sources Eliot identified as early as his essay "The Metaphysical Poets" (1921):

The poets of the seventeenth century, the successors of the dramatists of the sixteenth, possessed a mechanism of sensibility which could devour any kind of experience. They are simple, artificial, difficult, or fantastic, as their predecessors were: no less nor more than Dante, Guido Cavalcanti, Guinizelli, or Cino. In the seventeenth century a dissociation of sensibility set in, from which we have never recovered.[7]

Eliot attempted in his poems and his criticism to win back that unified sensibility. Already in *Prufrock* we have seen Dantean tendencies that were to remain central throughout his career. Characteristically, as we have seen, a male persona with deep sympathy for his fellow men and a strong sense of moral and social responsibility examines the lives around him and raises "overwhelming" questions. Eliot early and late proclaimed his emulation of Dante in these respects and others, but the unmistakably explicit poetic expression of that indebtedness and of the doctrine of the soul at its center did not come until the publication in 1929 of *Animula* and of the *Dante* book, in which Eliot quoted in English and Italian the *Purgatorio* passage on which *Animula* was based and clearly set down his attitudes toward and debts to Dante. Though many strong links tie *Animula* to *Ash-Wednesday* and other writings of the same period, the assumptions to which it gives clear statement had been implicit in Eliot's poetry as early as *Prufrock*. No other clues are as relevant to the reading of the entire body of Eliot's poetry.

Animula comprises not only a restatement of Dante's theory of the soul—his basic psychology, which Eliot called Aristotle's *De anima* "strained through the schools"[8]—but also the clear statement of the psychology and philosophy basic to all of Eliot's major poetry. *Animula* assumes and defines the attitudes toward the human soul, free will, and individual responsibility implicit in the poetry of both poets; it is therefore one of the best starting points for a study of Eliot. The poem is based on *Purgatorio* 16, in which Marco Lombardo answers Dante's questions about freedom of the will and about the nature of the soul.

Animula

Precisely at the middle of Dante's *Divine Comedy* (*Animula* is at the middle of *CPP50*), Dante the Pilgrim asks Marco Lombardo to explain to him whether the evil in the world is caused by "the heavens" or men. Marco responds that man has Mind and Free

Will, which can, if properly nurtured, completely gain the victory over stellar influence in his life. So man is responsible for the world's going astray. Evil leadership, not corrupt nature in each person, brings society's ills. Marco promises to explain why that happens; then follows the passage on which *Animula* is based. Eliot juxtaposed the Italian and English and placed single quotation marks around the first line of *Animula*, not only to acknowledge his debt to Dante but to make the reader look for even closer correspondences than just those of meaning:

> *Esce di mano a lui . . . l'anima semplicetta.*[9]
> 'Issues from the hand of God, the simple soul.'

In that first line (made up of the first halves of Dante's lines 85 and 88 in canto 16) Eliot has echoed not only the word order but also the actual sounds of Dante's Italian. This is no doubt one of the passages he said he had memorized in Italian and repeated to himself frequently. Marco's speech reads:

> From the hands of Him who loves her before she is, there issues like a little child that plays, with weeping and laughter, the simple soul, that knows nothing except that, come from the hands of a glad creator, she turns willingly to everything that delights her. First she tastes the flavour of a trifling good; then is beguiled, and pursues it, if neither guide nor check withhold her. Therefore laws were needed as a curb; a ruler was needed, who should at least see afar the tower of the true City.[10]

Eliot's ten-line adaptation of Marco's first sentence, beginning, " 'Issues from the hand of God, the simple soul'/To a flat world of changing lights and noise,/To light, dark, dry or damp, chilly or warm," gives us the same concept of the soul and the love or *amor* that motivates it as is seen in Dante and in Aristotle's *De anima.* Eliot later showed this same picture of the soul of a child in *The Cultivation of Christmas Trees* (1956), restating the theme probably because its importance in interpreting his works had been too often overlooked.

Like the simple soul, Dante fails to understand Marco's explanation fully and later asks Virgil to clarify it. Virgil partly does so, but warns him that reason is not enough to grasp the point, that Beatrice (since it is a matter of faith) will later expound it to him under the name of Free Will.

How the soul goes astray is indicated in Marco's second and third sentences (expanded by Virgil in that and the next canto), which are echoed in Eliot's next thirteen lines (11–23); the simple soul is seen as molded by its choices, its leaders, and its environment; it builds its own Karma. It "confounds the actual and the fanciful," and

> The heavy burden of the growing soul
> Perplexes and offends more, day by day;
>
> . . . .
>
> The pain of living and the drug of dreams
> Curl up the small soul in the window seat
> Behind the *Encyclopaedia Britannica*.

Consequently, the remainder of its life, as seen in lines 24–31, is disappointing—is not really life at all. Line 24 echoes line 1 (italics mine):

> Issues from the hand of *time* the simple soul
> Irresolute and selfish, misshapen, lame,
> Unable to fare forward or retreat,
> Fearing the warm reality, the offered good,
>
> . . . .
>
> Living first in the silence after the viaticum.

This doctrine of moral responsibility for our choices forms the deepest theme of Eliot's poetry and plays, and it is those other authors and writings dealing with such questions best that Eliot most frequently quotes or alludes to in his art and his criticism: Dante, Shakespeare, the Bible, St. John of the Cross and other Christian mystics, the *Bhagavad-Gita*, the Greek dramatists, Baudelaire, the Grail-quest myths, and Christian ritual. Improper choices are the chief failures of Prufrock, the waste-landers, the hollow men, and the unsuccessful characters in Eliot's plays. The proper choices, obversely, are the great triumphs of Dante's Arnaut Daniel (quoted in *The Waste Land*), the protagonists of *Ash-Wednesday* and the *Four Quartets*, Thomas in *Murder in the Cathedral*, Harry in *The Family Reunion*, everyone except (for the time, at least) Peter Quilpe in *The Cocktail Party*, and most of the characters in *The Confidential Clerk* and in *The Elder Statesman*. In fact, for Eliot as for Dante, it might be said that the essential requirement of Comedy is that the important characters (or rather the leading characters—all are important) learn to make those choices which direct their psychic movements toward higher loves.

The third and last section of *Animula* consists of six lines, a plea for prayer. The person addressed, who may be the reader or, more likely, Beatrice or Mary, is asked to pray for five persons whose lives were lost in different ways—who issued from the "hand of time" variously misshapen. All of these persons (and in the same order) are potentially present near the beginning of the poem.[11] None of them avoided confusing the actual and the fanciful, the imperatives of "is" and "seems," and they are consequently either dead or in a living death. For the dead, it is too late; but those still alive (like the reader) may yet receive life.

The last line of *Animula*, "Pray for us now and at the hour of our birth," slightly alters the closing lines of the *Ave Maria*:

> Holy Mary, Mother of God!
> pray for us sinners, now
> and at the hour of our death. Amen.

Eliot has put these last two lines of the *Ave Maria* into his own context, where they operate quite differently. His changing the last word to "birth" makes the prayer fit well with the theory of development—Dante's theory of education— built into *Animula*, prayers being needed at birth so we will not issue from the hand of time misshapen and lame. There is also the idea that death is an hour of beginning, another issuing from the hand of time; so birth in the last line may be the moment of death, the birth into a new higher order such as Socrates foresaw for himself in the *Apology* and *Phaedo*. Eliot's belief that prayers can assist souls of the dead (and that prayerful memory of the dead can assist the living) is attested in his East Coker memorial plaque. *Animula* depicts the soul as "living first in the silence after the viaticum" (final communion). Death would thus be the induction into a higher Christian order. These are universal patterns and beliefs which Eliot puts into various sets of terminology to remind us that he is dealing with not just Christian doctrine but universal human experience, experience that can be embodied in the terminology of all major religions or in the nonreligious vocabulary of psychology. He borrows this technique from Dante, who supports most of his important points by allusions to the Greek, Latin, and biblical traditions, as well as to his contemporary Italian scene in 1300 or thereabouts. Eliot similarly copies from Dante the taking of lines from the liturgy and from hymns, as well as from literature and life.

The concluding line of *Animula* subsumes all of the above meanings. The tone and mood of the poem are akin to those of *Marina*; each poem displays an unguarded honesty, a humility and an acceptance of one's own limitations that are rarely encountered. The role assumed by the author is that of Virgilian (and Dantean) moral guide, directing our attention to those considerations which may help us better understand our own psychic development and accept the responsibility for exercising proper choices, using our free will in proper directions, acting rather than letting life slip away unprofitably. Dante's scheme is accepted almost intact by Eliot—his aesthetic theories as well as his psychology and his attitude toward what is important in life.

Dantean Structure and *Amor Gentile*

Eliot began his *Collected Poems* (all editions) with *Prufrock*, in which (as early as 1910–11) he embarked on an ambitious scheme to make his complete works a Dantean structure. He began (see the "Observations" poems) with a trip through Hell; perhaps he intended to close with the Earthly-Paradise meeting with the Beatrice figure, or he may have aspired to the vision of *"l'amor che move il sole e l'altre stelle"* ("the Love that moves the sun and the other stars") of *Paradiso* 33. 144–45. Though the scheme, probably, was not completed in anything like the detail originally envisioned, that bold structure remains the framework of the whole corpus of his serious poems; and the resonances of the Dantean scheme with the developing pattern of his own life altered his conception and execution of the whole corpus. One can hardly unravel the central import of his works without examining the relation between his life and that Dantean conception as it appears in the poems. Fortunately, Eliot wrote enough on what Dante meant to him at various stages in his career to throw a great deal of light on the crucial questions, among them Eliot's interpretation and uses of the Lady who served as muse, earthly love, and intermediary to divinity in the writings of Dante, Guido Cavalcante, and the other Italian poets of their *dolce stil nuovo* (sweet new style). A. C. Charity summarizes the development of that tradition:

In outline then . . . the troubadours, as is well known, contributed a quasi-religious celebration of the lady and along with that a number of associated conceits, culminating in the *donna-angelo* which was to become practically a hallmark of "stilnovist" poetry. On those foundations it was the achievement of the Bolognese poet, Guinizelli, to construct, in a few poems, the framework of a more elaborate metaphysical context, and of Cavalcanti, Dante, and a few other Tuscan poets to add a closer, subtler, psychological attentiveness; so that from being, as *amour courtois*, a vaguely heretical cult or witty dissipation in the courts and castles of Provence, Love came in Italy, now in the form of *amor gentile*, to be considered (at least within this circle) as the beginning of religious wisdom and efficient cause of moral rectitude: the intellectual centre, at any rate in Dante's case, of a comprehensive vision of the world and man.[12]

Dante's Beatrice epitomizes this tradition.

The last eight lines of *Animula* seem to be addressed to Eliot's Beatrice-figure; it seems fair to ask how she relates to his own experiences. Sometime around the age of six or possibly seven, Eliot had, on meeting a girl, an experience which he later considered comparable to Dante's meeting with Beatrice in *La Vita Nuova*. He incorporated such an experience into his French poem *Dans le Restaurant* (1918) and commented on *La Vita Nuova* in his 1929 "Dante":

> In the first place, the type of sexual experience which Dante describes as occurring to him at the age of nine years is by no means impossible or unique. My only doubt (in which I found myself confirmed by a distinguished psychologist) is whether it could have taken place so *late* in life as the age of nine years. The psychologist agreed with me that it is more likely to occur at about five or six years of age. It is possible that Dante developed rather late, and it is also possible that he altered the dates to employ some other significance of the number nine. But to me it appears obvious that the *Vita Nuova* could only have been written around a personal experience. If so, the details do not matter: whether the lady was the Portinari or not, I do not care; it is quite as likely that she is a blind for some one else, even for a person whose name Dante may have forgotten or never known. But I cannot find it incredible that what has happened to others should have happened to Dante with much greater intensity.
>
> The same experience, described in Freudian terms, would be instantly accepted as fact by the modern public.[13]

The essay goes on to suggest that Dante "was following something more essential [more archetypal, I presume] than merely a 'literary' tradition."

In Eliot's comparable experience, the girl was probably Emily Hale, who seems to have served Beatrice-like poetic functions for him.[14] By the time he wrote *La Figlia che Piange* in 1911, he had both studied Dante and had a painful parting from some girl. A friend, likely aware of that parting, had told him to look up in an Italian museum a stele titled *La Figlia che Piange*—the girl who is crying—but, as mentioned in chapter 1, he had not found

it. Nevertheless, the statue gave him a blind for pretending unin-
volvement in the parting depicted in his poem *La Figlia che Piange*.

Back at Harvard, from 1911 to 1914, "he made a study of the
lives of saints and mystics, St. Theresa, Dame Julian of Norwich,
Mme Guyon, Walter Hilton, St. John of the Cross, Jacob Böhme,
and St. Bernard."[15] His poems and fragments of 1914 (identified
in Lyndall Gordon's *Eliot's Early Years*) show those preoccupations. In 1915 he married Vivien Haigh-Wood, no doubt hoping
that, like Dante's Beatrice, she could serve as his earthly love, the
muse of his poetry, and his mediator with divine love. The failure
of that marriage to develop into a healthy sexual and emotional
relationship is chronicled in *Lune de Miel* ([Honeymoon]—1917),
A Cooking Egg (c. 1919), the 1920 "Ode" thereafter suppressed,
and *The Waste Land* (1922).

By the time of *Gerontion* (1920), Eliot had to accept the fact
that Vivien was not going to serve the functions of Dantean Lady
for him. The 1920 "Ode" also indicated that the springs of his
poetry had dried up as a result of the breakdown of the marriage
relationship. By the time of *The Waste Land* (1922) he was looking through the tradition and through Dante for solutions to the
gnawing problem of what one does without the earthly Lady.
His Arnaut Daniel quotations (discussed in chapter 8) might be
taken to indicate that he thought himself far along through Purgatory; but still the *Waste Land* ending is ambiguous. He knew of
the *stil novist* potential of his own experience, but didn't seem
certain whether he could appropriate it. By *The Hollow Men*
(1925), directly addressed to this problem of the *stil novist* Lady,
he was allying his protagonist to Marlowe (not Kurtz) in Conrad's *Heart of Darkness*, having him wear deliberate disguises and
avoid such a meeting with the eyes of the lady as is consummated
in Dante's Earthly Paradise.

By the time of *Animula* and *Ash-Wednesday* (1927–30), however, he addressed a lady directly in prayer—probably a Beatrice/
Emily Hale figure (though the prayers may have been directed to
Mary, as the *Ave Maria* quotation suggests), Vivien having been
relegated to a role like that of Dante's wife, Gemma Alighieri. The

painful period of the *Landscapes* poems (1933-34) and the spiritual asceticism of *Murder in the Cathedral* (1935) preceded his writing to his friend Bonamy Dobrée in 1936, "I don't think that ordinary human affections are capable of leading us to the love of God, but rather that the love of God is capable of informing, intensifying and elevating our human affections...."[16]

The Dantean quest of his poems was concluded in the final image of *Four Quartets* (*Little Gidding*'s "the fire and the rose are one"—1942), but by that time Eliot's main attention had turned to the plays, in which the Dantean Lady does not figure in the same way. When he wrote of Baudelaire and of Pascal, Eliot emphasized the function of despair and suffering as Infernal moral illnesses that must precede one's Purgatorial discipline. Before man can be regenerated by religion, "the dying nurse" (*East Coker*) in "the hospital" of the world, those illnesses, those "fevers," must grow worse: as in Dante's *Inferno*, evil must be seen in all its horror and recognized as evil. Then only can Love be properly experienced in ever-increasing degrees.

In his 1950 talk "What Dante Means to Me," Eliot classed Dante with Shakespeare, Homer, and Virgil as one of the great masters to whom one slowly grows up. He pointed out that he had borrowed lines from Dante, set echoes of Dante in parallel to modern scenes for purposes of contrast and comparison, and consciously imitated Dante in the air raid scene of *Little Gidding*, which cost him more trouble than any other passage of similar length that he had written. That section, incidentally, has frequently been called Eliot's best poetry.

He went on to discuss three chief influences, which he summed up as the lessons of *craft*, of *speech*, and of *exploration of sensibility*. Of the first, the lesson of craft, he said that no poet of similar stature has been a more attentive student of the art of poetry than Dante. The second lesson taught by Dante's poetry—that of speech—is that as poet one should be the servant of his language rather than the master of it. He should refine and develop his language for those who come after him, which is the highest possible achievement of the poet's craft. This "purify[ing of] the dialect of the tribe" (*Little Gidding*) received Eliot's repeated attention and was memorably examined in the fifth section of each of the *Four Quartets*.

According to Eliot, the great poet should not be content to see and hear more clearly than ordinary men, but should perceive more than they and help them too to perceive it. The *Divine Comedy*, he said, expresses the full range of man's emotional possibilities, from despair to beatitude; it reminds later poets that they must similarly push back the frontiers of man's awareness.[17]

Eliot's works characteristically attempt, with considerable success, to express the almost inexpressible: the self-probings of many of his personae, the dawning moral awareness of Sweeney, the moral and spiritual struggles of Thomas in *Murder in the Cathedral* and of *Ash-Wednesday*, and the search for one's proper place in the universe in all of the major works.

Upon receiving the gold Dante Medal from the people of Florence in 1959, Eliot said he did not feel that he deserved it; he admitted, however, that he could not think of anyone who did.[18] The judgment might appropriately be left to readers of the "familiar compound ghost" section of *Little Gidding,* in which Dante's lessons of craft, of speech, and of exploration of sensibility are put to consummate use.

Chapter Four

Another Country

Eliot was awarded a traveling fellowship for the 1914–15 year, and spent some weeks of the summer in Germany, chiefly at Marburg. The start of World War I at the end of the summer, however, changed his traveling plans, and he went to England. In London, in the fall of 1914, he lived in the neighborhood of Russell Square, the setting of the brief poem *Morning at the Window* (1915).

He continued his studies at Merton College at Oxford in September. There he read Greek philosophy, the German phenomenologists Meinong and Husserl, and, "above all," Aristotle.[1] Eliot's interest in Aristotle was to be continually compounded and extended as it blended with his deep involvement in Dante. He also wrote poems at Oxford that year, chiefly Dantean observations marked by further sardonic evaluations, by sometimes bitter or ironic rejection of self and of social customs and institutions, by the side-thrusts of a clearly displaced set of personae attempting to salvage and come to terms with new identities. Even on the far side of the Atlantic, all was not well for art and artists, and Eliot was about to meet someone who knew it. On September 22, 1914, through his friend and schoolmate Conrad Aiken, he met Ezra Pound, who was to influence profoundly his life and his poetry, especially during the next eight years.

Whether by chance or design, Eliot's stay in England was to become permanent. Urged by Pound, he decided to settle there. Though he returned briefly to the States to discuss his plans with his parents in the summer of 1915, it would be 1932 before he saw America again, and by then he was to become a British subject.

Pound and Publication

Eliot's early education, his keen mind, his Harvard background, and his interests had already sent him along the paths Pound was advocating with his typical verve and impatience. The two poets were voluntary expatriates for similar reasons. If Pound's influence was not germinal, it did strongly reinforce tendencies already apparent in Eliot. By 1914, Eliot had written not only his *Smith Academy Review* and *Harvard Advocate* poems, but also most of those to be published through Pound's influence and connections within the next three years, culminating in *Prufrock and Other Observations* in 1917.

Of Pound's influence Eliot wrote:

My indebtedness to Pound is of two kinds: first, in my literary criticism; . . . second, in his criticism of my poetry in our talk, and his indications of desirable territories to explore. This indebtedness extends from 1915 to 1922, after which period Mr. Pound left England, and our meetings became infrequent.[2]

Pound had called Eliot, soon after their first meeting,

the only American I know of who has made what I can call adequate preparation for writing. He has actually trained himself *and* modernized himself *on his own.* . . . It is such a comfort to meet a man and not have to tell him to wash his face, wipe his feet, and remember the date (1914) on the calendar.[3]

Conrad Aiken had unsuccessfully tried for some time to help find a publisher for some of Eliot's poems; Pound was now to fare better, but not without a struggle. Of the poems that Eliot showed him, he picked out *Prufrock* as the one surest to succeed and to mark its author as different from any other poet then writing. After a prolonged campaign, Pound finally persuaded or perhaps bludgeoned Harriet Monroe, editor of *Poetry* (Pound was a contributing editor), into printing the poem. He had evidently suggested some changes in the poem, since he wrote Miss Monroe regarding the Hamlet passage, "It is an early and cherished bit and T. E. won't give it up, and as it is the only portion of the poem that most readers will like at first reading, I don't see that it will do much harm."[4]

After the impression created by *Prufrock*, Pound had less difficulty in helping, during 1915, to place a number of Eliot's other poems in *Poetry*, in Wyndham Lewis's effervescent periodical *Blast*, and in *Others*. He seems also to have been instrumental in Eliot's appointment as an assistant editor of the *Egoist* in 1917. And Pound himself published five of Eliot's poems in his *Catholic Anthology*—the first appearance in book form of any of Eliot's verse.[5]

The "programs" of Eliot and Pound dovetailed at a number of points, despite their marked differences in temperament. Each felt strongly about the value of tradition and the necessity of discipline in poetry; each considered Dante perhaps the greatest of poets and the finest model for a beginning poet to study.

Probably one of Pound's chief influences on Eliot's interest in Dante was to turn his attention to the Arnaut Daniel passage in Provençal (the only sustained passage in which Dante allowed one of his characters to speak in a tongue other than Dante's own) —the passage that Eliot was to cite and use so often in his later writings. Though even that interest may have preceded their acquaintance, it was very likely Pound's vigorous sounding of Arnaut Daniel's speech that impressed Eliot so deeply with it.

Certainly Pound's swashbuckling and uninhibited attempts to "educate the heathens" must have excited and appealed to the milder, more decorous younger poet (Eliot was twenty-six and Pound thirty in 1915). On one occasion, when Eliot tried in a poem to copy his friend's free-wheeling tactics, Pound admonished him, "That's not your style at all. You let *me* throw the bricks through the front window. You go in at the back door and take out the swag."[6]

Through Pound, Eliot became acquainted with many of the writers and artists who were to shape the thinking of their era, not a few of whom were kept inspired and even alive largely through the encouragement and assistance of the resourceful, energetic, and generous Pound. The list of artists who owed much to him before and during the 1920s is most impressive: Yeats, Joyce, Wyndham Lewis, the sculptor Gaudier-Brzeska, and Eliot, among others.

During the next year or two after meeting Pound, Eliot began writing reviews for philosophical journals; and he also completed his thesis, *Experience and the Objects of Knowledge in the Philosophy of F. H. Bradley* (not published until 1964), though he did not return to Harvard to take the examinations for his doctoral degree after the thesis had been accepted.

The young poet-philosopher, however, was hardly lost in books and study. On June 26, 1915, as already noted, after a decision made in "the awful daring of a moment's surrender" (*The Waste Land*), he married Vivien Haigh-Wood, a ballet dancer and daughter of the painter Charles Haigh-Wood. Eliot taught at High Wycombe Grammar School and then at the Highgate School for four terms. Part of this time the Eliots lived with Mrs. Eliot's parents in Hampstead and with Bertrand Russell in his London flat.

During the same period Eliot continued writing poetry, some of it in French; suffered the considerable financial difficulties likely at that time (according to Pound) to be the lot of anyone devoting himself to the arts; and finally took employment with Lloyd's Bank, where he was soon highly regarded. He remained there until, in 1925, he joined the publishing firm of Faber and Gwyer, later Faber and Faber, an association that lasted until his death.

He also did extension-lecturing,[7] editorial work, and a great deal of reviewing and writing for periodicals. Overwork seems to have produced poor health. In 1918, says Valerie Eliot,[8] his congenital hernia and tachycardia kept him out of the United States Navy. Eliot was an editor of the *Egoist* from 1917 to 1919, and he was also listed on the editorial committee for *Coterie* in 1919, along with Richard Aldington, Aldous Huxley, and Wyndham Lewis. In 1922, he undertook the editorship of the *Criterion*—which position he held until the discontinuance of its publication in 1939—and he built for it a reputation of unusual distinction. As an outgrowth of his friendship with John Middleton Murry, Eliot contributed numerous articles and reviews to the *Athenaeum*, which Murry edited from 1919 to 1921.

The October 1922 issue of the *Criterion* contained what was to become the most controversial and the most influential poem of the twentieth century to date: Eliot's *The Waste Land*, bluepenciled by Pound to about half the length of the original manuscript. But at just this time Pound was leaving England for Paris, and the close association of the two poets was coming to an end. As Eliot wrote in 1950, "There did come a point, of course, at which difference of outlook and belief became too wide; or it may have been distance and different environment, or it may have been both."[9]

Even after Pound moved to Paris in 1922 and the two saw each other much less frequently, great mutual respect for poetic abilities and accomplishments survived many differences in viewpoint and the passage of many years—hectic years for Pound in which his attacks on what he disapproved became more and more violent and sometimes aberrant. In World War II, he broadcast attacks on the American economic system for Mussolini; and after Italy fell to the Allies, he was charged with treason and incarcerated for some years at St. Elizabeth's Hospital, Washington, D.C., as mentally incapable of standing trial. It was partly through Eliot's efforts (along with those of many other writers) that Pound was eventually released to return to Italy for the remainder of his life. Disillusioned but widely admired, he died in Venice in 1972, having outlived Eliot by seven years.

At least twenty of the items in Donald Gallup's excellent bibliography concern Eliot's writings on Pound, and Eliot was far from alone in his estimate of Pound as one of the most capable poets of the twentieth century: in 1949 Pound was awarded the Bollingen–Library of Congress Award for the best poetry by an American citizen published during the previous year (his *Pisan Cantos*). Without their association, especially during the period from 1915 to 1922, Eliot's life and poetic career might have been far different. The spirit of camaraderie that had grown up between

Pound and Eliot, as well as Pound's championing publication of his poems and essays, no doubt stimulated Eliot's writing of poems at Oxford in 1915.

The Oxford Poems of 1915

In *The "Boston Evening Transcript," Aunt Helen,* and *Cousin Nancy,* the New England milieu is examined and rejected. In *Mr. Apollinax,* the rejection is broadened to include not only the cityscape and the social scene, but also Harvard faculty life, a career for which Eliot had been preparing and which his parents hoped he would still pursue. Professor and Mrs. Channing-Cheetah are being dismissed rather summarily in favor of their guest, a visiting British speaker based on Bertrand Russell, who as a visiting professor at Harvard the year before the poem was written had been impressed by his star pupil, T. S. Eliot, as much as Eliot had been impressed by him. The poem seems to suggest that the old world, where there is a better understanding of the vitality of art, provides a better atmosphere for the poet to live, thrive, and work in. The implicit conclusion that a poet, or painter, or musician should decamp for London or Paris was resisted by very few of the young artists of 1915.

In *Morning at the Window,* the reader's task is to identify with the "I" of the third line, looking down from a window at the waking but unattractive environment that twists not only the faces but also the souls of the people seen below.

> They are rattling breakfast plates in basement kitchens,
> And along the trampled edges of the street
> I am aware of the damp souls of housemaids
> Sprouting despondently at area gates.
>   The brown waves of fog toss up to me
> Twisted faces from the bottom of the street,
> And tear from a passer-by with muddy skirts
> An aimless smile that hovers in the air
> And vanishes along the level of the roofs.[10]

In the words and rhythm of the first line the reader hears the
rattling of the plates and the flat conversation that crosses the
breakfast tables. The "trampled edges of the street" testify to the
number of aimless, uninterested, and uninteresting existences passed
on this street.

But the deepest significance lies in the attitude of the observer
and the reader toward the lives of this street, both their own and
those seen in distorted snatches. Behind "the damp souls" is sensed
what Eliot called in *Preludes* "The notion of some infinitely gentle/
Infinitely suffering thing." And the words "damp," "twisted," and
"aimless" imply that these people deserve a more significant existence involving a scheme of moral order. In this poem, couched in
completely secular terms, is a doctrine of individual worth and of
human sympathy and the acceptance of responsibility.

Hysteria, the last of the Oxford 1915 poems, is in a form
more French than English, the prose poem. Baudelaire and Rimbaud, among others, had used that form effectively. Eliot used it
for a subject then in the forefront of psychological research, the
hysteria that had been the subject of Freud's early study. Eliot's
masterful reproduction of the rhythms and texture of hysteria make
it a very good exemplar of the genre. His sense of humor is evi-
dent, as well as an early hint of the great difficulties posed by his
wife Vivien's illnesses and problems.

Chapter Five

Merely Flesh and Blood: Poems 1919

The first of the 1919 *Poems, Sweeney Among the Nightingales,* will be dealt with in chapter 6. Two of the others satirize the church when its functions are improperly performed. These are *The Hippopotamus* (published in July 1917) and *Mr. Eliot's Sunday Morning Service* (September 1918). Both of them suggest what the proper functions of the church should be. Both contain excellent humor, but of different types.

The Hippopotamus

The Hippopotamus is written in nine quatrains, a stanza form consciously borrowed from Théophile Gautier's volume *Emaux et Camées* (*Enamels and Cameos*). In it both rapier and bludgeon are turned against devitalized religious institutions. The hippopotamus seems to represent at first the fallible individual human with all his limitations. The end suggests that the hippopotamus is the "True Church," mud-bound, whereas fallible man may ascend to heaven and be blessed by the choiring angels. The poem thus consists of an extended and shifting conceit. The references to the church are of two kinds: those to the earthly institutional church and those to the spiritual body. Surprisingly it is the first, the earthly church, that is represented by the capitalized label "True Church." By the poem's end, we are aware of the uncapitalized true church, the spiritual one that comfortingly hovers behind and above and before and between the literal earthly institutions and can perform the miracle of transmuting nervous shock into felicity—can, amid contradictory significations and various abuses, dissolve the strident Many into the quiet One. The poem clearly and strongly implies that the earthly church should reflect that spirit more faithfully, and that its functions are highly important to us.

Not all 1917 and 1918 readers reacted favorably to the poem; even yet some critics consider it blasphemous. Holders of such views should reread Eliot's discussion of blasphemy and humor in *After Strange Gods* (55–57). Eliot, many years later, is reported to have told a friend:

I first read *The Hippopotamus* at a Red Cross affair. Sir Edmund Gosse was in the chair—and *he* was shocked! . . . Arnold Bennett enjoyed it, and whenever we met always asked me when I was going to write another *Hippopotamus*! It is the only poem of mine that I know Joyce read: in Paris he told me, "I have been to the Jardin des Plantes (the Paris zoo) and paid my respects to your hippopotamus!" . . . Since that was written I have come to serve as a church warden and know the struggle to get money in when it is needed. If one lives long enough, one learns![1]

Mr. Eliot's Sunday Morning Service

Mr. Eliot's Sunday Morning Service is the other poem of all his pre-*Waste Land* poetry most explicitly focusing on the church. Here the tone is much less biting than in *The Hippopotamus*, but the technique is considerably more complex. The poem is also very funny, most of its humor resulting from its diction.

The poem cannot be appreciated in all its hilarious ambiguities without some checking of the multiple definitions of the various words used, since a number of them have both theological and botanical meanings that are relevant, in addition to their common meanings. Thus ambiguities, puns, and simultaneous meanings accumulate in this poem as (to a lesser degree) in *The Hippopotamus*. In a service like that seen in *Mr. Eliot's Sunday Morning Service*, even the words have lost their vitality and multiplicity of application. No longer the Logos or the Word, they are like the droning of bees heard at a distance.

In 1922, Eliot was to write, "Whatever words a writer employs, he benefits by knowing as much as possible of the history of those words. . . . The essential of tradition is this: in getting as much as possible of the whole weight of the history of the language behind his word."[2] As if in exemplification of his theory, he begins this poem with the twenty-letter jawbreaker "polyphiloprogenitive." To the dictionary term "philoprogenitive," meaning "prolific" or "loving offspring, especially one's own," Eliot added the prefix "poly-," meaning either "much, many, more than one" (as in polychromatic, polyandry); "more than usual, excessive," (polyphagia); or "in or of many kinds or parts" (polymorphous).[3]

Anselm Atkins points out in his excellent brief article "Mr. Eliot's Sunday Morning Parody" that this poem's structure and content are based on the Prologue of John's Gospel.[4] More precisely relevant is Origen's thirty-two-book commentary on John's Gospel. St. Jerome regarded Origen as the greatest teacher of the early church after the apostles; and Professor Henry Chadwick, writing for the *Encyclopaedia Britannica*, says that "the most striking literary feature of [John's] Gospel (and one of the reasons for its perennial fascination and intense power) is the artless form veiling a content of extraordinary subtlety. John loves words with many levels of meaning (cf., for example, 'lifted up,' 3:14; 12:32). The symbolism is especially attached to Jewish liturgical feasts. . . ." He adds that Origen preserved fragments of Heracleon's exposition of John's Gospel, "freely exploiting the evangelist's symbolism so that the work becomes an esoteric allegory."[5] The words of *Mr. Eliot's Sunday Morning Service* parody the Graeco-Latinate, polysyllabic diction of Origen and other theologians, thereby illustrating how those entrusted with the Word or Logos can, through disputatiousness and excessive verbiage, pervert their mission of producing more spiritual children. Philosophically, this process is described in the poem's second quatrain as "superfetation of το εν," *to en* being the Greek term for essential being, and "superfetation" the fertilization of an ovum during a pregnancy already in existence.

Origen's *Hexapla* is a clear example of superfetation of *to en*, since it set the Old Testament in six parallel columns (the Hebrew text and five Greek translations).[6]

The first words of John are repeated again in the second quatrain: "In the beginning was the Word./Superfetation of το εν,/ And at the mensual turn of time/Produced enervate Origen."

The phrase "the mensual turn of time" seems to imply that, like the poem itself, the process of superfetation is *mensurable*, having fixed rhythm and measure. But such overproduction, whether merely verbal, as here, or doctrinal, does "enervate"—"deprive of nerve, force, vigor, etc.; weaken physically, mentally, or morally; devitalize, debilitate." Origen was said by Eusebius to have castrated himself "so as to work freely in instructing female catechumens,"[7] and he was accused of various heresies. It is far from these words to the Word, the Logos, to *to en*, or to Christ and the other members of the Divine Trinity with which John was concerned. Despite his being a contemporary of Saint Paul, it is equally far from Origen to the Godhead and even farther from Origen's meanings to what the presbyters of this poem and the pustular penitents of the fifth quatrain now make of Origen's words—if they are even aware of them. And the worker bees, though infinitely removed from the Divinity, are some light years nearer to performing their proper fertilizing function, it is suggested, than the functionaries in some Sunday-morning services.

Eliot's next two stanzas introduce a painting of John baptizing Jesus, as described in John 1:29–34:

> A painter of the Umbrian School
> Designed upon a gesso ground
> The nimbus of the Baptized God,
> The wilderness is cracked and browned
>
> But through the water pale and thin
> Still shine the unoffending feet
> And there above the painter set
> The Father and the Paraclete.

The Paraclete is of course the Holy Spirit, usually seen, as in John, in the form of a dove. Critics disagree on the poet's attitude toward the Umbrian painting, but there can be no mistaking his positive attitude toward its subject, the unoffending feet of Christ being the dominant detail in the representation of John's baptism of him.

In contrast to the shining feet of Jesus, the next quatrain shows us the dark or sable functionaries of a church service: "The sable presbyters approach/ The avenue of penitence;/The young are red and pustular/Clutching piaculative pence." We are back into the "superfetated" diction that pervades all of the quatrains except the third, fourth, and sixth. "Piaculative" is not listed in Webster's Second Unabridged, but "piacular" is fruitfully ambiguous, meaning either "expiatory," *or* "sinful and requiring expiation." "Pustular" means simply "blistered and pimpled." It is perhaps significant that Origen was first ordained and then deposed as a presbyter.

The next quatrain, the sixth, is the most difficult to place, on the literal level: "Under the penitential gates/Sustained by staring Seraphim/Where the souls of the devout/Burn invisible and dim." Grammatically and syntactically this is puzzling. The period closing the previous stanza frustrates any attempt to look back for an independent clause to sustain the syntax, and even if the period at the end of the present stanza did not, the break in sense would frustrate any attempt to look forward to complete the sentence. Three interpretations seem to me equally possible, and probably all three are intended as simultaneous alternatives echoing the tensions of the entire poem. The word seraphim is derived from the Hebrew root *saraph*, to burn; it is associated with fervor of love, conventionally symbolized in the use of the color red to represent seraphim.[8] The "penitential gates sustained by staring Seraphim" may be an architectural feature of the literal church building envisioned, and perhaps, as Professor Grover Smith suggests, it is the souls of the presbyters that burn invisible and dim "like weak ghosts."[9] But the phrase "invisible and dim," as Mr. Smith himself points out, is borrowed from Henry Vaughan's poem *The Night*, based on the Nicodemus story in John 3:2-21, and in that poem the significance is quite different and positive: "There is in God—some say—/A deep but dazzling darkness.../.../Oh for that night, where I in Him/Might live invisible and dim!"[10] Possibly the souls of the devout are pictured or carved on or beside the penitential gates; perhaps, even, the pustular young penitents' souls burn invisible and dim, at least partly positive through their penitence.

We seem in the final two quatrains to have escaped the literal and degenerate ritual: "Along the garden-wall the bees/With hairy bellies pass between/The staminate and pistilate,/Blest office of the epicene." "Epicene" means neuter or the same for male and female. "Stamens" are male, "pistils" female. The bees, the painter, the Gospel of John, Origen's Commentary on it, the presbyters, and this poem are all engaged in the work of pollination, passing between what Mr. Smith calls "the stamen of the Logos and the pistil of humanity."[11] And indeed, that same service is the sacrament served us by Mr. Eliot in this poem.

We have been waiting for the Mr. Eliot of the title all through the poem, but it is Sweeney who appears: "Sweeney shifts from ham to ham/Stirring the water in his bath./The masters of the subtle schools/Are controversial, polymath." Probably Sweeney, in his bath instead of in church, looking at his feet through the water, has been reminded of the painting and the Gospel and of the divinity of the incarnate Word in which all creatures, all flesh (including the presbyters, the pustular penitents, and such a hippopotamus as himself) participate on the physical level and may participate, if devout, on the spiritual level as well.

The point of both *The Hippopotamus* and *Mr. Eliot's Sunday Morning Service*, as Audrey Cahill points out, is that the churchmen depicted are "'religious caterpillars' and 'sutlers,' following for what they can gain for themselves." Both poems are "reinterpretation[s] of Christ's own judgment on those who, like the Laodicean church, are neither cold nor hot"; they show the True Church "enjoying the spiritual and material comforts of its position without acknowledging that the sacramental principle of the Incarnation binds it to a hallowing of its life in every aspect." As a result, "human life is divided into two realms, the 'sacred' and the 'secular,' " and the church "fails to see the meeting point [as Sweeney does in his bath], or any possible connection, between the divine and the secular....

"There are many church-goers in Eliot's Waste Land, as there are many ecclesiastical dignitaries in Dante's Hell."[12]

Whispers of Immortality

Whispers of Immortality, another poem in quatrains, distills the essence of the appeal for Eliot of such writers as Webster and Donne, who "found no substitute for sense, to seize and clutch and penetrate." The poem implies that this thirst for experience, this "fever of the bone" which could not be allayed by any "contact possible to flesh," is what enabled these men to write so impressively. The second half of the poem presents the protagonist's speculations on Grishkin, who might be a close relative to Clavdia Chauchat in Thomas Mann's *The Magic Mountain*. Eliot's description of Grishkin—"Uncorseted, her friendly bust/Gives promise of pneumatic bliss"—plays ebulliently on the dual meanings of *pneumatic*. The first is taken from the Gnostics and from Origen (who was cited in *Mr. Eliot's Sunday Morning Service*): "Pneuma... the vital soul or the spirit;—variously interpreted as the animal soul mediating between the higher spiritual nature and the body, as the breath or life-giving principle, and as the spirit superior to both soul and body." The other and more common definition needs no elaboration in these days of inflatable plastics.

Grishkin's temptations are not only to earthly pleasure but also to a genuine grasp of experience; but the protagonist, more inclined to philosophy than to exploratory experience, will not seize and clutch and penetrate because "our lot crawls between dry ribs/To keep our metaphysics warm."

Poems in French

Le Directeur, one of four French poems presumably written in 1917, rejects not only the staid periodical *The Spectator* but also its director, smug in his reactionary conservatism. Short lines and repeated rhymes add ironic and laconic overtones to the picture.

In *Mélange Adultère de Tout* (1916–17)—a poem modeled on Corbière's *Épitaphe pour Tristan-Joachim-Edouard Corbière, Philosophe: Épave, Mort-Né*[13]—both the hollowness of accomplishments and the protagonist himself are cynically commented on.

In *Lune de Miel* (1916–17) the romantic European honeymoon tour outlined in Baedeker's guidebook is shown in the unsatisfactory light of an American couple only slightly aware at best of the glory that is (was?) Europe, but painfully aware of their expenses and the two hundred bedbugs sharing their accommodations at Ravenna. They ignore the nearby glories of the Cathedral of Saint Apollinaire. The *Ode* that was added to *Poems* (1919) in Eliot's 1920 volume *Ara Vos Prec* negatively evaluates a perhaps similar honeymoon.

Chapter Six

The King of Clubs: Sweeney Poems

Sweeney first appeared briefly and informally in 1918, as we have seen, in just two lines of *Mr. Eliot's Sunday Morning Service*: "Sweeney shifts from ham to ham/Stirring the water in his bath." Presumably even this vignette can be assimilated into their theologies by "The masters of the subtle schools/[who]Are controversial, polymath." The reader considers the three-way comparisons of the poem (of the devitalized presbyters, the life-propagating bees, and the shining, unoffending feet of Jesus in a conventionalized Umbrian bas-relief) and finds Sweeney's vigor and directness not wholly objectionable; the author does not completely reject Sweeney, any more than Yeats does his Crazy Jane. Usually when Sweeney appears, some degree of criticism against those who consider themselves greatly superior to him hovers in the background behind the sometimes gross figure that he cuts. So Sweeney in this poem takes on a slightly enigmatic character, but even so he contrasts both positively and negatively with such timid aesthetes as Prufrock who appear in the early poems.

Sweeney Erect

He is more clearly characterized in *Sweeney Erect* (1919), but the reader is allowed less sympathy with him. This poem is focused on desertions classical and otherwise, the latest and most "otherwise" being the one that Sweeney is about to commit. It is set in the distorted world of Mrs. Turner's "house." Presumably this is another version of the establishment of Mrs. Porter seen in *The Waste Land* and in *Sweeney Agonistes*. Doris appears in all three works, and the epileptic on the bed in *Sweeney Erect* may well be her friend Dusty.

In this world the classical stature and vitality of Homer's Odysseus, Nausicaa, and Polyphemus are weakly echoed by the "I" of the poem and by the apelike Sweeney and the epileptic who, for him, represents "the female temperament." Potential social tragedy is almost lost for lack of a proper audience, though the commenting persona suggests by calling them Nausicaa and Polyphemus that he rejects and will leave these people and this situation. He is presumably another Dantean watcher of the fruits of not only lust but also the ennui that Eliot, like Baudelaire, Laforgue, and the Elizabethan dramatists, observes, depicting residents of an inferno that he has passed through. Still, the reader missing the Dantean meaning may be misled by the fact that apparently, like Joyce's Stephen Dedalus, Odysseus is appearing in this company, even if he *can* transmute Beaumont and Fletcher and quote Emerson's definition of history as "the lengthened shadow of a man" to Sweeney's disadvantage. Such a reader should remind himself that Odysseus does not really appear here, that the observer may rather be a Homer figure. Even if Eliot's uses of Odysseus in *Prufrock* and *The Waste Land* and Joyce's in his works are taken to suggest that this protagonist is to be identified with him, we recall that Odysseus' values contrasted sharply with those of Polyphemus, just as Nausicaa's immature desire for him as husband contrasted with his experienced intentions.

Sweeney Among the Nightingales

Similar contrasts between the classical heroic and the hushed and shrunken scene of Sweeney in a bawdyhouse are found in *Sweeney Among the Nightingales* (1918). Mysterious identities, threats of violence, and whispers of intrigue create an oppressive, foreboding atmosphere. The setting reminds us of the "Circe" chapter of James Joyce's *Ulysses*. In fact, quite a few details of that book and of the "Nighttown" section of Joyce's *Portrait of the Artist as a Young Man* seem relevant to Sweeney in his various poems, which were written at a time when Pound and Eliot were championing Joyce and specifically *Ulysses* in the desperate struggle for publication in the face of moral indignation among almost all English-language publishers.

In *Sweeney Among the Nightingales* the reader is again allowed an ambivalent sympathy with Sweeney; in *Mr. Eliot's Sunday Morning Service* Sweeney compared favorably to "enervate Origen" for reasons involved in the present poem's setting, and now he compares favorably to Rachel of the murderous paws and to the other indistinct, threatening characters, four or possibly five of them, who lurk on the edges of our field of clear vision.

The chief classical symbols are those of stagnation, death (moral and physical), and sexual violation. These classical symbols merge and fuse into modern symbols.

> The circles of the stormy moon
> Slide westward toward the River Plate,
> Death and the Raven drift above
> And Sweeney guards the hornèd gate.

The horn and ivory gates comprise one of the many echoes from Virgil's *Aeneid* in these early poems. They are the two gates from which dreams issue to the world, true dreams from the gate of horn and false dreams from the gate of ivory. Just as the dreams issuing from the gate of horn are true, Death and the Raven are true symbols for the moral setting of this poem.

The foreboding of the line "Gloomy Orion and the Dog/Are veiled" indicates Sweeney's fear of some vague threat. He is there, having been tempted, having come for something, but is also frightened. He fears collusion among the vague, indistinct figures hovering on the edges of the picture, and feels that they may harm him or even perhaps kill him. The half-line "and hushed the shrunken seas" suggests the unheroic stature of this situation,

the wasteland moral terrain in which he finds himself. This terrain
seems to be a moral vacuum, but

> The nightingales are singing near
> The Convent of the Sacred Heart,
>
> And sang within the bloody wood
> When Agamemnon cried aloud
> And let their liquid siftings fall
> To stain the stiff dishonoured shroud.

The nightingales are presumably the prostitutes whose utterances
can hardly be dignified by the name of song, so that the same
sort of irony is involved in their singing as in Prufrock's "love
song." Agamemnon's cry, one of the most famous lines in Greek
drama, is from Aeschylus' play *Agamemnon*.[1] The dying cries of
Agamemnon when Clytemnestra struck him place Sweeney's situation against a genuinely tragic background. In that context we
see that Sweeney really may be murdered for his lusts, in spite of
his caution. Couple that with the Dantean and Christian doctrine
of the real worth of any individual's soul, and this flat situation
takes on tragic dimensions—and this situation is flat, not because
it is set in the twentieth century rather than the fourteenth B.C., but
because it is a moral wasteland; it can be found in every century and
in every place, and the clear intent of the poem is to make the
reader aware that in every place and time such wastelands must
be escaped if human life is to assume its proper dignity.

Sweeney represents a general axiom: Deal in acts like these,
associate with those who do, frequent this sort of setting, and you,
too, *lecteur*, will suffer the risk of violent and bloody passions. The
resultant purgation of pity and fear is further pursued in Eliot's
unfinished first venture into overt drama (or rather Aristophanic
melodrama), the projected play "Wanna Go Home, Baby?"—of
which only the two fragments entitled *Sweeney Agonistes* (1926)
and a synopsis and title page were written (see below).

F. O. Matthiessen sums up Sweeney's significance when he says that "the double feeling of [Eliot's] repulsion from vulgarity, and yet his shy attraction to the coarse earthiness of common life have found their complete symbol in Sweeney."[2]

Sweeney Agonistes

Although it breaks chronology, it seems advisable to go on to discuss *Sweeney Agonistes*, Eliot's first fragmentary published drama, while the Sweeney poems are fresh in the reader's mind. The importance of that unfinished play to Eliot's future development as a dramatist deserves great emphasis. We may recall that all of the Sweeney poems were highly dramatic, many a line reading like a stage direction, soliloquy, aside, or less often, one side of a dialogue in a play.

Eliot's first prose volume, *The Sacred Wood* (1920), had included an essay on the possibility of poetic drama and another entitled "Rhetoric and Poetic Drama." And any reader of the *Criterion* from 1922 onward could not fail to note Eliot's continued editorial interest in and emphasis on theater and dance as well as dramatic literature. He had also written about various English dramatists, Elizabethan and other, and about Seneca and Euripides, among classical playwrights. The dramatic nature of Eilot's poetry had long testified to such interests, and hardly anyone could be surprised when in 1926 there appeared *Fragment of a Prologue*, followed in 1927 by *Fragment of an Agon*, labeled then as from "Wanna Go Home, Baby?" In 1928 he wrote "A Dialogue on Poetic Drama"—later reprinted as "A Dialogue on Dramatic Poetry"—in which seven alphabetically designated speakers advanced various viewpoints related to the possibility of poetic drama.[3] In 1932, the two fragments were entitled *Sweeney Agonistes: Fragments of an Aristophanic Melodrama*.

Though it shows the wasteland picture of Sweeney's world among the nightingales, this first overt attempt at drama was written during the same period that produced the highly Christian poem *Ash-Wednesday*. As one of the participants in Eliot's "Dialogue on Dramatic Poetry" says of Restoration drama, so criticized for its por-

trayal of debauchery, "It assumes orthodox Christian morality. . . .
It retains its respect for the divine by showing the failure of the
human."[4]

Eliot's enthusiasm for the music-hall form of dramatic entertainment is well documented. That enthusiasm profoundly affected
the form of *Sweeney Agonistes*, which was interspersed with songs,
jazz rhythms, and abrupt transitions.

Eliot's 1923 article "The Beating of a Drum" had cited Aristotle's identification of poetry, music, and dancing—rhythm—with
drama.[5] Eliot there lamented the utter absence of rhythm from
modern drama (even verse drama) and its suppression in modern
performances of Shakespeare. He stressed that the catharsis or
purgation of drama is a ritual effect depending on rhythms, that
Charlie Chaplin, Leonid Massine, the juggler Rastelli, or the Mum-
mers' Play of St. George and the Dragon could be more cathartic
than a modern play such as *A Doll's House* because they used such
rhythms in a way that satisfied universal needs ignored by the
modern theater.

The important function of controlling rhythms in the circus,
the music hall, the minstrel show, and the burlesque theater was in
the capable hands of the jazz drummer, without whose rhythms
the bumps and grinds of burlesque, like its comic patter, would
have been merely gross and ludicrous. The drummer was crucial
to the life of all those forms; he set the pace of each act, built up
and released tensions and tempos at the proper points, and both
controlled and responded to the moods of the audience, pacing or
following the actors and making powerfully affective much that
would otherwise have been inane and unsuccessful.

A *Sweeney Agonistes* stage direction reads "Song by Wauchope
and Horsfall: Swarts as Tambo. Snow as Bones." Here is a music-
hall turn backed up by the traditional minstrel-show jazz drum-
mes, Tambo and Bones: Eliot was returning to the basic rhythms
of Greek Aristophanic comedy, as had Apollinaire's *Les mamelles
de Tirésias* in Paris in 1917.

"The Beating of a Drum" also emphasized the importance for
Eliot of Francis M. Cornford's *The Origin of Attic Comedy,* a book

used very importantly in all of his plays, including *Sweeney Ago-nistes*. Sweeney is, in fact, an Aristophanic *eiron* or ironical buffoon, *feigning* ignorance and self-deprecation, of the sort discussed by Cornford (as are also, later, the guardians in *The Cocktail Party*). According to Herbert Howarth, by the time of this first frag-mentary drama, Eliot had diligently over a period of some half-dozen years acquired

a list of requisites for a new poetic drama. He must entertain, and entertain with a crime story. He must involve the audience. His words must move the nerves like music and dance: pulse like a drum; use the repeated figures of the dance. They must be authentically speakable, as [Ford Madox] Ford had, long ago and more recently, insisted; but the speech must be managed with a deftness no contemporary poet had shown. He must convert to his purpose the song forms that cap-tivate English audiences. He must write comedy, and the more rather than the less because he intended a tragic reading of the world. [Richard] Aldington had prescribed an "Aristophanic levity" to render the crimes of 1919. [Laurent] Tailhade had caricatured the generation of 1900 in *Poèmes aristophanesques*. Though he aimed at tragedy, Eliot must work like Aristophanes.[6]

The publication in 1965 of Eliot's draft synopsis and typed title-page of "Homage to Aristophanes...Fragment of a Melo-comic Minstrelsy" was the key needed to arrive finally at confident conclusions regarding *Sweeney Agonistes*. That title-page clearly indicates the relevance of both the popular music-hall format and Aristophanic comedy, and the synopsis provides the link to Corn-ford's *The Origin of Attic Comedy* that makes possible the confi-dent identification of Aristophanes' *The Birds* and *Lysistrata* as Eliot's models for his fragments.[7]

The synopsis also introduces Mrs. Porter, of *Waste Land* fame, whose entrance is signaled by the nine knocks at the end of Eliot's agon fragment. Her murder after a debate with Sweeney precedes a succession of comic intruders or *Alazons*, Sweeney's scrambling eggs and distributing them, and Mrs. Porter's startling resurrection and reappearance. So the coffin in the card-reading scene and the other evocations of death relate to Mrs. Porter.

By October 1924 Eliot had completed and shown to Arnold Bennett sample pages and a scenario for the play.[8] No doubt the Aristophanic spirit of W. S. Gilbert had its influence on Eliot, as did the Aristophanic French theater of Apollinaire and of Jarry's *Ubu Roi*.

From 1917 on, Eliot used Sweeney frequently to express with sardonic, often ironic vigor a potent commentary on everyday life and ordinary men. It was natural, then, to use Sweeney as the central character when writing an Aristophanic play. And of course it was from Aristophanes, not Cornford, that he understood himself to be borrowing; Cornford simply offered ready-made some tools of analysis easily convertible to tools of composition. The sexual emphasis of *Lysistrata* and the theatricality of *The Birds* provided models, Sweeney having appeared among the nightingales in all but one of his previous outings. Reading Cornford's book, Eliot envisioned Sweeney as an Aristophanic buffoon, adjusted his nightingales to Cornford's other stock-character types, and replaced the Greek chorus with jazz drummers Swarts and Snow from the music hall, which also accounts for the abrupt transitions and sharp stylistic shifts of Eliot's fragments.

The title *Sweeney Agonistes* links the whole Sweeney series to the accounts of Samson both in the book of Judges and in Milton's *Samson Agonistes*. Milton's portrayal of Delilah, the Philistine temptress, is echoed in Eliot's portrayal of Dusty and especially of Doris Dorrance. Samson, of course, was not only figuratively but also literally blind through lust, his plight being the direct penalty for succumbing to the beguilement of two Philistine women. Of that lust, Milton's Samson says after his blinding,

> O indignity, O blot
> To honour and religion! servile mind
> Rewarded well with servile punishment!
> The base degree to which I now am fallen,

These rags, this grinding, is not yet so base
As was my former servitude, ignoble,
Unmanly, ignominious, infamous,
True slavery; and that blindness worse than this,
That saw not how degenerately I served.

(ll. 411–19)

Milton has Samson's father, Manoa, remind him that he violated "the sacred trust of silence...which to have kept/Tacit was in thy power." This fits well with Dante's and with Eliot's doctrine of Free Will and Temptation, of man's responsibility to guard the threshold of assent, as seen in *Animula*. Milton also shows the Philistines as morally blind when they unknowingly invite their own doom by requiring Samson to appear at their feast to the god Dagon:

So fond are mortal men,
Fallen into wrath divine,
As their own ruin on themselves to invite,
Insensate left, or to sense reprobate,
And with blindness internal struck.

(ll. 1682–86)

Milton's Aristotelian intent to purge his audience of pity and fear is, in the final lines of *Samson Agonistes*, attributed to God:

His servants he, with new acquist
Of true experience from this great event,
With peace and consolation hath dismissed,
And calm of mind, all passion spent.

(ll. 1755–58)

Given the stylization of the music-hall format seen in the interspersed songs of Eliot's agon, we must say that his motivations, entrances, and themes are more organic than Milton's. The rapid and powerful jazz rhythms of Eliot's fragments heighten the sense of foreboding that builds up even in the brief prologue fragment, in which the cast is introduced and the cards are read.

If the setting of *Sweeny Among the Nightingales* had seemed vague to some readers, certainly none should have been left in doubt as to that of *Sweeney Agonistes*: callers at "Miss Dorrance's *flat*" whistle below the window and call for a nose count:

> Wauchope: Hello dear
>   How many's up there?
> Dusty: Nobody's up here
>   How many's down there?
> Wauchope: Four of us here.
>   Wait till I put the car round the corner
>   We'll be right up
> Dusty: All right, come up.

Only Pereira, who pays the rent, seems unwelcome here. The moral vacuity of the characters and a strong sense of foreboding emerge in the card-reading of Dusty and Doris which precedes the arrival of their friends, customers, guests, or whatever. Between the two fragments, Sweeney has come on the scene and is accepted by the others; but, unlike Sam Wauchope, he seems unable to be "at *home* in London." For Sweeney has seen that in their world, as on his imagined cannibal isle, there is "Nothing at all but three things/... Birth and copulation, and death./That's all the facts when you come to brass tacks:/Birth, and copulation, and death." Wauchope and Horsfall seem typical wasteland characters in their song:

> Tell me in what part of the wood
> Do you want to flirt with me?
> Under the breadfruit, banyan, palmleaf
> Or under the bamboo tree?
> Any old tree will do for me
> Any old wood is just as good
> Any old isle is just my style
> Any fresh egg
> Any fresh egg
> And the sound of the coral sea.

They are likely, of course, to get cooking eggs rather than any fresh egg; and Doris, for her part, says she doesn't like eggs and never has. When Sweeney introduces the idea that life and death are the same—that birth and death, as seen in *A Song for Simeon* and *The Journey of the Magi*, are hard to distinguish—Doris, who drew the coffin (the two of spades), exclaims, "Oh Mr. Sweeney, please dont talk/...I dont care for such conversation/A woman runs a terrible risk." Sweeney alone of the characters seems to have some idea of the nature of the terrain in which they appear; in answer to their wrong questions, he repeats, "...that dont apply/But I've gotta use words when I talk to you," and again, "But if you understand or if you dont/That's nothing to me and nothing to you...."

These fragments were enough to reveal a remarkable gift of speech and pacing, of incision and intensity in the writing of drama. Moreover, the compelling jazz rhythms, the moral bankruptcy of the setting and situation, and the personal *angst* of the characters involved are almost overwhelming.

It is clear today that *Sweeney Agonistes* would have been at home in New York and London theaters of the 1960s and 1970s—was forty years before its time: Pinter's and Ionesco's plays share much with it. Many critics have regretted that Eliot did not pursue that vein of dramatic writing. But in drama, as in poetry, Eliot did not repeat himself; each new play was to explore new territory and technique, and considering what he accomplished in poetic drama, it is hard to wish he had done otherwise.

Chapter Seven

Ara Vos Prec

"And so I pray you (*ara vos prec*)," the shade of the Provençal poet Arnaut Daniel implores Dante in *Purgatorio* 26. 145–47, "... be mindful in due time of my pain." Eliot used Arnaut's words as the title of the London edition of his 1920 volume of poems. (The New York edition was titled simply *Poems 1920* because the publishers thought buyers would be put off by the Provençal title.[1])

Ara Vos Prec contains six poems not found either in *Prufrock and Other Observations* or in *Poems* (1919): *A Cooking Egg; Dans le Restaurant; Sweeney Erect; Burbank with a Baedeker: Bleistein with a Cigar; Gerontion*; and *Ode. Sweeney Erect* was dealt with in chapter 6 above. *Gerontion*, though first in the 1920 volume, will be dealt with last in this chapter, because it forms a proper introduction to *The Waste Land*.

A Cooking Egg (c. 1919)

A "cooking egg" is one no longer fresh enough to eat alone, and Eliot's poem *A Cooking Egg* apparently equates the protagonist's marriage with such an egg. Such a marital stalemate will be further explored in the "Game of Chess" section of *The Waste Land*. In the present poem, the "I" laments his lack of Honour, Capital, Society, and Pipit (who sits upright at a distance). In Heaven, he says, he will not need these things, since he shall hobnob with Sir Philip Sidney, Coriolanus, Sir Alfred Mond, Lucretia Borgia, Madame Blavatsky, and Dante's Piccarda de Donati.

In his Candide-like naiveté, he had thought in marrying Pipit that he was buying a penny world (a childhood-favorite candy?) to eat behind the screen with her—compare Candide and Cunegonde's explorations in Voltaire's *Candide*—but life as he envisioned it has not unfolded. Like the multitudes in a hundred ABC-chain restaurants, he complains of the disillusion of his life some distance from Pipit. His penny world, the visioned security of happy marriage, is gone like Coriolanus' eagles and trumpets, "buried beneath some snow-deep Alps." He no longer hopes in this life for perfection, but he would like Pipit to move closer.

Dans le Restaurant (1917)

One might speculate that the restaurant in this French poem is an ABC-chain café such as was referred to in *A Cooking Egg*. Its characters are the protagonist-customer and a rather unsavory old waiter who hangs over his shoulder and tells him of a deeply impressive seven-year-old experience strongly reminiscent of the first meeting between Dante and Beatrice in *La Vita Nuova*. The customer is outraged to find that his own highest experiences are much like those of the blubbering and repulsive waiter and sends him away. Both this part of the poem and the final stanza on Phlebas the Phoenician (later translated in *The Waste Land*) suggest that such experiences are archetypal: parallels may be seen in the colonnade and the hyacinth-garden episodes in *The Waste Land*, for example, and possibly in *La Figlia che Piange*.

Burbank (c. 1919)

Venice is the setting of *Burbank with a Baedeker: Bleistein with a Cigar*. The idealist Burbank, the chief character, is a tourist with his Baedeker guidebook that suggests and identifies the glories of Venice—"the great bronze horses over the doors of St. Mark's" and "Tiepolo's great frescoes of Antony and Cleopatra in the Pallazio Labia."[2] Burbank knows his literature and aesthetics as well as his Baedeker, but in his attempts to mediate between the ideal and his own "fever of the bone" (*Whispers of Immortality*), he has met Princess Volupine at a small hotel where "They were together, and he fell." The Princess's name suggests both "voluptuous" and "supine," and may remind the post-1922 reader of the Thames-daughter of Richmond origin who appears in section 3 of *The Waste Land*; at any rate, Burbank's fall is less heroic than that of Adam. Now by the dim, flickering light of "the smoky candle end of time," little glory is apparent from the narrowed perspectives of the fallen Burbank as he watches the "Princess" prepare to entertain her next customer, Sir Ferdinand—Klein. This name echoes the various contrasts between the ideal and the immediate throughout the poem. It reminds us that Burbank is no Antony to the Princess's watered-down Cleopatra, no Othello to her mock Desdemona.

Burbank meditates on these contrasts, watches the "lustreless protrusive eye" of Bleistein stare blankly at the scene of Canaletto's painting, considers "the proud winged lion on its pillar by the water-front" and the frescoes. Striving for a noncommittal position somewhere between such extremes, he muses on "time's ruins and the seven laws," wondering "Who clipped the lion's wings/And flea'd his rump and pared his claws?"

Most of the allusions in the poem—and this poem borrows and alludes as heavily as will *The Waste Land* later—are to works related to Venice. A line from the epigraph, "Nothing endures unless divine; all else is smoke" reminds us, if such a jog were needed, that Burbank, as well as Bleistein, lacks the stuff that endurance is made of—or perhaps not; perhaps it is only the experience and vision that created and that appreciate the more-than-beauty of the monuments that endure, not The Stones of Venice themselves.

Ode (c. 1919)

Ode appears only in *Ara Vos Prec*. Heavily based on Catullus' epithalamion (marriage hymn) Ode 61, it links marital failure with artistic decline, and parallels *Lune de Miel*, *A Cooking Egg*, and the "Exequy" fragment from the *Waste Land* manuscripts.

Gerontion (1919)

We may infer from its initial position in the 1920 volume *Ara Vos Prec* that *Gerontion* was the poem then most esteemed by the author of the new works included there—and perhaps the most recent. Eliot's letters to Pound show that in 1922 he considered using it as a prelude to *The Waste Land*, and its relevance to the dryness of that later, more widely analyzed poem has been suggested often.

Though cultural history is one of the poem's topics and the nature and efficacy of Christianity another, *Gerontion* is chiefly a personal poem, and the clarity and unity of its structure are obscured by failing sufficiently to relate those broader themes to the immediate experience of the persona who is its protagonist. The title means "little old man," and St. Paul's "old man" or "Adam" is relevant to the emphasis on Gerontion's search for right relationships both with "Christ the tiger" and with other persons in the natural world. Here, as in *The Waste Land* and *The Hollow Men*, Eliot (as did his mother earlier) uses traditional and biblical imagery of the seasons, of a spiritual waste land, of dryness, and of "water—the 'celestial fountain' and 'the healing flood'—[which] promises relief after long ordeals."[3]

The epigraph ("Thou hast nor youth nor age/But as it were, an after dinner sleep/Dreaming of both"—from Shakespeare's *Measure for Measure* 3.1) in one sense parallels the justly admired "History has many cunning passages" section. It is spoken by the Duke (disguised as a friar and serving a friar's function) to Claudio, a young man in jail, condemned to death under an obsolete law for fathering a child out of wedlock. In context, it does not address Claudio's age or his offense, but is rather a reminder that life passes us by—that we do not properly experience either youth or age because our attention is on the wrong things.

In form, the poem approximates a letter, as is suggested by the lines from Edward Fitzgerald's letters on which the beginning of *Gerontion* is based, by the *Ash-Wednesday* parallels, and by the documents of Sigismundo Malatesta (pondered on in Ezra Pound's *Malatesta Cantos*), who fought "knee deep in the salt marsh." The letter is addressed to a "you" who is asked to think of various things and to whom Gerontion says "I would meet you upon this honestly," explaining why "I that was near your heart was removed therefrom."

Like the later *Ash-Wednesday, Gerontion* is probably influenced by the *ballata* form of Cavalcante and Dante and their school, being a missive to the speaker's absent Lady. A likely referent, insofar as this poem may be autobiographical, is Vivien Eliot, the poet's first wife—taking the *Ash-Wednesday* parallels and its dedication to her as presumptive evidence.

In the first stanza the speaker calls himself "an old man in a dry month,/Being read to by a boy" (a near-quotation from Fitzgerald's letters). He is waiting for the rain that is so urgently desired in *The Waste Land.* He disowns any impressive history, having neither been "at the hot gates/Nor fought in the warm rain" nor has he "knee deep in the salt marsh, heaving a cutlass,/Bitten by flies, fought." These allusions are to the history of Sigismundo, as reflected in Pound's cantos. (Eliot's *Criterion* published an article on Pound's sources several years after *Gerontion* was written.[4]) On another level of meaning, since "hot gates" translates "Thermopylae," Gerontion has neither made a Thermopylae-like stand against his appetites nor had them fulfilled in the proper course of an adult love. The decayed-house metaphor which follows echoes the twelfth chapter of Ecclesiastes (a passage cited by Eliot in his notes to *The Waste Land*), in which a house is similarly used to represent the body and the senses.

As Mervyn W. Williamson suggests, "The elements which make up Western civilization are found in his [Gerontion's] being. For instance, Eliot has often insisted that Western civilization is essentially Christian and that one of its defects in our time is its loss of awareness of its religious roots."[5] Ezra Pound, in *Hugh Selwyn Mauberley*, called post-World War I Western culture "an old bitch gone in the teeth . . . a botched civilization."

Gerontion, of Greco-Roman, Judeo-Christian origin, lives in the decayed house of "the jew," who is descended (fallen, rather) from Abraham and from Christ (The Jew). Similarly, Mr. Silvero and the rest (including Gerontion) have fallen from the vitality of Heraclitus' *logos* passage on which the opening of John's gospel was based: "In the beginning was the Word." Mr. Williamson writes:

Like the "wandering jew" on the windowsill (obviously the well-known plant is suggested), the Jew is a wanderer in the modern world; his activity has been most closely connected with commercial centers such as Antwerp, Brussels, and London. Thus the term "jew" here is ambiguous, signifying both the ancient Hebrew culture from which Christianity sprang but which is now decadent, and the commercialism of the West which was "spawned" among the Renaissance Jewish merchants. . . . Both Jew and Christian have fallen from their former glory. . . . When the springs of religion have become exhausted, love becomes lust and finally lust loses its potency; the "woman," no longer a mistress, becomes a mere housekeeper. . . . Like Madame Sosostris in *The Waste Land,* she has a cold. . . . [As in *The Waste Land* and *The Hollow Men*], symbols of a fertile past have lost their potency and the inhabitants have become sterile.[6]

The Jew, the owner, may also represent four other things: first, if one insists on a literal level, the owner of the actual house that Gerontion rents in London; second, Christ (or God), the owner of both the body for which "house" is a metaphor and the soul that inhabits it, however unresponsive to God's claims Gerontion may at times have been; third, the Jewish international bankers who, Eliot evidently believed, participated heavily in the collapse of civilized Europe through World War I; and finally, that part of Gerontion influenced by Judeo-Christian values. I take it that all of these are demonstrably important and intertwined in this poem. James Joyce's treatment of Leopold Bloom in the "Cyclops" chapter of *Ulysses* similarly combines and emphasizes such themes and was probably familiar to Eliot at the time of writing *Gerontion.*[7]

The "old man ... being read to by a boy," like the epigraph, throws light on the apparent great disparity between Gerontion's age and that of the poet. Like the poet, Gerontion is really *nel mezzo del cammin di nostra vita* ("In the middle of the road of our life"—the opening line of Dante's *Divine Comedy*). Both the *old man* and the *boy* are aspects of Gerontion, metaphors in a psychological self-portrait. Though having neither youth nor age, he is an old man in the sense that he has lost his passion; he is being read to by a boy in the sense that his memories of all that passion persist, still tenant his house. M. L. Rosenthal writes that "[Gerontion] is an allegorical figure who represents the shrunken state of Western religious tradition and the morbid preoccupation of modern man with his own degradation. . . . Art, love, and religion seem to him debilitated and perverted by a selfish secularism."[8]

In lines 17–20, the theme of Christ is introduced in the "Word" or "*Logos*" passage that Eliot has used frequently (as, for example, in *Mr. Eliot's Sunday Morning Service* and *Ash-Wednesday*); and we are reminded of the beginning of Gerontion's life, as of the creation and, especially in this context, the birth of Christ. Eliot was consciously referring to a sermon of Lancelot Andrewes which speaks of "verbum infans," the word within a word, unable to speak a word—a passage cited by Eliot in his essay "For Lancelot Andrewes."

In the line " 'We would see a sign,' " we are reminded of Matthew 16 and John 6, in which Christ is asked for a sign that he is the son of God. In Matthew 16:4, he replies "A wicked and adulterous generation seeketh after a sign; and there shall no sign be given unto it, but the sign of the prophet Jonas." This could refer to the sign of the storm or of the fish, sent to Jonah, or the sign of Jonah's preaching, sent to the people of Nineveh; or of the gourd that God used to teach Jonah of the wrongness of his anger that Nineveh had been saved. It could also be the sign of the whole story, developing its themes of obedience to God's commands and acceptance of his will. In John, Christ replies that he is the sign. And in *Gerontion* again Christ is the sign, "The word within a word, unable to speak a word." And many other signs, Gerontion implies, are all about us; but wonders are desired, not signs. Yet Christ *is* a wonder, though rejected and unrecognized. So both in the individual life of Gerontion and in the life of Western culture, past and present, the sign is unrecognized and the nativity is followed by depraved May, the season of crucifixion; and the sacraments are perverted and parodied. "The Winter of the Nativity," writes Mervyn Williamson, "has become the Spring of the Crucifixion and Resurrection [as in *The Waste Land*], which is also the time celebrated in the Holy Communion."[9]

In Gerontion's experience the nearest things to the mysterious communion that could result from the proper acceptance of the divine in man, symbolized in Christianity and in all major religions by incarnation, are the overtures made "by Mr. Silvero/With caressing hands.../By Hakagawa, bowing among the Titians" (works of a painter who *did* understand); by Madame de Tornquist, who shifted the candles, having the scene arrange itself, as in *Portrait of a Lady*; and by Fraulein von Kulp, who turned and looked invitingly as she was about to enter her room.

The next section of *Gerontion*—perhaps justly the most widely admired lines in the poem—discusses the ways in which, like each of us, Gerontion has in his youth aspired toward a proper, fulfilling love, one which ideally would include both physical and spiritual love between a man and a woman. But his quest for such a love has had many cunning passages and contrived corridors and issues. History has deceived him with whispering ambitions and guided him by vanities. Perhaps his ambitions to educate and establish himself, to make a career in the world, have kept him from accepting the responsibilities of a love relationship, from giving of himself. Like Prufrock, he has been guided by concerns over what others might think, over his reputation and possible damage to his career; these have kept him from responding properly to the leads that might have produced such a love. History gave him, shall we say, *La Figlia che Piange* when his attention was distracted by the need to free himself from the limits of his youth and to breathe the artistic atmosphere of Europe, as in Henry James's story "The Jolly Corner." And history gave with such supple confusions through Mr. Silvero (clearly the wrong person), Madame de Tornquist (like the older woman of *Portrait of a Lady*, almost surely the wrong person), and Fraulein von Kulp, who turned in the hall invitingly, one hand on the door (in the wrong time and place, for the wrong reasons, when he had other concerns, scruples, or inhibitions).

We have F. O. Matthiessen's report of Eliot's saying in conversation that "the images here are 'consciously concrete'; they correspond as closely as possible to something he has actually seen and remembered."[10] Perhaps those cunning corridors and contrived passages were rather in his relations to the person addressed, the Lady, with the supple confusions arising out of his reactions to those other characters.

Now, with this Lady, history has given "too late/What's not believed in, or, if still believed,/In memory only, reconsidered passion." As a result, their love has not flowered as it seemed to promise. Their relationship has not matured and ripened, and he has lost beauty in terror, terror in inquisition, and consequently has lost his passion. But why should he need to keep it, since it has not led to the promised fulfillment, has not produced their closer contact?

Having seen the emptiness of all the substitute solutions, Gerontion meditates on and assesses his past and present quite intimately, and might be suspected of wanting to make an exhibition of himself. But he assures the addressee that "I have not made this show purposelessly/And it is not by any concitation [stirring up or excitation]/Of the backward devils" (presumably as in Conrad's *Heart of Darkness*). He meditates on his own history, the most important element of which is the quest of a proper love on a sexual-religious plane.

In the spring of his life, "the juvescence of the year," sprang "Christ the tiger." The Christian symbols for the Primal Love toward which Gerontion's *amor* might properly have been directed were not in his youth clearly perceived or experienced. His token participation in the devitalized and misunderstood sacraments of his "Christian" culture and in his Dantean-love model was shared with equally or more mis-oriented associates, and so he rejected both the divinity behind the rituals and the divinity in others which might have left him with some ghosts, holy or otherwise. Now much time has passed, as have many of the "supple confusions" of history which make of experiences often the opposite of our intentions and expectations, leaving us sadder but wiser. His hope of an earthly Beatrice is surrendered.

In the light of such knowledge comes a new Spring. Gerontion has accepted his place in life, his limits. Such a sign of Primal Love as Christ can be recognized and the lesser loves, the attachments to the appetites, are surrendered—devoured, perhaps, in fashion similar to the devouring of the leopards in the later *Ash-Wednesday*. Gerontion, then, in his draughty house, deliberates on the nature of his loves, higher and lower; and he explains to the person addressed the significance of their altered relationship. Eliot's purposes in this poem are to help that person understand Gerontion's reasons for turning away, to accept what *is*, and to help other readers understand not just Gerontion's plight and actions, his "desertion," but also the possibilities open to any person who sees the falseness of the *parodied* vitality, who can recognize and accept the signs as wonders without first wasting most of a lifetime tramping empty corridors. Gerontion is reconciled now to his place in the universal cycles, approaching the end of life and the dissolution or, he hopes, the transformation of death.

Like millions of others before him, like De Bailhache, Fresca, and Mrs. Cammel, he will be "whirled/Beyond the circuit of the shuddering Bear/In fractured atoms," but this is the universal fate, the proper pattern, and is common both to those who fight at the warm gates ("Gull against the wind, in the windy straits") and to "an old man driven by the Trades/To a sleepy corner"; and what is necessary now is to make the most of what remains. It is a small but difficult step—as *The Waste Land*, *The Hollow Men*, and *Ash-Wednesday* will demonstrate—from the avoidance of Beatrice's eyes in *The Hollow Men* ("Let me be no nearer") to the "Suffer me not to be separated" of *Ash-Wednesday*. The step needs continually to be reaffirmed, and Gerontion's prognosis is less confidently positive than that of the *Ash-Wednesday* speaker—but perhaps not. So the profit of what is past is protracted and shared through "These with a thousand small deliberations." Awareness of all this will not alter the universe: the spider and the weevil will continue their spinning and destruction. But the calm acceptance will be better than the vain pursuit of illusions, and Gerontion has surrendered his romanticism, seeing now the divinity in himself and in all humanity. Like Socrates or Lucretius, he waits for the death wind without fear and loathing; in Platonic or Christian terms, he hopes for a higher life after death, which he will regard as liberation from the dry brain and the decayed house, the life of the undistracted spirit rather than of the small deliberations.

No other Eliot poems were published before *The Waste Land* (1922) except *Song to the Opherion*, a *Waste Land* fragment now readily available in the *Waste Land Facsimile* volume as "Song" (with "for the Opherion" canceled) and briefly touched on in the next two chapters.

Chapter Eight

Different Voices: "Why Then Ile Fit You"

The Waste Land, the most influential and, at first, the most controversial poem of the twentieth century to date, was also for forty-some years the great literary mystery of its age.

Had the poem been published in the much longer version that was "lost" from the 1920s to its "discovery" in the 1960s, the meanings of the poem would not have been argued in so many hundreds of pages of criticism. Neither, probably, would it have become the critical and scholarly *cause célèbre* that, as James Joyce said, "ended the idea of poetry for ladies."[1]

Reworked to about half the original length by Eliot, with much help from Ezra Pound and some from Vivien, the version published in 1922 gained in poetic intensity but was much more cryptic and debatable (though it was possible, as the previous edition of this study shows, to arrive at essentially the same understandings of its meanings as are now much more demonstrably the author's intent).[2]

The poem as first published (hereafter called the 1922 version) must, since the 1968 "discovery," be considered against the backdrop of those long-lost drafts superbly edited and annotated by Valerie Eliot in 1971: *T. S. Eliot, The Waste Land: A Facsimile and Transcript of the Original Drafts, Including the Annotations of Ezra Pound* (hereafter called the *Facsimile* version).[3] This *Facsimile* version includes more than twenty passages (some of them complete sections) varying from a single line to passages of fifty-four, seventy, and eighty-three lines not found in the 1922 version. A brief

82

section-by-section consideration based on that 1922 version will follow some necessary general comments.

Eliot considered using *Gerontion* as prologue to *The Waste Land*, and that poem too is autobiographical. Gerontion, as we have seen him above, would make a not-at-all-inappropriate speaker for *The Waste Land*; he has known its themes and has hinted at the cultural and aesthetic awarenesses basic to its method. The Elizabethan dramatists who strongly influenced the verse-forms in *Gerontion* will appear in both the content and verse strategies of *The Waste Land*.

Though much of the technique of the poem had been seen in embryo as early as *Prufrock* and in more developed and involved form in *Burbank with a Baedeker, Mr. Eliot's Sunday Morning Service*, and *Sweeney Among the Nightingales*, the reader could in each of those poems follow a developing narrative of a sort. *The Waste Land*, however, like *Gerontion*, is a meditation by a speaker whose nature must be intuited from the materials, tone, and perspectives of the poem. The conscious links—the overt connections between the various voices making up the poem—are omitted and must be supplied by the reader via the inferences he can draw, which gradually make him aware of the precise center from which the poem is spoken. As in *Gerontion*, the basis of its technique and progression lies in a highly individualized consciousness.

The necessity to transcend one's self is a basic theme of the poem. Further, social responsibility is at the very core of the mythic and traditional elements combined in it. (Eliot's social consciousness is widely documented in such essays as *The Idea of a Christian Society* and in a number of his critical writings such as the 1917 "Tradition and the Individual Talent.")

The poem is essentially dramatic, and its appreciation depends on what Francis Fergusson calls "the histrionic sensibility."[4] Both the stage and the cast of the poem exist in the speaker's mind. It is true that we need sometimes to recognize the personages through whose voices he speaks, but always we need to recognize as well the tone and emphasis of his own voice speaking through them.

The Waste Land is addressed to twentieth-century readers. At times the protagonist directly addresses them; at other times he recalls from his own past or from his experience of literature, the other arts, and history, much as Gerontion did, elements which focus on or are analogous to events in his own psychic history. His memories, comments, and meditations are presented to the reader with varying degrees of directness; and these shifting modes of address seem to me to reproduce accurately the varieties of awareness normal to human experience.

The basic structural device of the poem is hinted in Eliot's original title, "He Do the Police in Different Voices." That title, a quotation from Dickens's *Our Mutual Friend*, alludes to Sloppy, a character who reads newspapers to his family, imitating the voices of various characters. Similarly, Eliot's poem gathers together many voices which the poet is "doing" for us in verse to match their utterances.

The voices of quite a number of "personages" are used in the poem, each of them having close and important connections with the struggle for psychic fulfillment or maturity. Although the protagonist identifies in varying degrees with each of these personages, he still seems always present as the filtering and uttering consciousness; the framework which gives each his proper place in the poem is not inherent in any one of them, though it may have an analogue in each one's history.

Eliot called the poem "the relief of a personal and wholly insignificant grouse against life."[5] I suggest that the "I" of the poem, despite the line "I Tiresias have foresuffered all . . . ," is Eliot himself; as more and more biographical material and especially Eliot correspondence becomes available, it is becoming clearer and clearer that Eliot's poetry is more highly autobiographical than has been generally recognized, comprising, as Lyndall Gordon demonstrates, a detailed selective spiritual record. "I Tiresias" in that line just quoted should be read "I, a Tiresias" or "I, speaking through Tiresias' voice"; and "what Tiresias sees" (in Eliot's note to the line) is what the poet sees, Tiresias not being different in kind from the other voices in the poem but being emphasized by Eliot because his is the voice that links (as that "I Tiresias" enables it to) the male and female understandings of all the other non-Christian voices in the poem.

Stephen Spender's excellent *T. S. Eliot* contains the best discussion I have found of the mythic method and its relation to the "many voices which say 'I' in *The Waste Land*." Citing Freud's theory that a maturing individual reenacts all the stages through which civilization has developed, he concludes that "the completely conscious and unrepressed individual would preserve in his mind a reflection in miniature of all the stages of the development of civilization. Part of his consciousness would be that which is symbolized by Tiresias." He pictures Tiresias at his remote end of time and us at ours, looking at each other's worlds. This, though Mr. Spender does not say so, is exactly the way in which Eliot used Rochefoucauld in *The "Boston Evening Transcript"*; and what Tiresias and Rochefoucauld had in common with biblical prophets, Dante, and Shakespeare was insight into the timeless truths of human nature and the cycles of life—the things that Eliot's wastelanders are blind to. To the extent that one sees these things *in any age or place*, one can recognize and may escape the Waste Land; all true prophets, seers, poets, and artists must see them, at least in part—not take their thoughts from the daily newspaper, "bound upon the wheel" of Fortune.

Mr. Spender points out the near-absurdity of accepting "the experiences of the modern 'I' " in the poem as "those of Tiresias," adding that "the deepest 'I,' that of a witness, a contemporary voice melting into that of the most ancient," is more the voice of an Old Testament prophet than of Tiresias. Tiresias, he says, may foresuffer the hyacinth-garden episode, but "the contemporary guilt-ridden voice" relating it is not his, nor is the weeping voice "By the waters of Leman" nor the exclaimer of "O city city...."[6]

The various voices of the poem are taken chiefly from a number of works involving the death/rebirth patterns on which the poem is balanced. The most pervasive of these, signaled by the title, is the coming of the water of life to the desert, the waste land of both biblical prophecy and the Grail-quest legends. This pattern

parallels another, the coming each spring of life-giving floods to
the Nile valley, traditionally foretold by the reading of the Tarot
card pack.

Other important death/rebirth patterns derive from the primitive
vegetative rites to which the Cambridge anthropologists admired
by Eliot (especially Sir James Frazer, Jessie L. Weston, Gilbert
Murray, and Francis M. Cornford) traced the origins of both Greek
drama and the Grail legends: the dismemberment and rebirth of
the scapegoat Year-god, buried or thrown into the Nile or another
river and later resurrected or "fished out" (compare the Fisher
King) and reassembled; the Grail-legend maiming (usually a
sexual wound) and eventual healing of the Fisher King, on whom
the health and fertility of his land and people depend (just as in
Oedipus Rex Tiresias, blind prophet of Apollo, knew that the
city's plague was brought on by Oedipus' crimes against the pro-
creative cycles)—only when the Fisher King is healed through
the appearing of a pure fool who asks the proper questions (as
in Wagner's *Parsifal*) can the land again become fertile. Other
such patterns are Tristan's healing by Isolde's arts and love; the
burial and resurrection of Christ and of the Christian in baptism;
the supposed drowning of Ferdinand's father, King Alonso, in
Shakespeare's *Tempest*, which eventuates in a real psychic resurrection for him; Dante's descent into hell, which eventually leads
up through purgatory to the earthly paradise as a prelude to his
ascent to paradise; the stealing of the Rhinegold treasure in Wagner's *Ring of the Nibelungs* tetralogy, eventually returned to its
rightful place; and the liberation from lust of Arnaut Daniel's purgation by fire, of Buddha's "Fire Sermon," of St. Augustine's
Confessions, and of the "Thunder Sermon" from which Eliot takes
the three commands Give, Sympathize, and Control.

The relevance of these patterns to the Christian scheme is developed by Miss Weston and summarized as follows by G. S. Fraser:
"The Christian interpretation of this traditional myth is the highest
one: the sacrificed king is Christ, as God Incarnate, and the barren
land which has to be reclaimed to fertility is the human heart,
full of selfishness and lust, choked with the tares of sin."[7] The

inevitability of "fish" and "fisher" symbolism is seen by reflecting on the high degree to which early peoples were dependent on rivers and seas, the fecundity and vitality of fishes, and the mysterious "grace" which brings the fish to the fisherman. Thus Buddha, for one example, was represented as sitting on the bank of the ocean of Samsara, casting for the fish of Truth to draw it to the light of salvation;[8] and Christ, for another, offered to make his disciples "fishers of men."

The Mythic Method

The poem relates all of these strands of meaning through the "mythic method" praised by Eliot in his 1923 review "Ulysses, Order, and Myth."[9] Each of these patterns involves a death-and-resurrection sequence, implying an awareness of positive potentialities growing out of the initial waste and barren condition. So rather than merely depicting the disillusionment of a generation and the aridity of twentieth-century culture, *The Waste Land* shows the anatomy of such deserts and then says, "That is not it, at all; here are desirable alternatives, proper eventualities for the individual enmeshed in those snares."

Most of Eliot's sources are identified in the famous notes added when the poem was first printed in book form two months after its initial publication in the *Criterion*. The printer needed additional copy to fill a signature; since Eliot had no other poems ready at that time, he submitted the explanatory notes on *The Waste Land* which now fill about five pages in the *Complete Poems and Plays of T. S. Eliot*. The notes have been the focus of much critical effort and comment, and Eliot, later calling the notes "bogus scholarship," regretted having appended them. One valuable function of the notes, nevertheless, has been to indicate some of the works that most importantly influenced the writing of the poem.

Many critics have written of the antitheses, the antinomies, and the contrasts in *The Waste Land*, which exist in abundance and are not just accidents of inclusion, but comprise a basic and indispensable aspect of the poem's technique, progression, and meaning. Many such polarities could be identified: universal-personal, male-female, conscious-unconscious, hope-fear, and others. But the technique of contradiction goes deeper in the poem's structure. Many of its symbols are what I should like to call "contra-symbols" because they simultaneously develop in antithetical directions. The symbol of water, for instance, is already present ambiguously in line nine of the first section: the shower of rain that comes over the Starnbergersee both heralds the summer and makes the speaker run for shelter.

The absence of water and the thirst for it enter in line 24, "the dry stone [gives] no sound of water"; in line 42, "*Oed' und leer das Meer*" ("Wide and empty the sea"), water is both a negative and a positive symbol: it may carry Isolde and her healing arts to the dying Tristan, but as yet it is vast and desolate. The fear of death by water is first made explicit by Madame Sosostris. Both sides of this ambiguous symbol are inconspicuously present in the game of chess: "The hot water at ten./And if it rains, a closed car at four"; and again the negative side is seen through the allusion to Ophelia, who drowned herself: "Good night, ladies, good night, sweet ladies, good night, good night."

In section 3, "The Fire Sermon," the river has both positive and negative connotations, suggesting both purity and pollution, both innocence and immorality. Mrs. Porter's soda water is contrasted with the ceremonial water of the Grail chapel as in Verlaine's *Parsifal*. This parallel-but-antithetical development is amplified in great detail throughout the poem. By section 4 both positive and negative meanings have intensified—water suggesting both the dissolution of physical death and the promise of resurrection in the Year-god ceremonies, Christian baptism, the Easter pageant, and the other chief symbolic patterns used.

The symbol of Philomel is another such contra-symbol: in its first appearance, again we see both positive and negative connotations:

> Above the antique mantel was displayed
> As though a window gave upon the sylvan scene

> The change of Philomel, by the barbarous king
> So rudely forced; yet there the nightingale
> Filled all the desert with inviolable voice
> And still she cried and still the world pursues,
> "Jug Jug" to dirty ears.

In context this passage suggests not only the beauty of a remote and picturesque artifact but also the cruel violation suffered by Philomel; her song, the "inviolable voice" ("twit twit") still sounds like "jug jug" to dirty ears. She next appears in section 3, "The Fire Sermon," after the contradictory references to Mrs. Porter and the quotation "*et O ces voix d'enfants, chantant dans la coupole!*" ("and O, those voices of children, singing in the choir loft!"): "Twit twit twit/ Jug jug jug jug jug jug/So rudely forc'd/Tereu." The irony of the reference to Verlaine's Grail ceremony in this context carries over into the song of the nightingale, at first positive, then negative. The next line, "So rudely forc'd," refers not only to Philomel but also to the use of Grail imagery in the "Sweeney and Mrs. Porter" context. The closing word of this four-line passage, "Tereu," suggests Tereus' act of violation, the fact that it is to be rued, and the sound of the bird's singing; for "twit twit," "jug jug," and "Tereu" were the three common representations of the nightingale's song in Elizabethan literature, where its moral meanings were emphasized as they are here.

Though Philomel does not appear again directly in *The Waste Land*, she is suggested in the other bird songs used and referred to at two levels of indirectness in the "*Quando fiam uti chelidon*" fragment ("When will I be like the swallow?") of the closing passage for the reader who is familiar with its context in the anonymous Latin work *Pervigilium Veneris*. As in the case of the water symbol, which by the end of the poem suggests the whole principle that Jung calls the "anima," the associations of the Philomel symbol have been expanded by the entire development of the poem: by the end she has come to suggest in all their varieties both violation through lust and purification through transformation. Fire, one of Eliot's dominant symbols, is similarly used

and developed as the symbol of both the destroying lust which must
be transcended and the purgatorial flames which purify.

Such contra-symbols are inevitable concomitants of the associa-
tive mythic method by which the poem develops in the mind of
the speaker. Its associational basis is not in ideas or images, but
in total states of a complex and individual consciousness that is
always aware of multiple implications. This sort of progression
is implicit in the poem's entire structure, but it is easy to miss,
since its recognition arises in the reader's empathic identification—
"You! *hypocrite lecteur!—mon semblable,—mon frère!*" The requirement of this identification necessarily limits the readership of
the poem, but it also allows degrees of compression and of subtle
complexity probably impossible to achieve by any other structural
technique.

Dantean Scheme and Intent

Eliot wrote in 1935 that he wanted literature to be unconsciously
rather than deliberately and defiantly Christian. This statement, of
course, refers to technique as well as to content. In the same essay
is expressed the view that reading does affect our moral and religious existence, and that the greatness of literature is not determined solely by literary standards: the poet's job is to present to
his readers (as Dante's Virgil does in *The Divine Comedy*) true
worldly wisdom, which will lead up to other-worldly wisdom, and
will be completed and fulfilled by it.[10]

As noted in chapter 3, Dante exerted a very strong influence on
Eliot's use of the Christian tradition, and especially on his use of
its rituals in *The Waste Land*: the crucifixion and resurrection;
baptism; and the burial ritual and liturgy, from which the first
section of the poem takes its title. (The Mass is dramatically embodied in the Earthly Paradise and Paradise sections of Dante's
Divine Comedy. Eliot followed that lead in writing *The Rock,
Murder in the Cathedral*, and especially *Ash-Wednesday*.)

The Dantean scheme and intent are central to the unity and to
the proper interpretation of *The Waste Land*. The most immedi-

ately obvious borrowings from the *Divine Comedy* are seen in the "crowd flowing over London Bridge" passage of section 1 and in the *"Poi s'ascose nel foco che gli affina"* quotation at the end of the poem. Dante's influence, however, permeates the whole poem, as a number of critics who compare it to Dante's *Inferno* have noted. Philo M. Buck, in his *Directions in Contemporary Literature*, writes of the "irrelevant waste and despair that knows not its emptiness" seen in *The Waste Land*, and he further points out that the purpose of Dante's *Inferno* is to make unregenerate humanity see, "with no veil to obscure, the ugliness of sin. Evil must be stripped of all its false allure and stand before the poet naked, grotesque, and unashamed, not that he may recoil at its horror and stand in judgement... but that he may suffer in mind and body the moral illness that is necessary before the discipline of Purgatory can be begun."[11]

This confrontation is precisely what the speaker of *The Waste Land* tries to accomplish for the wastelanders. The speaker, by recognizing its anatomy and significance, has passed out of hell, where no psychic postures except those observed are conceivable; and he has made the difficult transition into purgation of his damning tendencies—has exercised "the good of the intellect." He is aware of the antithetical poles of the poem's symbols, aware now of the depths of its negative implications but also the height of its positive dimensions. He is aware both of "the prison" (involvement with the profitless aspects of the immediate) and of "the key." And thanks to the collocation in his mind of Buddha's "Fire Sermon," Shakespeare's *The Tempest*, the three commands of the Hindu thunder myth, Christ's resurrection, St. Augustine's reversal, the Fisher King's restoration, and the other echoes in the poem, he is aware of the means needed to complete the transformation in his psychic focus to the high felicity of a properly ordered love. Hell, then, is represented in *The Waste Land* only through images. His contemporaries and readers, to whom the speaker addresses himself, are, like him, still living; and they have yet the possibility of putting the intellect to its good and proper use.

Eliot, like Dante, tries to stimulate his reader to do so by showing first—using language to communicate to the reader's bones and muscles—the feel of inferno, and then by introducing guides from literature and tradition, both classical and contemporary, who help one understand what he has seen and felt. And just as Dante has philosophical passages in which Virgil, Statius, Marco Lombardo, Beatrice, and others explain to Dante what he has already experienced so that he will understand it, will "use the good of the intellect," Eliot occasionally in the earlier poems and much more frequently in *Ash-Wednesday* and in the *Four Quartets* has written philosophical poetry aimed at the understanding of the reader as well as at his senses—the senses whose appeal the reader must transcend in order to escape inferno. The 1922 version of *The Waste Land*, however, omits all such explicit statements.

The speaker sees his contemporaries largely in those attitudes of soul symbolized in Dante's *Inferno* either by the trimmers— who "lived without blame, and without praise" and who are admitted neither to heaven nor the depths of hell (Dante's description of them is echoed in the lines "A crowd flowed over London Bridge, so many,/I had not thought death had undone so many")— or by the shades in Limbo who lived and died before Christianity and thus without baptism. Though they were virtuous, these latter shades occupy the first circle of Dante's hell (their description is echoed in Eliot's lines "Sighs, short and infrequent, were exhaled,/ And each man fixed his eyes before his feet"). But only if Eliot's Londoners are caught by death and frozen in such attitudes of the soul will they partake of hell.

The meeting with Stetson echoes the many passages in which Dante converses with the shades he and Virgil encounter in hell and purgatory, and the Arnaut Daniel fragment at the end of the poem focuses the relevance to *The Waste Land* of the Dantean scheme. (More often in this poem than in any other, Eliot demands of his reader for full understanding a familiarity with the broad context of his borrowed line; for he hopes to send those readers not already familiar with them on a tour through the works of literature most relevant to the paramount problems of the waste-landers.)

Dante the Pilgrim meets Arnaut Daniel in the seventh and last cornice of purgatory, where the lustful are purged. As he previously ascended the stairway to this cornice with his guides, the pagan Virgil and the Christian Statius, the latter has expounded to Dante the doctrine of the development of the soul which further clarifies Marco Lombardo's discourse (already examined above in connection with *Animula*). Statius has linked the soul's history closely to divine love and to the reproductive processes with their sexual basis. Through this discourse, Dante has been brought to understand the mode of existence of the shades populating Dante's hell, purgatory, and heaven.

Similarly, Eliot's reader, in order to understand the workings of *The Waste Land*'s imagery and structure, must become aware that the immediate scene, the "unreal city" of London, and the bodies of himself and his contemporaries are much less important than *their* souls.

Virgil's explanation of purgatory emphasizes the fact that Dante (like Eliot's readers) is still alive, and that full repentance before death can bring one to such an advanced stage of purgation as this—to the level of those in purgatory nearest their goal. For Arnaut is encountered shortly before the entrance to the Earthly Paradise at the top of Mount Purgatory. Dante has been allowed to experience these things before death, he says, through the grace of "a Lady above"—through unearned good fortune.

The shades in cornice 7 of the *Purgatorio* are divided into two groups: those who suffer for homosexual lust and those who, though their lusts were heterosexual, followed them "like brute beasts." (Both groups have also been included in *The Waste Land*.) This last conversation with a suffering shade in purgatory indicates approximately the limits beyond which, in Dante's scheme, the unchristian knowledge of Virgil cannot progress. It takes place on the narrow path where those who pass on between the flames and the cliff must go single file, alone; the nature of the progress beyond that point excludes help from outside; and it also requires the withdrawing of attachment to others or of love improperly directed toward them. And it is out of the searing flames that Arnaut addresses Dante.

This necessity of renouncing lust is also the message of Buddha's "Fire Sermon," which like the present passage is couched in fire imagery—though there the fire has only negative connotations; here it symbolizes both the burning flames of lust and the purging flames of proper love. Yet, though one must go alone to be plucked out of the first burning (lust) by the second (love), the plucking enables him to give, sympathize, and control, just as, when the two bands of shades pass in Dante's cornice 7, each of them quickly kisses one of those in the other group and hurries on. Of this sympathy, this properly directed love, their lust formerly made them incapable.

"What Tiresias sees," "the substance of the poem" according to Eliot's often-misinterpreted note, is therefore the necessity of pure concern for one's fellow-humans without the sins of lust that violate the proper natural order and make individuals incapable of genuine love. Like Dante's Virgil, though, Tiresias in *The Waste Land* lacks the Christian dimension; and he is able to point one only so far as the earthly felicity represented in Dante's scheme by the Earthly Paradise at the top of Mount Purgatory.

When *The Waste Land* appeared in 1922, Eliot already had given frequent hints of his preoccupation with Arnaut's speech, a passage earlier emphasized in Ezra Pound's *The Spirit of Romance*; and *Ara Vos Prec* (1920), as seen above, contained chiefly the observations of Dantean watchers of the fruits of improperly ordered love. The two lines beginning "Sovegna vos" occurred in one of the excised *Waste Land* passages;[12] "Sovegna vos" was used again in part 4 of *Ash-Wednesday*; and in his 1929 *Dante* book Eliot quoted Arnaut's speech both in Provençal and in English translation. Because a number of the Provençal phrases are scattered through Eliot's works, the speech bears repeating here:

I am Arnold, who weeps and goes singing.
I see in thought all the past folly.
And I see with joy the day for which I hope, before me.

And so I pray you, by that virtue
(*Ara vos prec, per aquella valor*)
　Which leads you to the topmost of the stair—
　(*que vos guida al som de l'escalina,*)
Be mindful in due time of my pain.
　(*sovegna vos a temps de ma dolor.*)
Then dived he back into that fire which refines them.
(POI S'ASCOSE NEL FOCO CHE GLI AFFINA.) [13]

As Arnaut and his fellow shades speak to Dante, they take great care not to step outside the painful flames which are purging them. It is crucial to note that their suffering is entirely voluntary. And this is not just a point of Dante's fiction: it is Thomistic doctrine. But more importantly, it is a psychological necessity known to the medical doctor as well as to the psychologist: the patient must will his own recovery—the bit can never be removed from the horse's mouth safely until he *wants* to go in the right direction, as in Plato's *Phaedrus*. What is involved in Dante's purgatory is not mere punishment, but the willing acceptance of the effects of misguided, defective, or excessive love which will make the sufferer aware of the improper nature of his past acts and will alter or erase his tendencies toward such acts. Thus at the top of Mount Purgatory he has achieved the regained innocence—not of ignorance but of understanding. And hence he recognizes the instant when his purgation in any one cornice of purgatory is complete, and nothing holds him back to suffer further if his own improper focus does not.

Such also is the nature of escape from Eliot's waste land; and, like Arnaut Daniel, Eliot's speaker has spoken out of the cleansing purgatorial fire only long enough to make clear to his hearers the nature of the place in which he has been met, of the ravages of lust in its most inclusive sense (the anatomy of hell), and of the process necessary to its transcendence—"Then dived he back into the fire that refines them." As Roy Battenhouse says, Eliot in his poetry made a vocation of diving back into the fire. [14]

The Burial of the Dead. Part 1 takes the title of the fu-
neral service in the Anglican *Book of Common Prayer*, also the
source of the "handful of dust" that evokes fear in part 1.

The fifty-four-line opening passage in the *Facsimile* version comprises an account of a night on the town by a voice that might be
Sweeney's or that of one of the acquaintances referred to in Conrad
Aiken's *Ushant*; it begins, "First we had a couple of feelers down
at Tom's place...." One of the characters mentioned is Gus Krutz-
sche, the pseudonym under which Eliot's *Song to the Opherion* was
published in 1921. The name seems to be based on that of Nietz-
sche, in addition to having the overtones of Petronius' Encolpius
("crutch" or "crotch"), as pointed out by Valerie Eliot.[15]

Next follows the famous "April is the cruellest month" passage
and then another broken image of "stony rubbish," the "Marie,
Marie" lines that seem to lament the lost vitality and zest of
youth. These foreshadowings of death, embittering the springtime,
make one wonder what life can grow out of such memories; the
lines expressing that question echo not only the book of Ezekiel,
but also the poem *The Death of Saint Narcissus* (*Facsimile*, pp. 90–
97), probably written as early as 1915. The red-rock image of both
poems seems to symbolize the solace of Christianity.

The hyacinth-girl episode then echoes the beginning and end of
Tristan und Isolde, recalling the emotions of a love before, just
after, and longer after its consummation, lost in distance—another
memory (this one of "the heart of light, the silence") to embitter
April.

The next voice, that of Madame Sosostris, reads an altered
Tarot card pack, trying to forecast the future and the structure
of the poem. She identifies the protagonist with the drowned Phoenician Sailor, Phlebas, in part 4. Two parenthetical quotations,
both deleted before publication, punctuate and qualify her readings: the first, "(Those are pearls that were his eyes. Look!),"
identifies the protagonist with King Alonso in Shakespeare's *The
Tempest*, promising a moral rebirth; the second, "(I John saw
these things, and heard them)," provides a New Testament parallel
to the protagonist's identification with Old Testament prophets,

especially Ezekiel, in part 1. Both quotations suggest a prophetic role for the protagonist, one that contrasts with the wicked-card-reading of Madame Sosostris.

The first-person "Unreal City" section parallels Dante's vestibule of the futile and his sighing Limbo to Eliot's workday-morning London Bridge scene. The "Stetson!" encounter (with Conrad Aiken?[16]) raises the question whether the Burial of the Dead will or will not lead to rebirth, and the final line, "You! *hypocrite lecteur!—mon semblable,—mon frère!*" implicates the reader, asking whether he too has buried his dead past and is undergoing a sea-change into something rich and strange.

A Game of Chess. Part 2, "A Game of Chess," depicts the stunting effects of improperly directed love or of lust mistaken for love. In this section we see the pawns moving about in two games that end not in checkmate but in stalemate. The first, the "nerves" passage, presents through a young man's consciousness a scene in an ornate marble-floored room where he and a young lady are marooned together. It may or may not be a hotel bridal suite. (Footsteps shuffle on the stairs, and the chambermaid will knock on the door in the morning.) She seems to be ill. (They will need a hot water bottle, and her nerves are bad.) He emphasizes the ambiguously symbolic artifacts of the room's decor (especially the mantel-painting of the metamorphosis of Philomel into the nightingale, after her raping by Tereus), the "withered stumps of time." He also emphasizes the lady's jewels, cosmetics, and perfumes, and his inability to share his thoughts with her. He wishes he were elsewhere.

Dido allusions and the lady's "Stay with me" raise the theme of desertion seen in such earlier works as *La Figlia che Piange* and *Sweeney Erect*. The protagonist feels that they "met first in rats' alley" (*Facsimile*, p. 11) and that he is now drowned, though he can remember the rebirth of "drowned" Alonso in *The Tempest*. The chess games in the Grail Castle (seeming to deal with proper courtship of and relations to a prospective mate), in Middleton's *Women Beware Women* (negative connotations), and Shake-

speare's *Tempest* (positive) supply the title of this section and
suggest the stalemating moves between the protagonist and *his*
lady. "In the Cage," the canceled earlier title (*Facsimile*, p. 11),
evokes, as Valerie Eliot's note points out, the Sybil at Cumae of
the poem's epigraph, hanging in a bottle and wishing to die.

Three other deleted poems of stunted loves from the *Facsimile*
are relevant: "Song," "Exequy," and "The Death of the Duchess."
The 1920 *Ode, Lune de Miel,* and *A Cooking Egg* seem also to
relate to the first of the two stalemates in "A Game of Chess,"
done in the protagonist's own voice. Joyce's *Exiles*, Conrad's *The
Return*, and Webster's *The Devil's Law Case* are also relevant,
but the chief parallel, as will be shown, is Webster's *The Duchess
of Malfi.*

"The Death of the Duchess" puts the "nerves" scene of "A
Game of Chess" in a somewhat clearer frame. The Duchess of
the title, as quoted lines show, is Webster's Duchess of Malfi; the
Waste Land lady is in some ways parallel to her.

Parts 1 and 2 picture the inhabitants of Hampstead very much
as *The "Boston Evening Transcript"* pictures proper Bostonians—
as taking their thoughts ready-made from the newspapers, as de-
humanized dogs and birds, having no words of their own. Against
such people each of the two stanzas contrasts "you and me,"
speechless for some different, unspecified reason, miserably alone
together.

If the people of Hampstead have nothing of their own to say,
what, the protagonist asks himself, have the two of them to say?

The Duchess has apparently found enough words to ask him,
"Do you love me?" What preceded, what prompted the question,
we are not told. He cannot find an answer, his thoughts having
tails but not wings. She combs her hair and awaits an answer.

He considers leaving, questioning what would happen if he
answered either that he did love her, or that he did not, and finds it
terrible that there is little difference between the outcomes. He

then concludes that it is time to go. At the comparable point in Webster's play, while the Duchess is combing her hair and (with her back turned) talking to her faithful, loving steward Antonio, secretly her husband, he and her maid Cariola sneak out of the room as a joke, leaving her talking, she thinks, to him; but her cruel brother Ferdinand, having treacherously procured a key to her chamber, enters quietly and overhears enough to betray her secret, for which he not long after has her murdered.

The second "Game of Chess" scene, a conversation in a pub at closing time narrated through the voice, Valerie Eliot says, of the Eliots' maid, deals with Lil's husband, Albert, about to return from World War I and expecting Lil to look "a bit smart."[17] Having taken pills to cause an abortion of her sixth child, she has never recovered. She is threatened with Albert's desertion, and the bartender's HURRY UP PLEASE ITS TIME operates on all the poem's levels of meaning. The section concludes with a reminder of Ophelia's abandonment by Hamlet and of her suicide.

The memories of these abortive "loves" comprise the stony rubble out of which it is to be hoped that the protagonist's roots, being stirred by spring rain, may send forth branches. Though the rebirth of Alonso and the possibility of the Grail Knight's success in his quest leave hope for the protagonist, he seems to have failed his initial test through inability to speak at the Grail castle in the hyacinth-garden episode of "The Burial of the Dead." Eliot cited Jessie L. Weston's *From Ritual to Romance* as the source of his Grail and vegetation rite references (including the poem's title). As yet, there is no indication in the poem of the releasing of the waters that will return the Waste Land to fertility.

The Fire Sermon. Section 3 takes its title from Buddha's "Fire Sermon," quoted in the notes of this study.[18] The reader who wishes to understand thoroughly the allusions and progressions of this section should read it, Saint Augustine's *Confessions*, and cantos 26–27 of Dante's *Purgatorio*. It will be seen that each of these focuses on the processes of escape from the total involvement in the life of the senses that we see reflected in the various scenes of misguided love suggested in *The Waste Land*. It is this broader reading of the word *lust* that is purged by Arnaut Daniel and by the speaker of *The Waste Land* in diving back into the fire of voluntary refinement.

In this third section suggestions of improper loves are mixed with intimations of vitality inherent in Spenser's *Prothalamion*, Shakespeare's *The Tempest*, and the voices of children in the choir loft of the Grail legends, presumably paralleled by the singing of the choir of angels or of the redeemed souls in Dante when another soul is redeemed from the barrenness of an improperly focused life. Yet the positive suggestions are attenuated: Elizabeth and Leicester, as seen in Froude's history, qualify the purity of the Thames scene in Spenser's *Prothalamion*; the sounds of both the horns and hunting in Day's *Parliament of Bees* and this poem's "horns and motors which shall bring/Sweeney to Mrs. Porter [a bawdyhouse madame] in the spring" prefigure slayings by boarhounds between the yew trees; and the sacrament of foot-washing is perverted to Mrs. Porter and her daughter washing themselves in soda water ("And so they oughter, to keep 'em clean").

As already noted, the song of the nightingale is ambiguously present in this section, both in its pure sound "Twit twit twit" and in the "Jug jug jug jug jug jug" that is perverted to dirty ears. The dual significance, the juxtaposition of proper and improper loves, creates an effect that is "So rudely forc'd./Tereu." Next comes the poem's second "unreal city" passage, the recollection of the perhaps homosexual overtures of Mr. Eugenides, the Smyrna merchant. This is followed by the seduction scene of the typist-home-at-teatime witnessed by Tiresias, who has foresuffered both male and female lusts and loves. The unperturbed if not unruffled typist, after the groping departure of the young man carbuncular, "smoothes her hair with automatic hand,/And puts a record on the gramophone." This arid suggestion of mechanical music is transmuted into the music of Ariel that crept by Ferdinand on the waters in *The Tempest*; it is associated with modern-London intimations of vitality, culminating in the "Inexplicable splendour of Ionian white and gold" of the Church of St. Magnus the Martyr.

Next come the songs of the three Thames-daughters, three London nymphs encountered by this modern Augustine-Aeneas when he first arrived in Boston-Paris-London-Carthage, to which he came "burning burning burning." But the song of the first Thames-daughter, echoing Dante's La Pia in *Purgatorio* 5.134 ("Siena made me, Maremna unmade me"), transmutes her memory, and the corrosive fires of the protagonist's lust are modulated into the cleansing purgatorial fires of Saint Augustine and of Dante's Arnaut Daniel in the final "burning" which follows "O Lord Thou pluckest me out." This overt statement by the speaker of the poem signifies that he is being plucked out of the waste land to a new life of properly ordered loves.

The opening passage of the *Facsimile* "Fire Sermon" was a seventy-two-line imitation of Pope's *The Rape of the Lock* depicting a dilettante lady identified as Fresca (mentioned earlier in *Gerontion*). There is also a seventeen-line insert to the "Fire Sermon." Fresca writes poetry when she can't sleep, but the protagonist is reminded of a minstrel show ("the rattle of the bones, and chuckle spread from ear to ear") and sums up her emotions as unreal but her appetites as real, commenting that that "same eternal and consuming itch" can produce anything from a martyr to a slattern, with many shades in between.[19] That this is not mere antifeminism, as some critics suggest, is attested in the *Little Gidding* lines "the intolerable shirt of flame/Which human power cannot remove."

Another deleted passage, "London, the swarming life you kill and breed," identifies the ills of the wastelanders: they know "neither how to think, nor how to feel,/But [live only] in the awareness of the observing eye." Buddha's "Fire Sermon" is the best explication of that idea; only through escaping the burning of the senses can one see the meaning of experience as the seers, prophets, and true poets do—can one "trace the cryptogram" within sense perceptions and see the meaning "in another world."[20]

The typist-home-at-teatime episode was longer and looser in the *Facsimile* version, but not significantly different in meaning, except for one final five-line stanza in which the protagonist's flying feet "up the ghastly hill of Cannon Street"[21] (later "up Queen Victoria Street") may evoke the "Elegy" lines, "God, in a rolling ball of fire/Pursues by day my errant feet." "Elegy" seems to add his lady to the other dead in "The Burial of the Dead";[22] as mentioned above, her death seems in "A Game of Chess" to have been of the spirit rather than the body, and his remorse is great. God's pursuit is positive, as is the echo of Ariel's song to Ferdinand ("This music crept by me upon the waters").

Death by Water. Section 4 briefly summarizes what happens after the burial of the dead, improper life: "the cry of gulls and the deep sea swell/And the profit and loss" are forgotten. Phlebas, the drowned Phoenician sailor, passes "the stages of his age and youth/Entering the whirlpool"; and the reader is reminded that the same state awaits him—the dissolution of death which, if the good of the intellect is used, can result not in simple dissolution in fractured atoms "Beyond the circuit of the shuddering Bear" (*Gerontion*) but in the rebirth suggested by the many strands of allusion in this poem.

The ten lines of "Death by Water" in the 1922 version were preceded in the *Facsimile* by a twelve-line comment on the dignity of sailors and a seventy-one-line account through a dead sailor's voice of his last voyage from the Dry Salvages to the Eastern Banks and then, driven northward by a howling gale past the point of no return, finally to shipwreck on an iceberg. This voyage strongly evokes three others: that in Coleridge's *Rime of the Ancient Mariner* (ambiguous) and those of Dante's (negative) and Tennyson's (positive) Ulysses. The "Remember me" line evokes both the ghost of Hamlet's father and Arnaut Daniel's "*Sovegna vos.*"

One other *Facsimile* poem, "Dirge," is related to "Death by Water." It is closely patterned on Ariel's song "Full fathom five thy father lies" in Shakespeare's *The Tempest.* It substitutes for "father" the name Bleistein, used earlier in *Burbank with a Bae-*

deker: Bleistein with a Cigar. Bleistein is a drowned Phoenician merchant, disintegrating in much more explicit detail than Phlebas. Though this poem differs markedly in tonal effects on a reader—being somewhat macabre and distasteful—it does not essentially alter the meanings of "Death by Water."

What the Thunder Said. Section 5 takes its title from the Second Brahmana passage on "The Three Cardinal Virtues," brief enough to be quoted in full:

1. The threefold offspring of Prajapati—gods, men, and devils (*asura*)—dwelt with their father Prajapati as students of sacred knowledge (*brahmacarya*).

Having lived the life of a student of sacred knowledge, the gods said: 'Speak to us, Sir.' To them he spoke this syllable, 'Da.' 'Did you understand?' 'We did understand,' said they. 'You said to us, "Restrain yourselves (*damyata*)."' 'Yes (*Om*)!' said he. 'You did understand.'

2. So then the men said to him: 'Speak to us, Sir.' To them then he spoke this syllable, 'Da.' 'Did you understand?' 'We did understand,' said they. 'You said to us, "Give (*datta*)."' 'Yes (*Om*)!' said he. 'You did understand.'

3. So then the devils said to him: 'Speak to us, Sir.' To them then he spoke this syllable, 'Da.' 'Did you understand?' 'We did understand,' said they. 'You said to us, "Be compassionate (*dayadhvam*)."' 'Yes (*Om*)!' said he. 'You did understand.'

This same thing does the divine voice here, thunder, repeat: *Da! Da! Da!* that is, restrain yourselves, give, be compassionate. One should practise this same triad: self-restraint, giving, compassion.[23]

In this fifth section of *The Waste Land* are given a number of analogous formulas for success in the quests of the poem's basic symbols. The first nine lines of the section place the themes in a Christian setting, putting us in Jerusalem just after the death of Christ and before his resurrection; the dryness and emptiness of this condition before rebirth is echoed in all of the patterns of the poem's various symbols. Here is the state of Gerontion, waiting for rain, being read to by a boy from the whole tradition, and looking back on his own renounced involvement in the life of attachment to the senses. As relief to the dry road winding among the mountains between rocks and in sand, without water, we have the mysterious figure who appeared to the disciples on the road to Emmaus, "the third who walks always beside you." For all ages, only when the life of temporal involvement is transcended, only when the towers and cities crumble as central psychic foci, only when the emptiness of the material and of man's pride in his accomplishments is seen, only when it is recognized that man's wells and cisterns are empty, can one approach the Grail chapel, hear the crow of the cock seen in a flash of lightning on the rooftree, and feel the damp gust that brings the rain so long awaited.

Then in a jungle setting owing much to Conrad,[24] we hear the rumble of the thunder and the three commands Give, Sympathize, Control—each then related in turn to the speaker's own life and to works of literature which he has experienced. The final stanza of the poem returns to the Fisher King who is sitting on the shore fishing, with the arid plain behind him. He asks himself if he shall at least set his lands in order. Then follows a group of quoted fragments which he says "I have shored against my ruins." *Shore* here has the dual sense of *shoring up* and of pulling *to shore*.

The first fragment, from the children's rhyme "London Bridge Is Falling Down," suggests the decay of the bridge to the Grail castle; it also suggests positive values: the purity of the children who sing it, and the Fisher King's overcoming of attachment to the immediate life of the senses in his surroundings. The second, *"Poi s' ascose nel foco che gli affina,"* suggests Arnaut Daniel's eager and willing diving back into the cleansing fire which will prepare him to enter the Earthly Paradise. The third, *"Quando fiam uti chelidon"* ("When will I be like the swallow?") is from the *Pervigilium Veneris* and—like the next, "O swallow swallow" from Tennyson—indicates longing for successful rebirth that will follow the obeying of the three commands of the thunder. The next, *"Le Prince d'Aquitaine à la tour abolie,"* as Eliot's notes indicate, is from Gerard de Nerval's sonnet "El Desdichado," and it relates to the Grail myths with which Nerval dramatically identified himself. It is the shoring of these fragments, as well as the method and content of the poem as a whole, that is referred to in the next quoted fragment, from Kyd's *Spanish Tragedy*, "Why then Ile fit you." This half-line repays closer examination than it has generally received, for it emerges as a key statement of Eliot's purpose in *The Waste Land*.

The line is striking in both works. In Kyd's play it is spoken by Hieronymo, Marshall of Spain, to the king's nephew Lorenzo and to Prince Balthazar of Portugal, the murderers of Hieronymo's son Horatio. In a war between their countries Balthazar, before the beginning of the play, had first killed Don Andrea, the lover of Bel-imperia, and then been defeated and captured by Horatio. When Bel-imperia then fell in love with Horatio, the envious Lorenzo and the lustful Balthazar treacherously murdered him. All this is secretly known to Hieronymo and Bel-imperia, but, since they dare not appeal to the villains' royal relatives for justice, they swear to help each other obtain revenge. At this juncture the murderers approach Hieronymo, who has previously entertained the court with a dumb show, to ask him a favor: will he present another play for the court? He replies, "Why then, I'll fit you; say no more"[25] and goes on to tell them that "it will prove most passing strange, and wondrous plausible to that assembly." He relates the plot, which reproduces essentially, though not too obviously, the relationships existing among themselves. Each of the actors, he says, must speak his part in a different language so that the audience (chiefly their fathers) shall catch the true meaning of the play. To Balthazar's protests that they will not be understood, the Marshall replies,

It must be so, for the conclusion
Shall prove the invention and all was good.
And I myself in an oration,
And with a strange and wondrous show besides,
That I will have there behind a curtain
[the body of his murdered son, Horatio]
Assure yourself, shall make the matter known.

Like Hamlet, Hieronymo has feigned madness to avoid alerting their fears; unsuspecting, they agree to humor him ("Hieronymo's mad againe") by acting the parts as he asks. When they inquire who shall take the part of the murderer, he replies, "O, that will I, my lords; make no doubt of it./I'll play the murderer, I warrant you,/For I already have conceited that." He carries out his promise to the letter when the play is presented, murdering them on stage before their fathers' eyes; and malevolently but heartbrokenly he reveals the true roles they have played.

So in saying "Why then Ile fit you," Hieronymo was saying not only "I'll supply your desire for entertainment," but also "I'll adapt my techniques to your circumstances," "I'll fit you into my intentions," "I'll alter my play to fit our purposes," and "I'll provide what is fitting to your deserts." And—the central theme of the play—Hieronymo, by focusing his whole psyche on vengeance, has fitted himself for the tortures of hell promised in the play's epilogue. His agonized and pitiless irony in the line borrowed by Eliot epitomizes the psychic effect of revenge central to the tragedy and etches itself indelibly on the reader's poetic sensibility.

Now let us see what Eliot has done with the line. He places it at the end of a poem which has not only as its subject matter but also as its form the processes of psychic progress. He is presenting a literary work to a reader who probably expects it to be roughly similar to many other poems he has read. The poet knows, though, that the reader will find this poem largely impervious to the usual approaches to poetry; he will be forced, if he wishes to experience this poem, to adapt his efforts to the form and techniques which Eliot has used. And in saying at the poem's end "Why then Ile fit you," he is promising to help fit the reader, through the poem and the patterns of experience necessary to the understanding of it, for possible success in his own quest.

Only by experiencing the works of art, literary and other, on which Eliot's poem draws, can the reader arrive at a truly comprehensive and detailed understanding of *The Waste Land* and achieve the state of the protagonist at the poem's end. The protagonist will fit the reader to put the Western traditions of literature, music, painting, architecture, and philosophy to what Eliot regards as their proper psychic or religious use. The poet-persona will provide entertainment, detective interest, and cultural instruction; but most importantly, he will help conduct the reader unawares down the hairy flank of Dante's Satan (*Inferno* 34) to that mysterious point at which he discovers that he is now climbing up toward the refining fire, having escaped his own waste land. The reader is reminded by this fragment that the aspiring psyche cannot focus on revenge or on the other dark lusts which separate it from other souls, but must dive eagerly into the refining flames.

What was in Kyd's play an impressive line has in *The Waste Land* entered fully into a new unity, and it has become a climactic statement of purpose which throws much light on the entire work. "Hieronoymo's mad againe," the subtitle to an early edition of Kyd's play, seems here to indicate that Eliot, like Hieronymo, though he mixes languages and confounds some of the expectations of his audience, does so not out of madness nor lack of skill.

The Waste Land ends with the reiteration of the three commands of the thunder: Give, Sympathize, Control. The state that follows obedience to the commands is indicated by the "Shantih shantih shantih" of the last line, somewhat akin to the "Selah" with which some of our Psalms end, and translated by Eliot as "the peace that passeth understanding."

Perhaps the *Facsimile* stanza "I am the Resurrection and the Life" should immediately precede the final fragments shored against ruins. It and the other sources cited for it by various critics probably all derive from the *Bhagavad-Gita* passage cited by Valerie Eliot.[26] It links the Eastern and Western traditions of Incarnation.

The "So through the evening, through the violet air" *Facsimile* passage supplied the inverted–towers lines.[27] These refer to the inverted values of postwar European civilization and of the waste land in all times and places. They also tie back to "The sound of horns and motors" in "The Fire Sermon." That line is adapted from Day's *Parliament of Bees*, in which the Plush Bee, determined

to make more show of his wealth than any rival, plans to build a
hive paved with clouds, sun, and moon and having for its ceiling

> Trees growing downwards, full of fallow deer;
> When of the sudden, listening, you shall hear
> A noise of horns and hunting, which shall bring
> Actaeon to Diana in the spring.

His world is topsy-turvy, like his values.[28]

I find convincing Stephen Spender's view that the maternal
lamentations and the hooded hordes, like Eliot's citation of Her-
mann Hesse's *Blick ins Chaos*, express the poet's deep concern over
the fate of refugees and sufferers in Europe after World War I.
I do not agree with him that the conception of the City of God
is lacking in *The Waste Land*: the Dante, Augustine, Buddha, and
Hindu references attest ample awareness of it.[29] Nevertheless, Eliot's
concluding sentence to "Thoughts after Lambeth" (1931) pre-
dicts that the world's experiment at forming a non-Christian but
civilized mentality will fail, but says we must patiently await its
collapse, "meanwhile redeeming the time: so that the Faith may
be preserved alive through the dark ages before us; to renew and
rebuild civilization, and save the World from suicide."[30] That prediction seems now, almost sixty years after *The Waste Land*, dis-
turbingly accurate.

If our civilization seems much farther now from achieving an
ideal society than in 1922, nevertheless, no individual is any more
doomed to the Waste Land than in Ezekiel's day, or Tiresias', or
John's, or Dante's, or Shakespeare's. *The Waste Land* and its meanings are not mired in history nor crucified on the calendar; it is not
showing the superiority of the past over the present, but is showing
the positive *and* negative potential of *every* time and place.
Escape is an individual matter, always available—but not easily,
as *Ash-Wednesday* and *Four Quartets* will demonstrate. In *The
Hollow Men*, it will seem to the protagonist beyond his energies.

Chapter Nine

Redeem the Dream

As D. E. S. Maxwell suggests, the waste land itself (not the poem) is "death's dream kingdom."[1] In *The Hollow Men*, this kingdom is contrasted with "death's other Kingdom" or "the twilight kingdom," which is the realm of Dante's earthly and heavenly paradises. This two-part division is based not on Dante's three canticles, but on the experience of the pilgrim in his relation to his lady Beatrice. The earthly paradise section of Dante's *Comedy* is indeed crucial to an understanding of either *The Hollow Men* or *Ash-Wednesday*: the meeting there with Beatrice is the turning point between the two kingdoms of death, and it is her eyes, or rather those of a lady analogous to her, that are feared and avoided, but desperately needed, in the "death's dream kingdom" of *The Hollow Men*. To understand thoroughly the implications of that meeting, one must also know Dante's *Vita Nuova*. Like most other major English poets, Eliot assumed his readers to be familiar with those two works of Dante. He speaks of "the system of Dante's organization of sensibility . . . the transition from Beatrice living to Beatrice dead, rising to the Cult of the Virgin. . . ."[2] It is in *La Vita Nuova* that we see Beatrice living and what she meant to Dante, who felt a voice within him, at their first meeting, cry, "Here beginneth the New Life." Beatrice, however, died early; and after her death, Dante was attracted to other loves. His affections strayed in various wrong directions until finally, in the middle of his life, he felt himself lost; or, as he says in the opening of the *Divine Comedy*, "I refound myself in a dark wood, where the proper road was lost" (my translation).

We find, however, in the *Divine Comedy*, that Beatrice, through

109

love and pity for him, has sent Virgil to guide him through hell (awareness of the nature of sin) and purgatory (self-knowledge) to the earthly paradise (regained innocence), where he will meet her again. Beatrice dead (his recognition of how much better he was under her influence) is the motive of Dante's self-development and self-mastery, the intermediary between Dante and the highest love, the love of God. When Dante meets Beatrice in the earthly paradise, he has already recognized in hell all that was debased in his former loves and inclinations; and in purgatory he has learned to turn away from the baser desires to the higher. In all this he was guided and counseled by Virgil and also, later, by Statius, who, unlike Virgil, was a Christian poet. Along the way these guides explained to Dante the nature of the soul and of love; but some things they could not explain. Beatrice, they promised, would be able to explain all such matters when he reached her. Eliot, like Dante, intends his poetry to perform similar functions for the reader.

The meeting between Dante and Beatrice, which takes place in cantos 30 and 31 of *Purgatorio*, is crucially alluded to in both *The Hollow Men* and *Ash-Wednesday*.

The Hollow Men (1924-25)

The persona of *The Hollow Men* defines himself in Dantean terms in sections 1, 2, and 4. The two epigraphs, "Mistah Kurtz—he dead" from Conrad's *Heart of Darkness* and "A penny for the Old Guy" (Guy Fawkes), suggest a pair of lost, violent souls that contrast with the hollow men. Kurtz in *Heart of Darkness* is called "hollow at the core," and yet his hollowness is less reprehensible than that of Eliot's hollow men insofar as he has at least made up his mind and acted, though wrongly. Marlowe, Conrad's narrator, describes Kurtz as "a voice"; he was a compelling speaker and writer who spouted idealisms of various sorts. Yet, when he traveled up the Congo River into the heart of Africa's darkness as an ivory trader, he succumbed to the whispering temptations of the jungle, to the primitive howling, the unsuspected appetites that Marlowe says may awake in any of us under such untrammeled conditions if we lack restraint; and he set himself up as a god among the natives, killing at will and participating in "unspeakable" midnight rites. By such means he extorted from his territory fantastic amounts of ivory—but, as the manager (another but less savory lost, violent soul) put it, his "methods" were "unsound."

He has failed to establish a satisfactory relationship with either of his ladies, his Intended back in Brussels or his black woman in the Congo—has abandoned both, so that both are remembered as stretching out their arms to him in unrequited longing. Finally, eaten up by jungle fever and his own insatiable burnings, Kurtz lies on a cot in the boat that is undertaking the impossible task of bringing him back to civilization; at the end, just before dying, he raises himself up, stares, and summarizes in a chilling, hollow voice the moral significance of what he has done: " 'The horror! The horror!' "

Eliot considered using these words as epigraph to *The Waste Land*, calling them "much the most appropriate I can find, and somewhat elucidative," but he was discouraged from doing so by Ezra Pound.[3] The "Mistah Kurtz" epigraph of *The Hollow Men* is spoken derisively by the cabin boy who reports the end of Kurtz's supremacy to the corrupt manager and his companions. It suggests here, as Eliot suggested elsewhere in reference to Baudelaire, that it is better to be a lost, violent soul like Kurtz or Guy Fawkes than to be one of Dante's trimmers—those who could not make up their minds to be either good or bad, and are not even allowed into hell proper but must perpetually chase banners hither and thither "as the wind behaves" in the vestibule of hell by the banks of "the tumid river" Acheron.

Guy Fawkes was a key figure in the Gunpowder Plot of 1605 which, in retaliation for harsh legal measures against Catholicism, was intended to blow up the House of Lords as King James opened the session of Parliament. When the plot failed, the key figures were executed. The day is still celebrated with fireworks in England, children carrying around straw-filled effigies of Guy Fawkes and begging pennies ("A penny for the Old Guy!") with which to buy fireworks. So here is another lost, violent soul and the source of the straw-filled-dummy image used in the poem as a symbol of the wastelanders with whom the persona identifies himself—as did not the protagonist of *The Waste Land*.

Three points in the Dantean scheme compose the moral ambience of *The Hollow Men*: the vestibule where the trimmers with their meaningless voices wander aimlessly; the reunion with Beatrice in the earthly paradise; and the multifoliate rose at the end of *Paradiso*. The two minor poems *Eyes that Last I Saw in Tears* and *The Wind Sprang Up at Four O'clock,* as well as *Song to the Opherion* and the nerves section of *The Waste Land*, are clearly and closely associated with *The Hollow Men*, the second having originally been published with parts 2 and 3 in the 1924 *Chapbook* as *Doris's Dream Songs*.[4] What emerges from the careful consideration of all these together is a protagonist who has participated in a separation scene (something like that of Eliot's early poem *La Figlia che Piange*) and whose life is now that of a hollow man, a dead man. When the dawn wind springs up at four o'clock, however, he is dreaming of another meeting with the girl from whom he turned away. Though their parting was final for this life, he dreams still of meeting her and reestablishing a satisfactory relation. Nevertheless, when he wakes alone, trembling with tenderness, "Lips that would kiss/Form prayers to broken stone." He realizes that such a meeting in this life is impossible, and he hopes only for a meeting like that of Dante with Beatrice. Such a meeting, though, entails the derision, the sharp rebuke which Dante suffered at Beatrice's appearance.

The tumid river in *The Hollow Men, Eyes that Last I Saw in Tears,* and *The Wind Sprang Up at Four O'clock* becomes the Thames of Conrad's *Heart of Darkness* and of *The Waste Land*, sweating tears and oil and tar. The memories of "sunlight on a broken column" and of the "tree swinging/And voices . . . in the wind's singing" of Dante's earthly paradise are qualified by the realization that these echoes are literary and are of a reality "More distant and more solemn/Than a fading star." So the "Lips that would kiss/Form prayers to broken stone," to the heap of broken images; the penitent attempts to find fulfillment in the ritual of the church at five o'clock in the morning. But this is the cactus land, so instead of the mulberry bush, *"Here we go round the prickly pear."* The ritual has lost its vitality. Even could the eyes be faced in dreams, even could grace restore the eyes with their rebuke and derision, this hollow man cannot bear to face the thought: "Between the idea [Dante's conception]/And the reality/ . . . Falls the Shadow." Perhaps this shadow suggests the rash act that grows out of boredom, as in Conrad's story "The Shadow-Line," and also the shadow of mortality which, in Dante's progress through purgatory, continually amazes the shades who have not crossed to death's other kingdom with direct eyes. And because Eliot's protagonist is hollow, stuffed with straw, he feels that, like Conrad's Marlowe, he will have nothing significant to say at his final moment—not the courage of Kurtz's "The horror! The horror!" and not the bang with which Guy Fawkes intended to end his world, but only the whimper of the fading Lord's Prayer: "For Thine is/ Life is/For Thine is the . . . ."

The Hollow Men ties together the worlds of Sweeney, *The Waste Land*, Dante, *Ash-Wednesday*, and the *Four Quartets*. The title *Doris's Dream Songs* signals the relations that emerge clearly upon careful examination. It is the waste-land world of *Sweeney Agonistes* that has been arrived at after the rejection, the division from "the eyes." The Dantean framework points forward to the later works; and yet the persona, recognizing all the possibilities of the lost, violent souls and of the blest souls as well, lacks the courage to be either. He prefers to join the souls of Dante's vestibule in "Behaving as the wind behaves." Stuffed with straw like the Guy Fawkes effigies, wearing "such deliberate disguises" as his scarecrow get-up, he avoids all significant actions or decisions.

Ash-Wednesday (1927-30)

In order of original publication, the parts of *Ash-Wednesday* are as follows: "Salutation" (1927, later part 2); *"Perch' io non spero"* (1928, later part 1); *"Al som de l'escalina"* (1929, later part 3); parts 4–6 added and the whole poem published under the title *Ash-Wednesday* (1930).

During that period, Eliot was very deeply involved with both religious and poetic questions, often overlapping each other. The fact that Eliot's poetry turned from the somewhat harsh negativity of Sweeney's world to the overtly religious topics of *The Hollow Men, Ash-Wednesday*, and the Ariel poems underscores his new preoccupation. In 1927 Eliot both joined the Church of England and became a British citizen, and we may assume that he participated in the church program of scripture study, which in each yearly course of the Christian calendar has one read the Psalms twelve times, the Old Testament once, and the New Testament twice. In such earlier works as *The Hippopotamus* and "Eeldrop and Appleplex" (1917) and *Mr. Eliot's Sunday Morning Service* (1918), his concern with theology and with the proper functions and rituals of the church had already been apparent.

The strong focus on Dante in his writings during this period helps to explain why these elements combined as they did in *Ash-Wednesday*: Dante had used the liturgy, the Christian calendar, the scriptural lessons, and hymns integrally in the scheme of his *Divine Comedy*; and he had combined with them the concept of the poet's craft as a striving after the proper sort of love, a part of his path toward God, and, equally important, the role of Beatrice, mediating between earthly and heavenly love. When we combine with this Dantean example Eliot's preoccupation with Anglican bishops (Andrewes and Bramhall), devotional poets (Crashaw, Herbert, and Donne), and Church historians, many of the strands of *Ash-Wednesday* emerge quite naturally. A number of the statements by the speakers in Eliot's 1927 "A Dialogue on Dramatic Poetry" are relevant, including these:

B: . . . We know too much, and are convinced of too little. Our literature is a substitute for religion, and so is our religion. . . .

E: . . . I say that the consummation of the drama, the perfect and ideal drama, is to be found in the ceremony of the Mass. I say . . . that drama springs from religious liturgy, and that it cannot afford to depart far from religious liturgy. . . . But when drama has ranged as far as it has in our own day, is not the only solution to return to religious liturgy? And the only dramatic satisfaction that I find now is in a High Mass well performed. Have you not there everything necessary? And indeed, if you consider the ritual of the Church during the cycle of the year, you have the complete drama represented. The Mass is a small drama, having all the unities; but in the Church year you have represented the full drama of creation. . . .

D: . . . The more fluid, the more chaotic the religious and ethical beliefs, the more the drama must tend in the direction of liturgy. Thus there would be some constant relation between drama and the religion of the time. . . .

C: To sum up: there is no "relation" between poetry and drama. All poetry tends towards drama, and all drama towards poetry.[5]

Ash Wednesday, the first day of Lent, is a day of fasting, contrition, and self-denial in which the Christian tries to renounce all other things and turn toward the things of God. In the Ash Wednesday service of the Anglican *Book of Common Prayer*, various scriptural readings are assigned as follows: Morning Prayer—Psalms: 32, 143; First Lesson: Isaiah 58:1–12; Second Lesson: Hebrews 12:1–14. Evening Prayer—Psalms: 102, 130; First Lesson: Jonah 3 and 4; Second Lesson: Luke 15:11.

Much of Eliot's imagery comes directly from these scripture lessons, in which the themes of "turning" and "turning again," of bones and dryness, and of birds are repeated so often as to be inevitably associated with the topic of Ash Wednesday. One example should suffice: In the Jonah reading, the King of Nineveh, having been warned by the prophet, proclaims, ". . . let man and beast be covered with sackcloth, and cry mightily unto God: yea, let them turn every one from his evil way, and from the violence that is in their hands. Who can tell if God will turn and repent, and turn way from his fierce anger, that we perish not? And God saw their works, that they turned from their evil way; and God repented of the evil, that he had said that he would do unto them; and he did it not."

Naturally the biblical imagery, including that of "turning," has permeated the offices and liturgy of the Anglican Church. In the penitential office used on Ash Wednesday, we read, "O most mighty God, and merciful Father, who hast compassion upon all men, and who wouldest not the death of a sinner, but rather that he should turn from his sin, and be saved; Mercifully forgive us our trespasses. . . . Turn thou us, O good Lord, and so shall we be turned. Be favorable, O Lord, Be favorable to thy people, Who turn to thee in weeping, fasting, and praying. For thou art a merciful God. . . . Spare thy people, good Lord, spare them, And let not thine heritage be brought to confusion."

Eliot's poem also quotes other phrases from the liturgy—some of them biblical in origin—such as: "Pray to God to have mercy upon us"; "Pray for us sinners now and at the hour of our death"; "Lord, I am not worthy but speak the word only"; "And after this our exile"; and "O my people, what have I done unto thee." Moreover, since Dante drew on the same sources in the earthly paradise and the paradise sections of his *Divine Comedy*, familiarity with the scriptural lessons and with the liturgy of the Anglican Church will illuminate both Eliot's *Ash-Wednesday* and Dante's influence on it. Far from being a collection of six loosely related poems, *Ash-Wednesday* is a disciplined expression of the experience of a particularly Dante-steeped penitent observing the Ash Wednesday rituals.

Another element from the traditions of the church heavily used by both Dante and Eliot is the imagery of what Eliot calls "the high dream"—the apocalyptic sort of imagery seen in the Book of Revelations, Daniel, Ezekiel, and Isaiah; in Dante's earthly and heavenly paradises; and in the eagle and leopard imagery of *Ash-Wednesday*. This sort of imagery, though rare in twentieth-century poetry, is still very much alive in the ritual of the church; it is also alive in many widely known Negro spirituals. It is the imagery of the Mass, and it is the most natural vehicle for the poet—Christian or not—who wishes to depict one celebrating the religious mystery of the incarnation of primal love in human flesh. These are the proper concerns of an Ash Wednesday penitent, and of the philosophical poets whom Eliot admires most—Dante and the writers of *The Bhagavad-Gita.*

Were Eliot's poetry didactic in the derogatory sense of that word, non-Catholic and non-Anglican readers might at this point turn away from the poem. Fortunately, however, as a number of critics have pointed out, Eliot in even his most philosophical and most religious poetry is setting before the reader authentic human experience—states, psychic actions, and realizations rather than labels and logical formulations. In this characteristic he may again be said to resemble Dante, who can be read with enjoyment and profit by a reader who rejects his theology, or who at least has reservations regarding it. Even in this most Christian of his poems, there is nothing narrow about Eliot's use of Christian symbols—indeed, he takes care to suggest through non-Christian symbols that the experience dealt with is paralleled outside the Christian persuasion.

Not surprisingly, the solutions to the chief critical problems of the poem grow out of the lines most likely to be noticed and questioned at a first reading—such lines as "Lady, three white leopards sat under a juniper-tree"; "Who walked between the violet and the violet"; "Because these wings are no longer wings to fly/But merely vans to beat the air"; "Till the wind shake a thousand whispers from the yew"; "But when the voices shaken from the yew-tree drift away/Let the other yew be shaken and reply"; and "While jewelled unicorns draw by the gilded hearse." And every one of these is greatly clarified by echoes of Dante, to whom we shall refer as we analyze the various sections of the poem.

I *"Perch' io non spero."*   Both the title of part 1 and its translation in the first line, "Because I do not hope to turn again," derive from a poem by Guido Cavalcanti (the friend to whom Dante dedicated his *Vita Nuova*), a *ballata* written in exile to Cavalcanti's Lady, whom he did not expect to see again before dying. Since the conception of the Lady seen in the *ballata* derives from the courtly love tradition of the Provençal troubadours via the Sicilian and Tuscan schools of Italian poetry—to which Dante, Cavalcanti, Pistoia, and other advocates of their "sweet new style" added the worship of the Virgin Mary—this *ballata* implies a relinquishing of aspirations toward both Cavalcanti's Lady and his poetic craft, of which she is the muse. His renunciation, like that in part 1 of *Ash-Wednesday,* suggests the state of Dante after the death of Beatrice; and it gives added significance to Eliot's dedication of his poem to the first Mrs. Eliot. The "Because I do not hope" line recurs near the end of part 1 and again, with a slight change, at the beginning of part 6.

Part 1 rejects three kinds of striving on the protagonist's part— that of his conscious will to control his fate, that (as poet-prophet) to rival such masters as Shakespeare and Dante, and that (as lover) toward his earthly Lady. To match these three renunciations, part 1 contains at least five triads of various sorts. The first three stanzas, each beginning "Because I . . . ," comprise one of the triads, summarized in the couplet "Consequently I rejoice, having to construct something/Upon which to rejoice."

In renouncing the poet-prophet's striving, the protagonist compares himself to an aged eagle (the eagle was known to Dante and to his contemporaries as the bird that could look at the sun without being blinded—the poet can look at the truth more steadily than most of his fellows). The transition from Beatrice living to Beatrice dead fuses the three sorts of renunciation, and at any rate the three spirits are not separable except as an expedient of analysis: in the poem, as in life, they merge and intertwine.

Dante's *Vita Nuova* and *Divine Comedy* study the journey from earthly love to the highest felicity in the attainment of the deified Lady, and the use in Eliot's earlier poetry of purgatorial symbolism— along with such symbols as Tristan and Isolde and the Holy Grail— may be taken to indicate an earlier, more optimistic period in which the poet felt greater faith in his art and his love as a means of attaining such felicity. Now, however, he knows that such aspirations are possible only for one place and one time, for Dante in 1300, perhaps again in one time and one place for himself or some other poet, but not with any sense of permanence. Since this is true, the speaker says, "Consequently I rejoice, having to construct something/Upon which to rejoice/And pray to God to have mercy upon us." Such efforts and such confident aspirations as were seen in the earlier poetic attempts form a proper stage in the artist's development ("The vanished power of the usual reign"); but they cannot be permanent, "Because one has only learnt to get the better of words/For the thing one no longer has to say, or the way in which/One is no longer disposed to say it" (*East Coker*). Realizing all this, and aiming toward the relaxed and humble acceptance of his proper place in the scheme of things, the *Ash-Wednesday* penitent prays for mercy: "Let these words answer/For what is done, not to be done again/May the judgement not be too heavy upon us." And because his will and his craft are no longer seen as wings to fly, because he realizes it is not by his own concentration and exertion of will that the proper state can be reached, he prays, hoping to accept his limitations and his present state, "Teach us to care and not to care/Teach us to sit still."

The state suggested by this first section is one of deep humility growing out of awareness of one's actual and one's proper relation to the universe. The turning away of all three renunciations symbolizes the turning to God which permeates the scriptures and liturgy traditionally connected with Ash Wednesday, and the protagonist does not hope to turn again away from God to a reliance in himself and his capacities.

II "Salutation." The second section begins

> Lady, three white leopards sat under a juniper-tree
> In the cool of the day, having fed to satiety
> On my legs my heart my liver and that which had been
> contained
> In the hollow round of my skull.

The three sorts of striving renounced in part 1 seem to be the diets of the three allegorical white leopards; the three strivings reside in three different organs. They may be matched to Dante's three-part psychology (in *La Vita Nuova*) as follows:

> Vital spirit—heart—striving of the conscious will;
> Animate spirit—brain—striving of the poet-prophet;
> Natural spirit—liver—striving for the earthly Lady.

Eliot's emphasis on the proper roles of the artist and artistic aspiration is further seen in the epigraph originally attached to part 2: "The Hand of the Lord Was Upon Me:-*e vo significando.*" The Italian clause occurs in *Purgatorio* 24. 52-54, where Dante explains to the poet Bonagiunta of Lucca his "sweet new style (*dolce stil nuovo*)": "When Love inspires me I take note, and I write in that mode (*e vo significando*) which he dictates within."[6] Both the sense of the passage and the explicit references in the context relate it to Dante's Lady.[7] The passage occurs on the sixth cornice of purgatory in a context highly relevant to *Ash-Wednesday*, between the encounters with the two yew trees of that cornice.

The first half of the epigraph comes from the dry bones passage of Ezekiel 37, and it ushers in the imagery of the higher dream, of bones and leopards and Ladies (as of the eagle in part 1). Eliot applied the term "high dream" to the divine pageant accompanying the appearance of Dante's Beatrice, and its strict parallel in *Ash-Wednesday* is in the line "While jewelled unicorns draw by the gilded hearse." Both he and Dante are here echoing the pageant of the Mass—in which the protagonist of Eliot's poem is participating.

So Eliot's epigraph attests the faithfulness of the heightened imagery to the poet's inspiration, as well as his submissiveness, and also the relevance to this section of the love of the Lady in all her ramifications. He is claiming for his poem the highest inspiration, derived from Primal Love.

The humility and submission of part 1 are equated to the dry bones lying in the sand and scattered. The value of the renunciation is suggested in the brightness of the bones. The leopards suggest Dante's three beasts (leopard, lion, and wolf), the leopard being identified with sins of incontinence.

The juniper tree under which the leopards sat suggests the juniper under which Elijah sat in I Kings 19: having overcome and slain the priests of Baal, Elijah has been forced by Jezebel's threats to flee into the wilderness. He sits under the tree and implores, "Now, O Lord, take away my life; for I am not better than my fathers." His attitude is similar to that of the penitent of our poem, and further details suggest the forty-day Lenten season, the communion, and the final vision of God. He falls asleep and is twice wakened by an angel who commands him to eat of a cake baked there on coals and to drink from a cruse of water. This sacrament sustains him through forty days spent on Mount Horeb, the mount of God, without further nourishment. Finally, after a strong wind that breaks the rocks, an earthquake, and a fire, God reveals himself in a still small voice telling the prophet to go and anoint not only new kings over Syria and Israel but also a new prophet to take his own place.

In the Ezekiel account, God asks, "Shall these bones live?" He commands Ezekiel to prophesy to the bones and promises to reassemble them and clothe them in flesh, make them live again, and place them in the land of their inheritance according to His previous promises. In *Ash-Wednesday*, "That which had been contained/In the bones" replies, chirping with the burden of the grasshopper of Ecclesiastes 12, a passage also relevant to *Gerontion* and *The Waste Land*:

Remember now thy Creator in the days of thy youth, while the evil days come not, nor the years draw nigh, when thou shalt say, I have no pleasure in them. . . . And the doors shall be shut in the streets, when the sound of the grinding is low, and he shall rise up at the voice of the bird . . . and the almond tree shall flourish, and *the grasshopper* [my italics] shall be a burden, and desire shall fail: because man goeth to his long home, and the mourners go about the streets. . . . And moreover, because the preacher was wise, he still taught the people

knowledge. . . . The preacher sought to find out acceptable words . . .
even words of truth. . . . And further, by these, my son, be admonished:
of making many books there is no end; and much study is a weariness
of the flesh. Let us hear the conclusion of the whole matter: Fear
God, and keep his commandments: for this is the whole duty of man.

"The burden of the grasshopper" comprises the renunciations of
Ash-Wednesday, part 1.

The protagonist proffers his deeds to oblivion (as Jonah is
reluctant to do in the Jonah 4 Ash Wednesday scripture lesson),
and this compliance recovers those parts of him which the leopards
reject. The song of the bones is patterned on Saint Bernard's prayer
to the Virgin Mary in *Paradiso* 32 and 33. Beatrice has done all
she can for Dante by leading him to the point of gazing on the
multifoliate rose of the whole company of the blest, the Church
Triumphant, and she has made him aware of the symbolic nature
of much that he has seen. Having served to the limits of her usefulness for Dante's aspirations, she has been replaced by the shade
of the contemplative Saint Bernard. As Dante warms to the intense
love that radiates from Mary and is mirrored all round by the
blessed souls, Bernard prays to Mary to fit Dante to look directly
on the vision of God, the Primal Love. Bernard's prayer is answered,
and the *Divine Comedy* closes on Dante's attempt to figure dimly
the vision of the Primal Love then revealed to him—what Eliot in
Selected Essays terms "to my mind, the highest point that poetry
has ever reached or ever can reach" (1950, p. 212).

Part 2 of *Ash-Wednesday* closes with the bones singing "We are
glad to be scattered, we did little good to each other," and with their
acceptance of dryness and separation as the land of their inheritance,
the earthly Lady has been surrendered according to the adjusted
vision of the higher dream.

III *"Som de l'escalina."* The title *"Som de l'escalina,"*
originally attached to the third section, again focuses our attention
on the late cantos of *Purgatorio*, specifically on the exchange between Dante and Arnaut Daniel, already referred to in chapter 8.
It is Arnaut who, in the lines most often used by Eliot, asks to be

remembered when Dante reaches "the topmost of the stair." *"Sovegna vos"* ("Be mindful [in due time of my pain]")—from the same speech—will appear shortly in part 4 of *Ash-Wednesday*.

This title identifies the vantage point from which the penitent's "blind eye" recreates in part 3 the climbing of the three purgatorial stairs which are close echoes of two details in Dante: the three steps of penitence to St. Peter's gate of purgatory—*confession, contrition,* and *satisfaction*—and the three classes of improperly ordered love on which the structure of purgatory is based—*distorted, defective,* and *excessive* loves.[8] Their immediate source is probably in the three steps to the high altar and the turnings of the Mass ceremony.

The three strophes of *Ash-Wednesday* part 3 bring the protagonist almost to the top of the stairs, to the point at which he is about to make the passage to the earthly paradise—or to partake of the sacrament of the Mass. Having almost completed the purgation of his improperly ordered loves, he looks back and remembers the process by which he has come to this point; and at this moment his faith and humility are expressed in the line from the Mass, taken from Matthew 8:8, "Lord, I am not worthy but speak the word only." This "word" suggests the words of the angels who admit Dante and his companions to each cornice of purgatory, without which none can proceed. Whoever is admitted to the last stair has disciplined his appetites and ordered his loves; he has reached a condition in which his own inclinations are the surest guides to proper conduct.

The third stair seems to involve the purgation of excessive love: of avarice, gluttony, and lust. Its imagery is highly sexual. However, these distraction themes, these unwilling memories, are fading; and the protagonist experiences a strength beyond hope and despair, a strength which allows him to resign himself for the entry to the earthly paradise—to life at its best on this earth. I suggest that Eliot's poem does not exclude what C. S. Lewis, in *The Allegory of Love*, refers to as "a love which reaches the divine without abandoning the human and becomes spiritual while remaining also carnal."[9] However, the death of Beatrice in *La Vita Nuova* and Dante's exile suggest reasons for Dante's eschewing such a solution; and Eliot's protagonist has similar reasons for renouncing the blessed face.

The seeming regression of part 3 from the paradisal echoes of Bernard's "Queen of Heaven" prayer in part 2 clarifies the protagonist's subtle awareness of the levels of symbolism and imagery that are part of his poet-penitent quest for felicity. Only symbolically has he experienced what Dante is talking about in the end of *Paradiso*, and the desire to savor the sensations of such an experience is perhaps the form of gluttony that detains Forese, Bonagiunta of Lucca, and our protagonist on the sixth cornice of purgatory for a time. An excessive savoring of involvement in the sensual aspects of both their experiences and their craft of poetry is the "burning" of Buddha's "Fire Sermon." The surrendering of "word" for "Word" is one of the most difficult renunciations for the poet.

IV.   The fourth section recreates the earthly paradise setting of Dante's meeting with Beatrice; cantos 28–33 of *Purgatorio* will shed more light on its meanings than any amount of explication, and should be read with *Ash-Wednesday*. The protagonist's Beatrice-figure is addressed in the first eleven lines. Her appearance, like that of Beatrice, parallels the uncovering of the host, the sacramental elements, in the Mass. She makes the fountains spring up and redeems the time and the dream. The last eight lines echo Dante's bliss shortly before his ascent to paradise. Eliot is restoring with a new verse—his own—the ancient rhyme of Dante; he is also restoring with the new heavenly verse—the higher dream—the ancient earthly love. The *Ash-Wednesday* penitent is aspiring to Dante's Beatrice-dead experience and is praying to his God-bearing figures for their favor and help.

Part 4 concludes with the reminder, from the "Salve Regina" of the liturgy, that Mary stands as a link to the Word, the divine image, which shall follow: "Turn then, most gracious advocate, thine eyes of mercy towards us. And after this our exile, show unto us the blessed fruit of thy womb, Jesus."[10] Eliot uses only the line "And after this our exile."

V. The fifth section begins with the well-known incantatory consideration of the Word, culminating in the lines "Against the Word the unstilled world still whirled/About the centre of the silent Word," and continuing in the next strophe in the self-aware but not self-conscious "Where shall the word be found, where will the word/Resound?" passage. Such echoing and balancing of tensions is carried on throughout part 5, a section which owes more than just a text to the sonorous sermons of Lancelot Andrewes.

That text of the Word or Logos has been used frequently in Eliot's poetic career: as "The word within a word, unable to speak a word,/Swaddled with darkness" in *Gerontion* (1920); as "In the beginning was the Word./Superfetation of *to en*" in *Mr. Eliot's Sunday Morning Service* (1918), implying the Greek origins in Heraclitus and before; as the present passage in *Ash-Wednesday* and "the Infant, the still unspeaking and unspoken Word" of *A Song for Simeon* (1928); in *The Rock* as "Knowledge of words and ignorance of the Word" and "Where the word is unspoken/We will build with new speech" in chorus 1, "Much is your reading, but not the Word of God" and "the time-kept City;/where My Word is unspoken" in chorus 3, and "Then it seemed as if men must proceed from light to light, in the light of the Word [after the Incarnation]" in chorus 7.

And finally, in *Burnt Norton*, appears "The Word in the desert," as well as the Greek epigraph from the Logos passage of Heraclitus that reads as follows: "This Word [Logos] is from everlasting, yet men understand it as little after the first hearing of it as before. For though all things come to pass according to this Word, men seem wanting in experience when they examine the words and deeds I set forth, distinguishing each thing in its nature and showing how it truly is. But other men know not what they do when awake, even as they forget what they do in sleep. . . ."[11] The Gospel of John opens with a newer version: "In the beginning was the Word, and the Word was with God, and the Word was God. The

same was in the beginning with God. All things were made by
him; and without him was not anything made that was made. In
him was life; and the life was the light of men." Lancelot Andrewes
may very well have been responsible for this King James version
of John. (He was one of the committee of translators.) At any rate
it is echoed in the sermon from which Eliot quotes the lines "The
word within a word, unable to speak a word," which he calls an
example of Andrewes' "flashing phrases which never desert the
memory."[12]

Eliot's Word passage at the beginning of part 5 of *Ash-Wednesday* closes with the suggestion of the profound reorientation
achieved by Dante in *Paradiso* when he realized that what had
seemed to him the farthest and widest sphere was really the still
center of the universe, with the discordant, unstilled world whirling about it at a great distance. But "For those who walk in darkness . . . who avoid the face," conditions for finding the Word are
not propitious, we are told in the next strophe. Eliot's veiled sister,
the Beatrice-figure, is asked to pray for those about to partake of
the divine revelation, those about to spit from the mouth the
withered apple seed, the last vestige of Eve's guilt in eating of the
Tree of Knowledge and of Persephone's partaking of the pome-
granate in the underworld—both of which are explained by Dante's
Matilda as relevant to the earthly paradise. As well as the protagonists's acceptance of celibacy, this emptying of the mouth suggests
the whole pattern of confession, contrition, and satisfaction which
prepares the Ash Wednesday communicant to take in his mouth
the sacred Elements—now already revealed on the altar.

The two earlier repetitions of the Good Friday reproach, "O
my people, what have I done unto thee," spoken by God to his
rebellious people in Micah 6:3, suggest the difficulty in the
whirling world of proper orientation to the Word, as well as the
undeservedness of Christ's rejection by men. In the Micah passage,
God enumerates the blessings He has given and concludes, "O my
people, remember now . . . that ye may know the righteousness

of the Lord." It is this positive note that is suggested by the "O my people" that concludes part 5.

The "word" of this part of the poem is not only the divine Word but also the poetic word. It is only in Dante's poetry that the final meeting with the Lady leads to the unattenuated vision of Primal Love. It is only in poetry or after death that the felicity depicted by Dante can be achieved. The vision of Dante is good only for one time and one place, and, though the protagonist of *Ash-Wednesday* has chosen the veiled sister, he is terrified and cannot surrender; he affirms before the world and denies between the rocks—the last blue rocks of part 5, which suggest the stairway to the earthly paradise on which Dante, Virgil, and Statius spend the night after the dark shadows have closed in around them. On the next morning comes the long-desired reunion.

VI.   The opening of part 6, substituting "Although" for "Because," surrenders even the causal emphasis of *"Perch' io non spero."* Again "I do not hope" is repeated three times, reminding us of the three spirits renounced and of the protagonist's inability to correct his own state. Here he wavers in the twilight between birth and dying, the years which, he hopes, are bearing away the sensuous attachment to earthly things—attachment to lesser loves. It is also the dreamcrossed twilight between the dying out of the renounced appetites and the spiritual birth hoped for. In this ambivalent state he asks for the blessing of the priest ("Bless me father"). He confesses that, although he does not wish it, the images of the rejected objects of the appetites, of the unordered loves, still recur to him. Still "the lost heart stiffens" and "the blind eye creates/The empty forms between the ivory gates." But the nearness of success is indicated: these are *empty* forms, seen at the ivory gates from which, as in Virgil's *Aeneid*, the *false* dreams issue. The rocks of this place are "blue of Mary's colour," the color of grace.

The three dreams that cross in this purple twilight reiterate the three rejected spirits, the leopards, and the stairs; they further echo

Oedipus' "place where three roads meet" and Plato's similar references in the myth of the soul's experiences after death in the *Phaedo.* The yew-tree references suggest *Purgatorio* 32 and the unbearably sweet singing from the Tree of Knowledge, of Man's proper nature after Christ the griffon has reunited to the Tree the chariot pole (his cross, traditionally of yew wood).

The penitent has seen the anatomy of hell, has recognized the nature of his improper impulses; he has heard the voices crying examples of temperance and gluttony from the two yews of cornice 6, where his poet-acquaintances purge the excessive attachment to the life of the senses that seems an occupational hazard for them. His struggle is not to be won unequivocally before death, but it can be won through the humility and acceptance of Ash Wednesday and through the grace figured in the Ladies, to whom the final prayer of the poem is offered. "Our peace in His will" (*"e la sua volontate é nostra pace"*) was spoken by Piccarda de Donati in Dante's *Paradiso* 3, as she explained that though there are degrees of blessedness in heaven, each spirit there accepts his own place without jealousy or discontent. *Ash-Wednesday* closes with the prayer that immediately precedes the receiving of the Eucharist, "Suffer me not to be separated/And let my cry come unto Thee."

It will be found on reflection that the main differences between *Ash-Wednesday* and *The Waste Land* are in the exclusiveness of the Christian imagery used and in the degree of self-revelation— and not in religious content. The protagonists of both poems are chiefly concerned, in Dantean terms, with the difficult transition from purgatory proper to the regained innocence of the earthly paradise, after the recognition of the anatomy of hell has been accomplished. In *The Waste Land*, of course, there is greater emphasis on communicating the recognition of hell to the reader; in *Ash-Wednesday* the central focus is on the surrender of self, the humility of prayer—on the re-creation of the meditating Ash Wednesday communicant. The themes, symbols, and attitudes seen in this poem will dominate most of Eliot's remaining poetic production as well as *The Rock; Murder in the Cathedral*; and, to a lesser extent, the other plays.

Ariel Poems

During the period from *The Hollow Men* (1925) to *Ash-Wednesday* (1930) were published four Ariel poems (the name given by the Faber firm to a series of Christmas poems): *Journey of the Magi* (1927), *A Song for Simeon* (1928), *Animula* (1929, discussed in chapter 3), and *Marina* (1930). The first two poems have personae—comparable to Gerontion—who in each case contemplate the significance of the incarnation, the birth of Christ, which has put an end to one era and begun another, combining birth and death.

The Journey of the Magi (1927). The title *The Journey of the Magi* suggests also the epic journey of the hero myths, for after rigorous trials the hero is initiated, but then he must return to his own world and try to make the hard adjustment of living with and communicating his knowledge to the uninitiated. The Magus says,

> I had seen birth and death,
> But had thought they were different; this Birth was
> Hard and bitter agony for us, like Death, our death.
> We returned to our places, these Kingdoms,
> But no longer at ease here, in the old dispensation,
> With an alien people clutching their gods.
> I should be glad of another death.

A Song for Simeon (1928). The title character of *A Song for Simeon* is found in the biblical story of Joseph and Mary's bringing Jesus to Jerusalem to dedicate him to the Lord (Luke 2: 25–35):

And, behold, there was a man in Jerusalem, whose name was Simeon; and the same man was just and devout, waiting for the consolation of Israel: and the Holy Ghost was upon him.

And it was revealed unto him by the Holy Ghost, that he should not see death, before he had seen the Lord's Christ.

And he came by the Spirit into the temple: and when the parents brought in the child Jesus, to do for him after the custom of the law,

Then took he him up in his arms, and blessed God, and said,

Lord, now lettest thou thy servant depart in peace, according to thy word:

For mine eyes have seen thy salvation. . . .

After blessing them, Simeon said to Mary,

. . . Behold, this child is set for the fall and rising again of many in Israel; and for a sign which shall be spoken against;

(Yea, a sword shall pierce through thy own soul also,) that the thoughts of many hearts may be revealed.

In the poem, Simeon foresees the Roman oppressions and the crucifixion; and he asks to be granted the peace of death before those things occur. Old and tired, he says: "Not for me the martyrdom, the ecstasy . . ./Not for me the ultimate vision./Grant me thy peace." He also repeats the parenthetic "(And a sword shall pierce thy heart,/Thine also)." Like Gerontion's, "this show" has not been made purposelessly; and yet this sign that he has seen, this unspoken Word, will be rejected by many.

Marina (1930). In *Marina* we have one of Eliot's most appealing and best-loved poems. We need not recognize any of its echoes of either Shakespeare's *Pericles* or Seneca's *Hercules Furens* to find its tone and imagery free, open, and compelling. The reader familiar with *Pericles* will recognize that Eliot has strikingly recreated the tonality of the remarkable recognition scene in act 5 of that play. The Latin epigraph from Seneca—spoken by Hercules as he comes out of a fit of madness in which, though he does not yet realize it, he has killed his children—seems to add a rather cruel qualification to the felicity of the poem. Yet, even though the song of the woodthrush may be "the deception of the thrush" (*Burnt Norton*), I would connect that deception to the earlier, unfulfilled aspirations of Pericles' youth. For we remember that in *The Waste Land* it is the hermit thrush singing in the pine trees that is longed for as a sign of the much-desired water; in *Marina*, however, the song is real, the face is real, the pulse is real; and all previous suffering fades to insignificance.

So the epigraph, on second thought, seems to suggest the contrasting vices of the incestuous Antiochus and his daughter, the murderously jealous Dionyza and her compliant husband Cleon, the hired murderers, pirates, and panderers of the play, all of which Shakespeare sets against the unwavering virtues of Pericles, his daughter Marina, and his wife Thaisa. The former vices seem to be referred to in Eliot's enumeration of five of the cardinal sins. "Those who sharpen the tooth of the dog" suggests the concupiscence of a number of Shakespeare's characters. "Those who glitter with the glory of the hummingbird" suggests Antiochus' persistence in his incestuous relation, and "Those who suffer the ecstasy of the animals," the inhabitants and the patrons of the brothel from which Marina escapes unsullied. But all of these "Are become unsubstantial" by the grace of the reunions with Marina and Thaisa. "No more, you gods!" says Shakespeare's Pericles. "Your present kindness makes my past miseries sports. You shall do well that on the touching of her lips I may melt and no more be seen." This last sentence suggests the resignation of the end of *Marina*. Both the heavenly music that Shakespeare's Pericles hears, the music of the spheres, and the trembling, unbelievable surmise of fulfillment have gotten into Eliot's verse.

We may hope that the long-tortured poet had found—however briefly—such bliss as informs *Marina*, in a foreshadowing of the happy second marriage that crowned his career and elicited the peace and joy of *The Elder Statesman*.

The boat imagery of the poem is similar to that of Rimbaud's *Le Bateau Ivre* [The Drunken Boat]; the boat is the speaker Pericles himself—another of Eliot's Old Man personae. Pericles' decline is referred to in the lines "Bowsprit cracked with ice and paint cracked with heat" and "The rigging weak and the canvas rotten." The "this" that he made "Between one June and another September" is Marina, his daughter. Now, though his "garboard strake leaks, [and] the seams need caulking," Marina, a new ship, will live on beyond his time. And Pericles is quite contented to "Resign my life for this life, my speech for that unspoken." Here, in perhaps the most sustained ecstasy of Eliot's poems, the deadly sins, "meaning Death," are "reduced by a wind,/A breath of pine, and the woodsong fog."

Chapter Ten

Cry What Shall I Cry?

The great felicity of *Marina* could not cancel out other pressures in Eliot's life that were drawing to a head. Perhaps his most difficult times lay ahead of him, times requiring emotional discipline of the most stringent kind. The two *Coriolan* poems and *Minor Poems*, especially *Landscapes*, will particularize that statement.

Coriolan (1931)

The two poems entitled *Coriolan* consider the qualities of a proper hero and statesman as contrasted with both the unheroic qualities of the mob and the pride of Shakespeare's Coriolanus, not a proper statesman and eventually a traitor, though he has been a considerable hero. Another contrast with the proper statesman is seen in the petty committees and commissions, complete with all the details of minor statesmanship that erode the heroism of the public servant and, by forcing the compromises of which Shakespeare's Coriolanus is incapable, bow and dim the fierce spirit and the aggressive virtues of the hero.

Eliot considered *Coriolanus* one of Shakespeare's two most assured artistic successes (the other being *Antony and Cleopatra*). It provides a link between a number of Eliot's works: *A Cooking Egg*, the suppressed 1920 *Ode, The Waste Land*, and the two parts of *Coriolan*.

Three other sources seem to me crucially important in Eliot's *Coriolan* poems. The first is Isaiah 38 and 40 in which the prophet is admonished to prophesy to his society. The second is Charles Maurras's *L'Avenir de l'Intelligence*, which "opens with an ironic account of how each new tawdry journalistic triumph is now

133

greeted in the streets with procession and applause."[1] Eliot's third
major source is canto 6 of Dante's *Purgatorio*, from which both
Dante's opening image of soldiers dicing and a central theme are
taken.

I *Triumphal March*. In *Triumphal March* we see the hero
Coriolan still loyal, but chafing against "the rank-scented many";
because of his pride and self-interest, he has the potential of becoming a traitor later on. The poem shows him coming back from
war, receiving the adulation of the public, having demonstrated his
heroic qualities in battle. The emphasis is on the artificial pageantry,
the interminable wait for the significant moment when the ob-
servers can see the hero, and also on the hero himself:

> There he is now, look:
> There is no interrogation in his eyes
> Or in the hands, quiet over the horse's neck,
> And the eyes watchful, waiting, perceiving, indifferent.
> O hidden under the dove's wing, hidden in the turtle's breast,
> Under the palmtree at noon, under the running water
> At the still point of the turning world. O hidden.

The speaker of those lines is obviously impressed by the hero's eyes
but fails to see through them to the character that will make
Shakespeare's Coriolanus betray his country through inability to
abandon the ways of war and deal with the peaceful citizens. The
citizens are more interested in the sausage that may come in handy
later than in either the details of the pageant or the concerns of war
in which Coriolan won his glory. The unbending pride that makes
him see himself as infinitely above the commoners and ultimately
above the state is his undoing in Shakespeare's play. His mother,
in fact, is the only person whom we see him treat as an equal in
that play.

The irony of the poem is doubled: Coriolan sees the true role
of the hero and statesman no more than the common people watching the procession see what is behind his eyes. Chiefly they see
"Stone, bronze, stone, steel, stone, oakleaves, horses' heels/Over the

paving," which they quickly forget in their small chatter about "young Cyril," originally intended by Eliot as the central character of a whole series of poems. Taken to church on Easter, Cyril mistook for the tea-time bell the communion bell signaling the revelation of the Host and "said right out loud, *crumpets.*" Similarly, all of the people in this poem have missed the significance of the life-giving ritual. "Don't throw away that sausage,/It'll come in handy," says one of them. We have Richard Eberhart's word that Eliot told him this sausage was "of Aristophanic origin, besides being phallic."[2]

II *Difficulties of a Statesman.* In *Difficulties of a Statesman*—not published separately as *Triumphal March* had been before both appeared as *Coriolan*—the time of the triumphal march is past and the details of administration are galling the hero. The poem begins with Isaiah's "Cry what shall I cry?" presumably paralleling Shakespeare's act 3 in which Coriolanus' pride keeps him from accepting the political reality of his relation to the common people and working through the accepted procedures with them. Having hoped for heroic and vigorous action, he is now faced with committees and commissions and secretaries; and the efforts of the committees to establish perpetual peace are opposed by the fletchers and javelin-makers and smiths, who have even formed their own committee. "Where are the eagles and the trumpets?" he cried in *A Cooking Egg*, and answered "Buried beneath some snow-deep Alps." His former vision of the proper composure of a statesman is attenuated: "O hidden under the . . . Hidden under the . . ." (Eliot's ellipses). Rather than Gerontion's "dull head among windy spaces," Coriolan calls himself "a tired head among these heads." Shakespeare's Coriolanus, we remember, refused to placate "the mutable, rank-scented many"; his nature was "too noble for this world; he would not flatter Neptune for his trident." Coriolanus' fierce pride was earlier spurred on by his mother, Volumnia, of whom he asks: "Cry what shall I cry?" How, Eliot's hero asks, can he cope with these situations? What can he cry, what can he write, say, or do to help his city?

The frogs that "croak in the marshes" have a literary parallel in Aristophanes' *The Frogs*, where Dionysus, the god of drama, is going to Hades to find a playwright who can help the city of Athens in its difficulties.

Five-Finger Exercises (1932)

The five poems entitled *Five-Finger Exercises* are, like the later *Old Possum's Book of Practical Cats* (1939), delightful parodies on other poets as well as exercises in various devices and forms of verse. Nevertheless, the content of the first three of these five is serious and reflects the religious concern of the period from *The Hollow Men* to *Ash-Wednesday.* Grover Smith lists a number of probable sources for the poems' echoes and allusions.[3]

The first exercise, *I. Lines to a Persian Cat,* is set in Russell Square, that lovely green space of flowers, walks, benches, and big trees bounded on two sides by the British Museum, Senate House of the University of London, and the building at 24 Russell Square to which, for his last forty years, Eliot went to work. Here may be seen "the songsters of the air," dear to bird-watcher Eliot. "The quick eyes of Woolly Bear" also see the owners of Persian cats, Pekes, Pollicles, and Yorkshire terriers, stirring sharp desires that will not be indulged. "Woolly Bear" will sit in the broken chair of his situation wondering *"When* will time flow away?"

In *II. Lines to a Yorkshire Terrier,* the tree is not green but "crookt and dry." The protagonist of *The Death of St. Narcissus* (1915) "wished that he had been a tree" but is now "dry and stained/With the shadow in his mouth." Like the natural forces that shriek aloud from a black sky, threatening a Yorkshire terrier, the sharp desires and quick eyes threaten the "I" of this second *Exercise.* The terrier is "safe and warm/ Under a cretonne eiderdown," suggesting the comforts of religion and acceptance, but since the field and the tree are yet cracked and brown, cramped and dry, the speaker must, like the terrier, pause and heave up his prior paws (saying grace like the child of Herrick's *Another Grace for a Child*), and then let the quick eyes and sharp desires sleep endlessly.

III. Lines to a Duck in the Park shows us a would-be Grail Knight, such as Percivale in Tennyson's *The Holy Grail*, who faltered, however, in his quest when after many nights in the open as "a bed-mate of the snail and eft and snake," he grew "wan and meagre" and then was reunited with the love of his youth, who made the quest fade in his heart.

Frank Morley's recollections on Eliot (in Tate's *T. S. Eliot: The Man and His Work*, p. 95), besides supplying numerous delightful insights into the poet's life and times, throw light on Eliot's selection of a subject for *IV. Lines to Ralph Hodgson Esqre*. Hodgson's dog, Pickwick, would probably have been encountered at Morley's Pike's Farm, where Eliot stayed after his return from the States in 1933 and must have visited earlier. This and the last of the *Five-Finger Exercises, V. Lines for Cuscuscaraway and Mirza Murad Ali Beg*, contrast the popular, jovial Poet-Epicure Hodgson with the dour self-portrait of Mr. Eliot, "with his features of clerical cut,/ . . . and his conversation . . . restricted to . . . If and Perhaps and But."

In all five of these 1932 poems, the strain of the breakdown of Eliot's marriage to Vivien comes through intensely.

Landscapes (1936)

Eliot's title *Landscapes* and his use of Roman numerals with the individual titles indicate that he saw as a related group his five additional inclusions in *Minor Poems: I. New Hampshire, II. Virginia, III. Usk, IV. Rannoch, by Glencoe,* and *V. Cape Ann*. Several critics have pointed out that in various ways these lyrics prefigure *Four Quartets*. Grover Smith mentions their "emotional relaxation" and musicality; indeed, Eliot first published *New Hampshire* and *Virginia* under the title *Words for Music*. Ann Brady refers to "Eliot's development toward *Four Quartets* in the use of place for lyric subject matter." Helen Gardner points out themes shared by the two groups of poems: children's voices, stillness and heat, legendary and historical motifs, and memories of New England boy-hood. She also acknowledges that some of the above elements appear in *Five-Finger Exercises*, and of course some appeared in much earlier Eliot poems.[4]

As to what ties the five lyrics together, several critics have pursued George Williamson's observation that "from each place he [Eliot] distils an essence which concentrates a state of mind and thus becomes accessible to a spiritual history."[5]

The *Landscapes* were written during and after the year (1932–33) that Eliot spent in the United States following an absence of seventeen years. In that period the holocaust of World War I and its aftermath and his disastrous first marriage to Vivien had been followed by the deaths of his father and then his mother. In 1927, as noted above, he had become a British subject and a member of the Anglican Church.

Before leaving London he had decided on a permanent separation from Vivien—a decision probably not yet shared with her.[6] Here was a very necessary but very difficult major break with his past life, and at the same time a return to the New England of his youthful summers and of Milton Academy and Harvard University days.

I. New Hampshire. A snapshot in the Houghton Library[7] shows Eliot and relatives on a 1933 New Hampshire picnic that could be the setting for the first landscape poem, *New Hampshire.* The poem evokes happy springtime memories ("between the blossom- and the fruit-time") with birds hovering over. But the reminiscing gives way to the present: "Twenty years and the spring is over;/To-day grieves, tomorrow grieves,/Cover me over, light-in-leaves;/ . . ." Joy, nostalgia for the lost simple innocence of youth, and the awareness of regained innocence are all strongly present in the poem's last four lines.

New Hampshire and the whole *Landscapes* sequence have strong parallels in *The Family Reunion.*[8]

II. Virginia. Traveling to Charlottesville, Virginia, to give the Page-Barbour Lectures in April 1933 (published as *After*

Strange Gods: A Primer of Modern Heresy, 1934), Eliot could
hardly have forgotten the contrast drawn in *The Education of
Henry Adams* between the moral rigor of New England and the
lush moral laxity of the Washington, D.C., area, which he had
echoed in *Gerontion* (1920). The lost felicity and continued grief
suggested in *New Hampshire,* as well as the necessity of communicating to Vivien his decision to leave her, might constitute
the "iron thoughts" of the second *Landscapes* poem, *Virginia.* His
attempts to still his will have not been completely successful: "No
will is still as a river/Still." But no new decision is planned: "Iron
thoughts came with me/And go with me. . . ."

III. Usk. In July 1935, Helen Gardner reports, the Frank
Morleys took Eliot to Wales, the setting of the third Landscape
poem *Usk,* originally titled "Usk Valley. Breton."[9] Nancy Hargrove
quotes a letter from Valerie Eliot regarding the poet's statement
that "an understanding of 'Usk' depends partly on the immediate
evocation of the scenery in *The Mabinogion.*"[10] The Vale of Usk,
west of the Wye Valley in the southeast corner of Wales, is the
site of the ruins of King Arthur's seat at Caerleon, the setting of
early Arthurian legends of the Grail quest (as drawn on in the
Breton lais and the works of Mallory, Tennyson, and others).

The line "Gently dip, but not too deep" is from George Peele's
Elizabethan play *The Old Wives Tale,*[11] a fertility play in the
classical Greek tradition, one that also incorporates the folk motifs
of *The Three Heads at the Well* and "The Grateful Dead" as
tests of character and choice which determine what sort of married
life one shall have. In Peele's context, the line "Gently dip, but not
too deep" suggests that beauty is irrelevant to happy mating and
that haste, shrewishness, prudery, and stubborn pride guarantee a
bad married life, whereas deliberateness, respect, affection, and un-
strained acceptance of sex as natural bring happiness, offspring, and
wealth in marriage. The quest to rescue a noble lady from a con-
jurer in Peele's play parallels similar quests and also Grail quests
both in *The Mabinogion* and in other Arthurian accounts.

To hazard an interpretation, the questing speaker of *Usk* and his lady have perhaps gone to the well for the water of life; the advice "Gently dip, but not too deep," it would appear, was ignored or a pitcher (pitchers?) broken; one (or both) of them caused the golden head to weep, and now "iron thoughts" ensue.

IV. Rannoch, by Glencoe. Driving north from Crianlarich, Scotland, across Rannoch Moor to Glencoe, one traverses awesome scenery—rugged, sparse, somber, and breathtaking. From Rannoch Station the trail stretches along Loch Laidon toward the long, narrow pass of Glencoe, where a simple Celtic cross marks the site of the massacre of the MacDonalds in 1692 by the Campbells and English soldiers.

Riding the train from Rannoch Station to Tulloch, one sees crows, vultures, deer, and, if fortunate, a stag or two: "Here [in the bitter winters] the crow starves, here the patient stag/Breeds for the rifle." And in many a Scottish and English great house the number of antlers displayed testifies to both the patient breeding and the accuracy of the rifle.

Here memory is strong. Resentment of the treachery is long. Eliot referred to the American Civil War as the greatest American disaster, saying the country had never recovered from it and perhaps never would.[12] The Glencoe massacre may be paralleled: "Pride snapped,/Shadow of pride is long."

The poem may be only a comment on the attitudes of the men of Glencoe. More likely, it is a comment on the parallel feelings of the speaker, who finds that having, he thought, given up pride of specific sorts (*Ash-Wednesday*, 1930), the attitudes that accompanied pride may persist. Decisions determinedly taken may assimilate slowly.

V. Cape Ann. The last of the five *Landscapes* is ostensibly focused on various birds found on Cape Ann—or rather on a bird-watcher enjoying them. The guide to birds of New England that Eliot used as a boy on Cape Ann is in the Hayward Bequest at King's College, Cambridge. He commented that he was a devoted bird-watcher but always arrived in Massachusetts after the nesting season.[13]

The verse is subtly matched to the rhythm and tone of each of ten Cape Ann birds observed at various times and places. The delectable and varied encounters suggest various sweet experiences, hopes, and expectations earlier in life (*New Hampshire*), before the advent of "iron thoughts" (*Virginia*). As in *Usk*, one can hardly give up the hope of "the white hart behind the white well," since, as on Rannoch Moor, "memory is strong." But in the end one must resign this land (one's being) "to its true owner, the tough one, the sea-gull." Then, like the series of *Landscapes*, "the palaver is finished."

Lines for an Old Man

The last of the *Minor Poems, Lines for an Old Man*, uncharacteristically borrows from Mallarmé a hostile, hissing tone and directs it toward those too dull to grasp the poet's wit.

Chapter Eleven

The Second and Third Voices

Eliot's plans for his first play, "Wanna Go Home, Baby?," produced the two *Sweeney Agonistes* fragments examined above (chapter 6). All of his subsequent plays were to be first directed by E. Martin Browne, whose indispensable book *The Making of T. S. Eliot's Plays* throws much light on their writing and interpretation, quoting liberally from successive drafts and sharing many reminiscences of the two men's consultations before and during each production.[1] Those theater experiences were to bring Eliot with each play a surer grasp of the realities of the theater and the reactions of an audience, as anyone will discover who is involved in comparable productions of any two successive Eliot plays.

The Rock

Eliot's interest in poetic drama was given added stimulation by the commission to write the words to the religious pageant-play *The Rock* (1934). Frankly didactic, it was written "on behalf of the Forty-Five Churches Fund of the Diocese of London." The pageant explores on several levels the meaning of the building of a church. It crosses the boundaries of time and makes coexistent on the stage the Saxon king and his subjects as they hear of the Christian faith from the monk Mellitus, first Bishop of London; Rahere, a monk of King Henry's time who was also a London church-builder; the Israelites who rebuilt Jerusalem; the martyrs of the Danish invasion; Blomfield, a Bishop of London who built two hundred churches; some departing crusaders; and the twentieth-century workers who also are laboring against many difficulties to build a London church.

All of these serve to show that never has the work of the church been easy or unopposed. The Rock, a seerlike figure whose first entrance borrows from that of Tiresias in Sophocles' *Oedipus Rex*, stands on a pinnacle watching the building of the church and speaks the "I have known two worlds" passage quoted in chapter 2. The speech includes the lines:

> There shall be always the Church and the World
> And the Heart of Man
> Shivering and fluttering between them, choosing and chosen,
> Valiant, ignoble, dark and full of light
> Swinging between Hell Gate and Heaven Gate.

Promising success in the campaign to build forty-five new London churches, the Rock concludes:

> And the Gates of Hell shall not prevail.
> Darkness now, then
> Light.
>
> Light.

The book of words that Eliot wrote conformed to a committee-written scenario, and the poet was careful to point out that, except for one scene and the choruses, he was responsible for only the words, not the plot, and that much of the whole had been rewritten with the expert advice of E. Martin Browne. Despite that disclaimer and the fact that only the choruses (entirely his own work) are reprinted in *The Complete Poems and Plays, 1909–1950, The Rock* is extremely interesting and "somewhat elucidative" in tying together and explicitly stating themes found both in previous poetry and in the shortly-to-appear *Murder in the Cathedral*. In its speech patterns and rhythms *The Rock* also looked forward to the plays to come, and its use of the chorus foreshadowed that which in *Murder in the Cathedral* was to impress at least one critic as "the greatest choral poetry yet written in English."[2]

The audience is reminded by this pageant-play, as later by *Mur-*

der in the Cathedral, of the continual necessity to do the work of the church in the face of adversity: "Remembering the words of Nehemiah the Prophet: 'The trowel in hand, and the gun rather loose in the holster.'" In context, this line effectively mediates between history or tradition and the present; such mediation was to remain a frequent and successful technique in all of Eliot's future plays.

Both *Sweeney Agonistes* and *The Rock* were affected by the music-hall revue, which Eliot considered the appropriate form for modern poetic drama. In 1920 he wrote, "Possibly the majority of attempts to confect a poetic drama have begun at the wrong end; they have aimed at the small public which wants 'poetry.' . . . The Elizabethan drama was aimed at a public which wanted *entertainment* of a crude sort, but would *stand* a good deal of poetry; our problem should be to take a form of entertainment, and subject it to the process which would leave it a form of art. Perhaps the music-hall comedian is the best material."[3]

Murder in the Cathedral

With the 1935 Canterbury Festival performance of *Murder in the Cathedral*[4] in the Chapter House where the murder had taken place in 1170, Eliot was revealed as an assured and powerful dramatic poet. Such an emphatic success was not wholly predictable, nor was the precise nature of the subject matter of this play: martyrdom. As Leonard Unger says, "The alienation of Prufrock *et al.* is remodeled into the alienation of the saint; yet the predicament of Prufrock would not become the predicament of Becket— if it had not."[5]

In *Murder in the Cathedral*, though he was again writing on commission for the church, Eliot was the sole author; not just the book of words but the total conception was his. This allowed him to produce a tight artistic unity in which no element is extraneous nor merely repetitive. Probably the author found his subject while working on *The Rock*, and certainly he profited greatly by the experience of working on the productions of both works with E. Martin Browne. This experience was to produce great differences among his future plays. From each he was to draw specific lessons and apply them to the next; in each he attempted something significantly different. To the practicing dramatic poet, this was dictated by a logic of necessity not inevitably apparent to one only interested in reading or in seeing the plays. In the early plays Eliot intentionally kept the audience aware that they were listening to poetry. Each of the later plays was to be written at a lower and lower level of poetic intensity, until the author could say of *The Cocktail Party* that it was questionable whether it contained any real poetry at all—obviously a great exaggeration.

The fact that *Murder in the Cathedral* was to be performed before an officially Christian audience in a cathedral and as part of a Christian festival had much to do with both the choice of subject and the treatment given it. These factors made it plausible, for instance, to follow the classical unities of place and action rather closely, and made it natural to use a sermon as interlude. They also importantly influenced the character and the use of the chorus and suggested the direct involvement of the audience, so effectively achieved through the use of the Knights' speeches, the sermon, and the choruses. The presence of a pulpit and the physical limitation of the single entry to the Canterbury Chapter House (situated behind the audience and far from the wingless playing area) evoked from Eliot (and Browne?) techniques that heightened audience involvement and response.

Like *Burnt Norton* (1936) this play is concerned with the "enchainment of past and future/Woven in the weakness of the changing body" and with the still point of the turning world where past and future are gathered. Both are concerned with "abstention from movement; while the world moves/In appetency, on its metalled ways/Of time past and time future." But in the play, all this was channeled through the one vividly individualized character,

Thomas. The play goes behind the mere facts of his martyrdom
to show us the inner experience and its meaning. It makes of
Thomas, a particular individual, a symbol of the meaning of all
martyrdoms and of the life of the church in its struggle against
the world, as well as a symbol of the meaning embodied in the
particular consecrated place that is Canterbury Cathedral. It makes
the audience consider these questions: "What *are* we, what *should*
we be, and what *can* we be?" Like *The Rock*, it reminds the
spectators that their struggles and their responsibilities echo those
of the church in all times. It further reminds them that only by
getting beyond involvement with the particular occurrence can one
discover the meaning that gives peace and fulness to an experience.

The plot of *Murder in the Cathedral* may be summarized as follows: The chorus of women of Canterbury and the three priests
receive word that Thomas, their archbishop, is about to return
after seven years in exile. They express doubts and forebodings as
to what shall follow, calling his reconciliation with the King un-
certain. As the women lament his return, which may upset their
small routines, and the priests urge them to welcome the archbishop, Thomas himself enters. He makes it clear that his return
was opposed and awaited by many enemies, and that they will soon
descend on him; he adds, "Meanwhile the substance of our first
act/Will be shadows, and the strife with shadows," just as the
First Tempter enters. This figure from the past tempts him with
pleasures of the past, to which Thomas replies:

> Men learn little from others' experience.
> But in the life of one man, never
> The same time returns. Sever
> The cord, shed the scale. Only
> The fool, fixed in his folly, may think
> He can turn the wheel on which he turns.

The First Tempter leaves and the Second Tempter enters to offer
the chancellorship which Thomas once held, if only he will give up
his archbishopric. "No!" says Thomas,

> . . . shall I, who keep the keys
> Of heaven and hell, supreme alone in England,
> Who bind and loose, with power from the Pope,
> Descend to a punier power?

and the Second Tempter leaves. The Third Tempter comes to offer "a happy coalition of intelligent interests"—those of Thomas and of the barons—against the King. He is also dismissed and an unexpected Fourth Tempter appears. His temptation is that Thomas shall become a martyr for the wrong motives—his own eternal glory and pride. Recognizing his own desires in this, Thomas almost despairs: "Is there no way, in my soul's sickness,/Does not lead to damnation in pride?" After the Tempters, Priests, and Chorus have echoed the welter of impulses, fears, and forebodings implicit in the situation, the Chorus implores, "save yourself that we may be saved," and Thomas sees his way clear. He has vanquished this last and greatest of the Tempters, and he will now avoid doing the right deed, martyrdom, for the wrong reason, pride. Thomas's comedy is now complete, and the interlude and act 2 serve to complete those of the Chorus, Thomas's Canterbury-sermon audience, and the twentieth-century audience of Eliot's play.

The interlude between parts 1 and 2 is a Christmas sermon on the nature of the peace heralded at Christ's birth and of the martyrdom that falls the lot of some of those who achieve that mysterious peace: a martyrdom "is never the design of man; for the true martyr is he who has become the instrument of God, who has lost his will in the will of God, and no longer desires anything for himself, not even the glory of being a martyr." As the sermon continues, Thomas's congregation expands to include the modern audience and to prepare them, as it did the humble folk of Thomas's Canterbury, to understand the meaning of his death.

In part 2, the Chorus signifies acceptance of its part in Thomas's martyrdom, and then the four knights who will murder him make their first appearance. They make their demands and accusations and almost attack Thomas, but leave when the priests and attendants intervene. Several weeks later (December 29, 1170) they return and kill Thomas, who accepts his death willingly in spite of his priests' attempts to hide him.

The knights then address the audience and try to explain away their guilt and implicate the audience in it. They plead their disinterestedness and sacrifice, Thomas's reversal of his policies after the king had caused him to be made archbishop, and the necessity of protecting the State against the pretensions of the church. Finally the Fourth Knight, Richard Brito, argues that Thomas had determined to die a martyr and is really guilty of "Suicide while of Unsound Mind."

The Chorus, however, and the priests, reject the knights' reasoning and dismiss them to their empty fate, accepting and rejoicing in the significance of Thomas's martyrdom, which renews the sanctity of their time and place and delineates the contrast between the life of the world and the life of the church, between which hovers the soul of man.

Murder in the Cathedral might be called the most obviously successful of Eliot's plays. The consistent purpose of the play is to share revitalization of a whole world-view with the audience. As already suggested, the audience is irresistibly drawn into the action and made to feel co-responsible for it. What Eliot shares with his audience is not philosophy nor theology in the abstract, but the emotional and muscular feel of belief in a world-view that has divine incarnation and Christian martyrdom as its most significant and perpetual truths. The play emphasizes the necessity of perpetually renewing the awareness of the mysteries which comprise the links between the world and the church.

The choruses in this play represent an advance over those of *The Rock*, for the lines spoken are matched to the general character of the women of Canterbury, but the members of the chorus are not distinguished one from another. When Eliot collaborated with George Hoellering in making a film of *Murder in the Cathedral*, lines of the chorus were assigned to individual women seen in the film at their daily tasks as they spoke. (Eliot and Hoellering in the prefaces to their 1952 book *The Film of Murder in the Cathedral*[6] provocatively discuss the problems of adaptation from stage to film.) There is some individualization of the priests in the play, but there is more of the knights and of the tempters who accost Thomas. The knights and tempters link the levels of the play's meanings. Though quite plausible on the literal level, both groups step back and forth between levels of meaning. The tempters seem even more real on the psychological plane, and indeed in the film the Fourth Tempter was represented only by a voice (that of the poet himself) that is listened to and challenged by Thomas as he wrestles with wrong motives and finally vanquishes them.

That the play should have been an overwhelming success at the Canterbury Festival with a Christian audience is not surprising; a greater testimony to its dramatic and poetic virtues is the success it achieved in commercial and educational theaters throughout the world. But as Eliot said, it was hardly a repeatable success; much of what fused together so vividly in it had necessarily to be abandoned in the next play—one not less impressive, though less acclaimed. *The Family Reunion*, though it lacks the monolithic unity of *Murder in the Cathedral*, also expands the potentialities of the English dramatic tradition, but in different directions.

The Family Reunion

In *The Family Reunion* (1939) Eliot explored, as the title and use of the Eumenides indicate, the meaning of the family curse that was so integral a part of the great Greek tragedies—but a part that the modern audience is at first likely to find puzzling and either irrelevant or anachronistic. The effect of *The Family Reunion* is to recreate the relevance, to make the curse meaningful in twentieth-century terms. The play even goes a long way toward reconciling and tempering the seeming injustice of the biblical curse that the sins of the father shall be visited on the sons to the third and fourth generations. This is accomplished by portraying the emotional inevitability of the recurrent psychic pattern of those violations against familial and reproductive cycles which underlie the curses on the houses of Atreus, Thyestes, and Harry Lord Monchensey.

In "The Three Voices of Poetry," Eliot writes of: first, "the voice of the poet talking to himself—or to nobody"; second, "the voice of the poet addressing an audience"; and third, "the voice of the poet when he attempts to create a dramatic character speaking in verse; when he is saying, not what he would say in his own person, but only what he can say within the limits of one imaginary character addressing another imaginary character."[7] Eliot says that not until 1938, after the completion of both *The Rock* and *Murder in the Cathedral*, did that third voice begin "to force itself upon [his] ear." This points to both a strength and a weakness of *Murder in the Cathedral*: its entire structure was organized in a mind identifying with the mind of Thomas, producing rare psychological penetration and powerful orchestration of tone, also making possible the kaleidoscoping of time and strong audience-empathy. At the same time, it produced a stylized rather than realistic play, a poetically heightened superrealism entirely appropriate to its themes. As a result, it contains only one vividly realized character, the voices of the others being projections of his consciousness of them rather than their own full voices. *The Family Reunion* was to present more fully the individual voices of characters to whom the protagonist relates.

The play is set in Wishwood, the English country house of the Monchenseys. For the first time in eight years, they are having a family reunion. Three of them, Arthur, John, and Harry, have not yet arrived. The Chorus is composed, from time to time, of Ivy, Violet, Gerald, and Charles, sisters and brothers-in-law of Amy, Dowager Lady Monchensey. Agatha, another sister, shows herself almost from the start to be more perceptive and less blinded by petty immediacies than the rest. Mary, the daughter of a cousin and the youngest member of the family present, seems also freer of the misconceptions and myopia of the others.

Before Harry arrives, it is made clear that he married eight years ago against the wishes of the family and has not been back since. His wife has died about a year previously, the conditions of her disappearance from shipdeck in a storm not being very clear. At Harry's appearance, we see that all is not well. He believes that he murdered his wife, and now for the first time he sees the Furies that have pursued him since her death. The family is convinced that he is suffering delusions of guilt.

Agatha and Mary understand more of their and Harry's problems than he does, and for a moment Mary has given Harry again the hope that he thought was forever gone, but the reappearance of the Furies breaks their rapport. As the play progresses, the nature of Harry's malady and the significance of the specters appearing to him becomes clearer through his discussions with Dr. Warburton (the family physician) and especially with Agatha. She tells him of her affair with his father, the origin of the curse he will now have to expiate, and as he comes to understand, he accepts the specters as not Furies but Eumenides ("the all-seeing kindly ones") and says he will seek rather than flee them from now on. He prepares to leave. Not only Harry, but also Agatha, Mary, and his mother, Amy, have reached the point at which illusions are falling away and new starts must be made. Amy, though, is too old and tired; with understanding comes death. She leaves behind Agatha and Mary, wandering in "the neutral territory/Between two worlds" —that into which Harry has crossed and that in which the rest of the family continues unaware of the other.

To some extent, Eliot's play is based on Aeschylus' *Oresteia* trilogy (*Agamemnon, The Choëphoroe, The Eumenides*), the only surviving complete trilogy from the golden age of Athenian drama. Eliot did not, however, follow closely or slavishly the patterns of Aeschylus. Harry Lord Monchensey is comparable to Orestes, but his expiation of the curse through suffering has begun before the death of his mother. Indeed, we could hardly call Harry's decision to leave Wishwood a matricide in spite of Dr. Warburton's previous warning that any shock might cause Amy's immediate death (as Harry's departure does). In fact, Harry, Agatha, and Mary believe

that his leaving is absolutely essential to the expiation of the family
curse. And Downing, Harry's chauffeur (Krishna, the charioteer?)
and the first person able to see the Eumenides, has foreseen the
necessity of their leaving, just as he foresees that Harry will not
need him or anyone else much longer.

It remains doubtful whether Harry has actually committed any
murder. "Perhaps," he says, "my life has only been a dream/Dreamt
through me by the minds of others." And of his wife's drowning,
he adds, "Perhaps/I only dreamt I pushed her." Agatha replies,
"So I had supposed." Probably he is guilty only of the desire to
get rid of her, just as his father was guilty only of the desire to
murder Amy. And yet it is the desire, the intent, the psychic posture
involved in the curse, to which the Furies or the Eumenides are
related. The act itself, as Harry points out, is the accident of a moment, seeming almost unrelated to the continuing identity of the
actor:

> It is really harder to believe in murder
> Than to believe in cancer. Cancer is here:
> The lump, the dull pain, the occasional sickness:
> Murder a reversal of sleep and waking.
> Murder was there. Your ordinary murderer
> Regards himself as an innocent victim.*
> To himself he is still what he used to be
> Or what he would be. He cannot realize
> That everything is irrevocable,
> The past unredeemable.
> *[cf. Raskolnikov in *Crime and Punishment*]

But whether or not he *indulged* the impulse, the murderer can
escape it only through the slow purgational movement of a psychic
reorientation whose magnitude is measured by the fact of the
Eumenides' appearing; and a single lifetime is likely to be too
short to make such a transition, human nature and nurture being
what they are. Only when Athena steps in is Orestes' expiation fulfilled, and only with the help of Mary and Agatha is Harry brought

to understand not only the nature of the curse but also the nature and use of the Eumenides, whom he will henceforth hunt rather than flee ("Then dived he back back into the fire . . .").

At the beginning of the play, Harry thinks of himself as alone with his problems and as solely capable of understanding and facing them. He feels that all his life has been determined by his mother Amy and that he has been prevented from living for himself, as he now insists on doing. Later, when Agatha tells him about his father and her affair with him, he sees himself as reunited to the family and as one who has fulfilled a pattern, a curse on the whole family, fulfilled earlier by his father—perhaps not for the first time. In realizing this Harry understands that the Furies which plague him are the measure of his unhealthy impulses, the necessary agents of expiation, and that only by accepting the natures of himself and his family can he successfully escape from what he has been, can he "unknot the knot," "uncross the cross," "make straight the crooked," and end the curse.

The other characters of the play (who see only one world) try, as Harry tells them, "to think of each thing separately/Making small things important, so that everything/May be unimportant." Later they say in chorus, "We have suffered far more than a personal loss—/We have lost our way in the dark." Like Tennyson's Ulysses to his son Telemachus, Harry will leave to his brother John the unimaginative, unchallenging job of running his estate. Harry's repeated insistence that none of them can understand his problem, his decision, or his language leads Agatha to protest that, whatever he has learned, he must remember that there is always more; and Mary says that she thinks she could understand, but he would have to be patient.

As in *Murder in the Cathedral*, Eliot in *The Family Reunion* has the members of the chorus vitally involved in the plot. They are Harry's aunts Ivy and Violet and his uncles Gerald and Charles. Their concerted speeches, in which they express their unenlightened condition and the emotions that go along with it, are punctuated by individual lines in which they characterize themselves or one another. The sentiments expressed are usually of foreboding and futility. In their final speech, the "We have lost our way in the dark" line is completed after individual lines by "But we must adjust ourselves to the moment: we must do the right thing." The final incantation on the nature of a curse and of redemption from it is chanted not by the Chorus but by Agatha and Mary. Its concluding lines emphasize what Agatha has already suggested: that it is not only the living but also the dead for whom the curse is expiated; that Harry, as she told him earlier, may be "the consciousness of your unhappy family,/Its bird sent flying through the purgatorial flame." In the same speech she told him that all of them have written "not a story of detection,/Of crime and punishment, but of sin and expiation." (This, of course, is what Dostoyevsky really wrote too in his *Crime and Punishment*; any other reading must ignore the role of Porfiry Petrovitch, the epilogue, and the underlying structural principle of the novel and its unity.) She tells him that though he may not yet have known "what sin/You shall expiate, or whose, or why, . . . the knowledge of it must precede the expiation."

At the end of the play we are left in the dark as to exactly what form Harry's expiation will take after he leaves; and yet it does not matter. As Dostoyevsky says in the epilogue to that most gripping of psychological novels, *Crime and Punishment*, "But that is the beginning of a new story—the story of the gradual renewal of a man, the story of his gradual regeneration, of his passing from one world into another, of his initiation into a new unknown life. That might be the subject of a new story, but our present story is ended."[8]

The Eumenides are suprapersonal, representing the moral forces that are unbalanced by the wrong tendencies involved in the curse on Harry's house, the sin which must be expiated and the forces demanding its expiation before balance can be restored. And the "loop in time" which has brought Harry back face to face with that issue has also placed him in a position to expiate the curse and to free the family of it just as Orestes was able, finally, to free his.

Eliot in this play has largely avoided Christian symbols: "The public at large beat a path, it is true, to *Murder in the Cathedral*. But most of them went as sightseers, ready to forget their own standards when these were burlesqued in the murderers' Erastian apologies, but in a spirit which regarded as historical not only the events, but also the Christian values and standards of the play. In *The Family Reunion* Eliot has deliberately made impossible any such facile acceptance of the reality of the supernatural. He has sought to confront the modern world with the necessity of redemption at its starkest, without benefit of clergy," writes C. L. Barber.[9]

The use of the Eumenides has called forth more criticism than any other aspect of the play. Eliot agreed that it is very difficult to stage properly the scenes in which they appear. Nevertheless, they fit well with the stylization of the trancelike speeches of Harry, Agatha, and the chorus; with the explicit shifts in levels of meaning; and with the anti-literal tone that recurrently emerges—elements not necessarily derived from Greek tragedy. They effectively stop any tendency of the audience to interpret the play realistically at the literal level or to ignore the degree of reality attached to psychic and moral—religious—life. It even seems to me that the audience need supply no knowledge of the Greek use of the Eumenides in order to grasp their significance in this play. The play in its own terms justifies their use.

I became certain that they were not a weakness but a highly unusual strength of the play in the 1979 London production, in which the Eumenides appeared as huge, awesome, white, ghostlike superhuman figures. The total emotional impact was almost more than I could bear at several moments, but I have never experienced a more powerful Aristotelian purgation of pity and fear in a theater. I admit that I came away convinced that only a superb cast of English actors can make the play that effective—that the Monchenseys are indelibly English.

Though much in the play is likely to be missed in a first viewing by an auditor unaware of the life of the psyche, unfamiliar with the themes that Eliot characteristically handles and the Dantean frame of reference, *The Family Reunion* represents a remarkable achievement; it makes not only understandable but also relevant to twentieth-century life the Greeks' use of the family curse and its role in any individual's quest for identity and felicity. The play may appeal to a more limited audience than *Murder in the Cathedral* or *The Cocktail Party*, but for those familiar with the whole body of Eliot's works, it is a play likely to be esteemed more and more on each encounter. Like *Crime and Punishment*, its relevance is greatest for the guilty—but all of us share Harry's problem; *The Family Reunion* can tell us so and help us unravel it.

Chapter Twelve

Where Every Word
Is at Home

Throughout his career, Eliot admired more than any other poetry
the great philosophical poems of both the Western and Eastern
traditions. His writings repeatedly quote or allude to Dante's *Divine
Comedy* and the Hindu *Bhagavad-Gita* as the best such poetry. His
own crowning achievement is in this genre, comprising not one
masterpiece but four: *Four Quartets.* The first, *Burnt Norton*
(1936), was written, as already noted, during the period following
The Rock and *Murder in the Cathedral.* Some of its parts were
originally intended for *Murder in the Cathedral.* The second, *East
Coker,* was published on Good Friday of 1940, the year following
the appearance of *The Family Reunion* and the demise of the
Criterion. The third, *The Dry Salvages,* was written in 1941, and
Little Gidding first appeared in 1942 when all four were published
as *Four Quartets.*

Helen Gardner's *The Composition of Four Quartets* contains
much previously unpublished material, reproduces many sections of
various drafts of the *Quartets,* and is an invaluable source of information and interpretations.[1]

Long before 1948, when Eliot received the Nobel Prize for
Literature, *Four Quartets* had been hailed by critics as his greatest
poetry, and *Little Gidding,* the fourth quartet, is so markedly con-
clusive that it would be hard to imagine what more the poet could
have written in the poetic veins and modes explored throughout
the entire body of his poetry and crowned in the *Quartets.*

In these poems Eliot openly expresses in his own voice his deepest feelings and concerns.

We rarely understand immediate experience. The central focus of the *Quartets* is on grasping the meaning of our experiences—on the moments when we learn who we really were and why we did what we did in some earlier experience. Because we usually have erroneous conceptions of ourselves and tend to rationalize our desires to preserve those erroneous self-conceptions, every moment has the potential of "a new and shocking valuation of all that we have done and been" (*East Coker*); "We had the experience but missed the meaning" (*The Dry Salvages*); we suffer "the shame of motives late revealed, and the awareness/Of things ill done and done to others' harm/Which once [we] took for exercise of virtue" (*Little Gidding*).

The moments of illumination are like Joycian epiphanies; they are also moments of Incarnation, when our wills conform to God's—when the Hindu Atman indwells in us. Saints may grasp the meaning steadily; most of us do so only sporadically, occasionally.

Each *Quartet* examines a moment in the author's life when he felt that he understood his place in the whole scheme of things. The four locations that supply the titles are places where Eliot had such experiences. The first, Burnt Norton, in the Cotswolds, is very close to Chipping Campden, a town where Eliot stayed in the 1930s with the uncle and aunt of Emily Hale; he wrote later that he had come to feel more at home there than he had felt anywhere for twenty years.

The whole poem-cycle is introduced by the epigraphs to *Burnt Norton*, two fragments from Heraclitus. The first translates, "But though the Word [Logos] is common, the many live as though they had a wisdom of their own"; the second, "The road up and the road down are one and the same." These point to central themes of all four poems: the doctrine of the Logos, the Word—the capitalized *Word* which fuses into the uncapitalized *word* of the poet that, if right, has its own tongue of fire.

The main theme is one emphasized in Eliot's writings from 1917 onwards. It is also a perception structurally implicit in Dante's *Comedy*: the necessity of detaching oneself from total involvement in the transient life of the senses and of seeing behind the accidents of time the whole panorama of simultaneous moral order; the need to see in the happenings of one's own life and in the myths, tales, and literature of our culture—classical, biblical, and modern—the emotional, psychic, and religious truths reflected in the postures of the souls involved in them. As Eliot wrote in 1929, "The *Divine Comedy* is a complete scale of the *depths* and *heights* of human emotion; . . . the *Purgatorio* and *Paradiso* are to be read as extensions of the ordinarily very limited human range. Every degree of the feeling of humanity, from lowest to highest, has, moreover, an intimate relation to the next above and below, and all fit together according to the logic of sensibility."[2]

The Word, or Logos, or Love, stands for the organizing principle of the total scheme that is grasped at rare moments of illumination or seen steadily by the saint. And in *Four Quartets*, as throughout Eliot's poetry, the task of grasping the whole scheme is closely related to the poet's task of understanding, finding words for, and communicating his relation to and his role in the scheme. As with Dante, the proper "making" of the poem is a form of right action and a part of the religious duty of the poet. Hence we see in the fifth section of each quartet some study of those problems of the poet; and we see throughout the quartets the continual recurrence of concern with the word, capitalized or uncapitalized. Hence also the concern with the incarnation, the "impossible union" of the divine and earthly spheres; with the simultaneous expanse of "the sea" which makes up the whole scheme, and "the river" of man's experience in time, so that incarnation and Christ become symbols of the moment of illumination and of the life of the saint that burns in every moment.

Burnt Norton

The germ of *Burnt Norton* was, Helen Gardner says, a thirteen-line speech written in late 1935 as an " 'unnecessary' attempt [later cut] to liven up act 1 of *Murder in the Cathedral.*"³ Like *The Waste Land, Five-Finger Exercises, Landscapes,* and the other quartets, *Burnt Norton* is composed of five sections, comparable to five movements of a musical work. Eliot wrote to John Hayward that he was weaving together in each quartet three or four themes that only seemed unrelated.⁴ Like the first two *Landscapes* and the *Five-Finger Exercises,* as Helen Gardner points out, the *Quartets* are "Words for Music" (the title under which *New Hampshire* and *Virginia* were originally published).

Eliot identified the beginning of *Alice in Wonderland* as one of his sources and also his poem *New Hampshire* and an Elizabeth Barrett Browning poem which Helen Gardner identifies quite convincingly as *The Lost Bower.*⁵

The chief "idea" of section 1 of *Burnt Norton* is contained in the repeated couplet that ends it: "What might have been and what has been/Point to one end, which is always present." This couplet first occurs after a more conventional consideration of attitudes towards past, present, and future. Though in Dante's purgatory and in *Ash-Wednesday* it is conceivable that one can "Reedem the time, redeem the dream" and "Redeem/The unread vision in the higher dream," in *Burnt Norton* we are told that "if all time is eternally present/All time is unredeemable." The title of the poem and its setting are taken from a deserted house and garden which Eliot wandered into with Emily Hale in the summer of 1934.⁶ On the literal level, the visitors seem to look around the house, to disturb the dust on a bowl of rose leaves, and then to walk out into the formal rose garden and to the empty pool. This deserted garden echoes Swinburne's "The Forsaken Garden" and the dead lovers there evoked. The garden and the "first gate" leading to it are referred to again in *The Family Reunion*: Agatha says to Harry (part 2, scene 2), "I only looked through the little door/When the sun was shining on the rose-garden:/And heard in the distance tiny voices/And then a black raven flew over./And then I was only my own feet walking/Away, down a concrete corridor/In a dead air." After each of them tells of the torment that followed a moment of ecstasy and continued until they found release from their prisons, Harry says, "I was not there, you were not there, only our phantasms/And what did not happen is as true as what did happen,/O my dear, and you walked through the little door/And I ran to meet you in the rose-garden."

The similarity to the imagery of *Burnt Norton*, part 1, is striking; and both throw light on the meaning of parts 1 and 5 of *The Waste Land*. In the hyacinth-girl episode of *The Waste Land*, the phrase "heart of light" follows the sexual experience that so strongly echoes *Tristan und Isolde*: "—Yet when we came back, late, from the Hyacinth garden,/Your arms full, and your hair wet, I could not/Speak, and my eyes failed, I was neither/Living nor dead, and I knew nothing,/Looking into the heart of light, the silence."

In *Burnt Norton*, as the couple looked down into the drained concrete pool, suddenly "the pool was filled with water out of sunlight,/And the lotos rose, quietly, quietly,/The surface glittered out of heart of light,/And they were behind us, reflected in the pool./ Then a cloud passed, and the pool was empty." The moment of extreme felicity results in *The Waste Land* from the hyacinth-garden embrace. In *Burnt Norton* the moment of illumination in which moral and psychic truth may be grasped—in which the distinctions between past, present, and future are erased and in which all the implications of various experiences are simultaneously present—grows from recognition of "what might have been," which leads to new understanding of what has been.

Here, at a moment in time, time has been conquered, but such perceptions cannot be sustained by humankind, and the voice of the bird distracts to the immediate surface. Yet this perception of the nature of love, whether based on past experience in time or speculation on what might have been, points to one end: the Love, or Logos, or Word that orders the entire universe and moves the individual soul to move and act, the motive which is always present.

Part 2 is a many-faceted consideration of the moment of illumination, the moment in and out of time in which the pattern is

grasped, as will be further considered in part 5. This is the moment in the rose-garden;[7] the moment in the arbor of *Dans le restaurant* and *The Waste Land*, section 1, where the rain beat; and the moment in the draughty church at smokefall of *The Waste Land* and *Little Gidding*.

The opening lines of section 2 of *Burnt Norton* have proven the most puzzling to a number of critics: "Garlic and sapphires in the mud/Clot the bedded axle-tree." In *Burbank with a Baedeker*, Eliot wrote, "The horses, under the axle-tree/Beat up the dawn from Istria/With even feet." Though Venetian frescoes were the immediate literal referent in *Burbank*, both passages seem to suggest the chariot of the sun and the wheeling of the days and seasons. In Milton's "On the Morning of Christ's Nativity" we read that at the birth of Christ "The sun himself withheld his wonted speed,/And hid his head for shame,/As his inferior flame/The new-enlightened world no more should need;/He saw a greater sun appear/Than his bright throne or burning axle-tree could bear."

In this light, Eliot's imagery suggests a parallel between the incarnation of the Word in Christ's birth and the moment of illumination in which the total pattern is grasped. Garlic suggests the human and sapphires the divine natures in either the mud of the "handful of dust" that is man or the mud of the stable of Bethlehem; at any rate, the glory of the incarnation slows the chariot of the sun; clots the axle-tree, stopping its movement; draws together all things in a newly perceived pattern. Read with the hindsight of familiarity with *The Family Reunion*, "The trilling wire in the blood" that "Sings below inveterate scars" suggests the family curse, the understanding of which frees Harry and Agatha for their moment of new illumination; and it is this understanding that reconciles "forgotten wars" (for example, the English Civil War of *Little Gidding*, part 3).

The remainder of part 2 explores in relatively simple terms the still point where past and future are gathered, the moment of illumination. So part 2 has given us "variations on a theme."

Part 3 considers the two ways suggested by the second epigraph from Heraclitus: the way up and the way down to the moment of illumination. An incomplete version of the way down is explored first in the London subway imagery that recurs in *East Coker*. In the first half of part 3 are echoed the "unreal city" sections of *The Waste Land*, and also of *The Hollow Men*, showing us again the "trimmers" who are "distracted from distraction by distraction" on the bank of "the tumid river." This semi-darkness of the twittering subway world is not the vacancy of the mystic's negative approach to illumination, which requires, as we see in the last half of part 3, that we descend lower into "the world of perpetual solitude." This descent is comparable to the devouring by the leopards in part 2 of *Ash-Wednesday*, and again the three spirits of Dante's *Vita Nuova* are suggested in the triad "Desiccation of the world of sense,/Evacuation of the world of fancy,/Inoperancy of the world of spirit." This is the way down, and the way up, we are told, is the same. It consists in the action of the saint who is involved in the experience of the world but who, like Thomas in *Murder in the Cathedral*, succeeds in divesting himself of his own will—or rather succeeds in conforming his will to that of God so that he no longer tries to turn the wheel but rests at its still center.

Part 4, a brief lyric as in each of the quartets, brings us briefly back to the garden of part 1. "Time and the bell have buried the day." This is the Angelus, the evening bell, and the black cloud that passes "carries the sun away." The questions "Will the sunflower turn to us, will the clematis/Stray down, bend to us; tendril and spray/Clutch and cling?/Chill/Fingers of yew be curled/Down on us?" suggests the *Waste Land* passage "What are the roots that clutch, what branches grow/Out of this stony rubbish?"

Part 5 clarifies the nature of the rose-garden moment by emphasis on patterns in music and speech, including poetry. The attempt to find the meaning is always attacked by voices of temptation, by the distractions of involvement with the life of the senses. We are told that "Only by the form, the pattern,/Can words or music reach/The stillness," and the stillness is the conception of

the total pattern of the music, though we can hear it only one note
at a time, or of the poem, though we hear it only one word at a
time. When deeply enough understood, it becomes (as in *The Dry
Salvages*) "music heard so deeply/That it is not heard at all, but
you are the music/While the music lasts."

The second section of part 5 relates this concept of pattern to
the rose-garden moment. "The detail of the pattern" may be seen in
"the figure of the ten stairs" of the Christian mystic St. John of the
Cross and his negative approach to illumination. We have, then,
the contrast between the desire that operates in time and is movement and the love that operates in eternity and is itself unmoving,
though it is the cause and the end of all movement. And when,
"sudden in a shaft of sunlight," one has seen the view of eternity,
then all else, we are told, seems only "the waste sad time/Stretch-
ing before and after." The task of both poet and Grail-seeker is the
quest for the Word.

East Coker

As the author explained in a letter written shortly after the
poem, "The title [*East Coker*] is taken from a village in Somerset
where my family lived for some two centuries. The first section
contains some phrases in Tudor English taken from 'The Gover-
nour' of Sir Thomas Elyot who was a grandson of Simon Elyot
or Eliot of that village. The third section contains several lines
adapted from 'The Ascent of Mount Carmel.' "[8] He also indicated
the likelihood of influence by Gerstärker's *Germelshausen*. Other
relevant sources are the motto of Mary Queen of Scots, *"En ma fin
est mon commencement"* ("In my end is my beginning"), and the
Eliot motto *"tace et fac"* ("Be silent and act"), which, as Elizabeth
Drew points out, "could be interpreted 'We must be still and still
moving.' "[9] Eliot published the poem on Good Friday, 1940, and
referred at the end of part 4 to Christ's Passion and the Eucharist:
"Again, in spite of that, we call this Friday good."

Returning to visit the home of his ancestors, as Eliot did in 1937, the poet seeks his beginnings. In poetry reminiscent of book 1 of Lucretius' *De rerum natura*, he considers the recurrent cycles of time to which he will, like his ancestors, be subject. He associates the decay of the houses and people in imagery that again, as in *Gerontion*, echoes Ecclesiastes:

> Old stone to new building, old timber to new fires,
> Old fires to ashes, and ashes to the earth
> Which is already flesh, fur and faeces,
> Bone of man and beast, cornstalk and leaf.
> Houses live and die: there is a time for building
> And a time for living and for generation
> And a time for the wind to break the loosened pane
> And to shake the wainscot where the field-mouse trots
> And to shake the tattered arras woven with a silent motto.

The second strophe of part 1 recreates his approach to the village; the third, the life of the people who once lived there, dancing happily "in clumsy shoes,/Earth feet, loam feet, lifted in country mirth/ . . . Keeping the rhythm in their dancing/As in their living in the living seasons." The poetry is warm and lucid, full of movement. The rhythm of the dance is continued in the movement of the sea, the wind, the day: "Out at sea the dawn wind/Wrinkles and slides." The poet is "here/Or there, or elsewhere. In [his] beginning."

Part 2 of *East Coker* is an attempt to understand the significance of the pattern—a rational questioning of what it adds up to. But this mode of exploration is "not very satisfactory," and no answers to the questions of the first strophe emerge. When the details of time are marshalled and put into an equation, they seem to cancel one another out rather than adding up to a pattern. Late November fights spring; summer heat and snowdrops, destructive fire and the ice-cap, all whirl in a vortex. The attempt to arrive by such means at the still moment of knowledge of the pattern is doomed to failure like the "hollyhocks that aim too high/Red into grey and tumble down. . . ." Starting again, the poet echoes Gerontion's disillusionment with the knowledge derived from experience, knowledge which "imposes a pattern, and falsifies." Such attempts at understanding are constantly shifting: new patterns emerge in each moment, "And every moment is a new and shocking/Valuation of all we have been." This is man's fate, and it is not only *"Nel mezzo del cammin di nostra vita"* ("In the middle of the way of our life") but "all the way" that we find ourselves in a dark wood as Dante did. The approach through knowledge is rejected: "The only wisdom we can hope to acquire/Is the wisdom of humility: humility is endless." Like the dancers and houses, we too shall disappear; but in the surrender to the still point of the turning world, the humble acceptance of Love for the Word that is and was in the beginning, lies the achievement of the saint or the moment in the rose-garden that *is* for Eliot satisfactory.

Part 3 continues and transmutes this disillusionment with the inevitable passing of all houses and people, all of whom, even if not—like Milton's Samson—blinded for their lust, go into the dark: "O dark dark dark." All of them, like Gerontion's de Bailhache, Fresca, and Mrs. Cammel, are "whirled/Beyond the circuit of the shuddering Bear/In fractured atoms" into "the vacant interstellar spaces." So, in contemplating this village, the poet says to himself, "Be still, and let the dark come upon you/Which shall be the darkness of God." This darkness is the humility which can surrender the rational modes, the efforts to turn the wheel—can surrender even the hope, love, and faith that would be misguided, since it must be the gift of grace and can neither be forced nor earned. When that surrender is achieved, then come the freeing images of the rose-garden moment:

> Whisper of running streams, and winter lightning.
> The wild thyme unseen and the wild strawberry,
> The laughter in the garden, echoed ecstasy
> Not lost, but requiring, pointing to the agony
> Of death and birth.

In such moments, one sees himself as he is. In such surrender is the reconciliation of time with the eternal pattern, the merging of word and Word, power and Power (see *Ash-Wednesday*, 5). The final strophe of part 3 says the same thing again in the terms of St. John of the Cross, describing the way down to mystic union with God.

Part 4 renders in Christian and Dantean terms, and especially in the imagery of Good Friday, the combined positive and negative ways, the way up and the way down, fused inseparably. The "illness" of the poet and reader is questioned by the probe wielded by the bleeding, nail-torn hands of Christ. This probing resolves the enigma of unsatisfactory actions motivated by the dissatisfaction of the patient and reflected on the fever chart. It is this dissatisfaction, the disease, of which the church, "the dying nurse," reminds us; and it is only the disease—the awareness of unsatisfactoriness—that can, if it grows bad enough, point us toward the final cure. Our hospital, the earth, is endowed not only by Adam, who invented the disease, but chiefly by Christ, the ruined millionaire who gave up heavenly glory to make possible the treatment and cure. And if we are fortunate, the disease will become so bad that we die of it: become dead to the involvement in the transient things of whose unsatisfactoriness God's universal and inescapable scheme continually reminds us—if we do well. As infatuation with the life in time dies out, the chill ascends as it did for Socrates in Plato's *Phaedo* "from feet to knees" and "the fever sings" as it did for Agatha and Harry in *The Family Reunion* "in mental wires." The sickness grows so bad that something must happen: the purgational suffering that leads to a new orientation must be not only accepted but sought, so that the Furies may be transmuted into the Eumenides.

Part 5 of *East Coker* is a consideration of the poet's own history and of his changed awareness of his direction and significance. In it he is "in the middle way," still "on the edge of a grimpen," having spent twenty years as poet trying to reconcile the word with the Word; twenty years raiding the inarticulate "with shabby equipment always deteriorating/In the general mess of imprecision of feeling"; trying to find, "By strength and submission, [what] has already been discovered/Once or twice, or several times, by men whom one cannot hope/To emulate" (Shakespeare, Dante, and the writers of the *Bhagavad-Gita*, perhaps); and trying to do all this "under conditions/That seem unpropitious." But perhaps his lot is no worse than theirs was; perhaps the changes in language and in modes of awareness and environment represent neither gain nor loss. As Krishna will tell us in other words in part 3 of *The Dry Salvages*, "For us, there is only the trying. The rest is not our business."

In the last strophe of *East Coker* is recorded a very significant shift from the attitude of *Burnt Norton* toward the moment of revelation. The effect of growing old is to make the world stranger and its "pattern more complicated/Of dead and living. Not the intense moment/Isolated, with no before and after,/But a lifetime burning in every moment/And not the lifetime of one man only/But of old stones that cannot be deciphered." As this happens, here and now cease to matter and love becomes "most nearly itself." For these reasons old men ought to be explorers; they have learned "to care and not to care," to "be still and still moving/Into another intensity." These lines suggest the successive expansions of Dante's awareness in the *Divine Comedy*, for, at first blinded by the greater brightness of each succeeding angel of the cornices of purgatory, he is later able to look at the ever-increasing brightness of Beatrice, of each new heaven, later of St. Bernard and then of the Virgin Mary, and finally of the Godhead itself. Such a destination can be reached even through "the dark cold and the empty desolation" and "the vast waters" of Gerontion's conclusion. In the light of these new awarenesses, the poet can say with simplicity and conviction that "In my end"—in these new awarenesses and orientations—"is my [real] beginning."

One further point needs to be emphasized before leaving *East Coker*: the inadequacy of "understanding" that Eliot emphasizes in this poem can easily be "understood" as the poem is read and then ignored in the summing up or in afterthoughts on the poem. Eliot echoes the lesson built into every canto of Dante's *Divine Comedy*, the lesson that knowing is a partial mode of awareness, and that simply to "understand" is of little benefit unless the awareness penetrates to the unconscious motives and to the heart and the muscles—unless the unpremeditated action is altered in its quality by an inner change in the whole psyche. It is this awareness that drew Eliot throughout his career to the Elizabethan dramatists and to the Metaphysical poets. And though I may have talked in this chapter as though the illumination of the rose-garden moment and of the saint were mental acts, if they are no more than that they are nothing. This is implicit in *East Coker*. And such awareness is what age adds to our rereadings of the great masters "if we do well."

The Dry Salvages

The Dry Salvages adds to the *air* which stirred the dust on the bowl of rose leaves in *Burnt Norton* and to the soil or *earth* of *East Coker*, another of the four elements of Heraclitus: the *water* of the river and the ocean. Again, the poem takes its title from the name of a specific place. As Eliot tells us in a note following the title, "(The Dry Salvages—presumably *les trois sauvages*—is a small group of rocks, with a beacon, off the N.E. coast of Cape Ann, Massachusetts. *Salvages* is pronounced to rhyme with *assuages*. . . .)" As a youth, Eliot sailed past them each time he set out from Eastern Point, near Gloucester, Massachusetts (as in the excised voyage of *The Waste Land*'s "Death by Water"[10]).

Part 1 of the poem contrasts the river within us and the sea all about us. The rhythm of the masculine "strong brown god" of the river "was present in the nursery bedroom" in St. Louis; and, though it suggests the individual life in time of Bergson's *durée* with its concomitant limitations, it is the "reminder/Of what men choose to forget." Though in one sense it contrasts with the sea of all human experience, which is not flowing but universally co-existent, at another level its reminder parallels and its rhythms and cycles parallel the larger pattern of which the sea as well is a part. Through the sea's many voices and its "time not our time," "Older than the time of chronometers, older/Than time counted by anxious worried women/Lying awake, calculating the future,/Trying to un-weave, unwind, unravel/And piece together the past and the fu-ture,/Between midnight and dawn," we come to understand who and where we are through the salt on the briar rose and fog in the fir trees. As in *Marina*, this imagery suggests the felicity of the moment of awareness, measureless felicity. This dichotomy of river and sea can be transcended in the glimpse of the over-all pattern.

The first stanza of part 2 of *The Dry Salvages* names some of the forms of agony that are a part of man's life in time and also a part of the eternal scheme: the soundless wailing, the silent wither-ing of flowers, the drifting wreckage, and the prayer of the bone on the beach. These are the results of "the calamitous annunciation" of God to Adam and Eve in Genesis 3:16–19. First God said to Eve, "I will greatly multiply thy sorrow and thy conception; in sorrow thou shalt bring forth children; and thy desire shall be to thy husband, and he shall rule over thee." Then He said to Adam, "Cursed is the ground for thy sake; in sorrow shalt thou eat of it all the days of thy life; Thorns also and thistles shall it bring forth to thee: and thou shalt eat the herb of the field; In the sweat of thy face shalt thou eat bread, till thou return unto the ground; for out of it wast thou taken: for dust thou art, and unto dust shalt thou return." From this annunciation comes the "fear in a handful of dust" of *The Waste Land* and of *Ash-Wednesday*.

After that annunciation there is no end to "the trailing/Conse-quence of further days and hours" for man, or of the speaker's particular days and hours. This section of *The Dry Salvages* mixes personal with general and universal comments, and we need not attempt to sort them out since they all "Point to one end, which is always present" (*Burnt Norton*). A Gerontion-like figure, having rejected the subtle temptations of history, has renounced what was held as most permanent. "The final addition" to that endless sum is "The unattached devotion" of Gerontion and of Pericles "In a drifting boat with a slow leakage" before the meeting with Marina—"The silent listening to the undeniable/Clamor of the bell of the last annunciation." Perhaps this is Donne's parting bell, which "tolls for thee," and also the bell clanged by the unhurried ground swell of the time "Older than the time of chronometers" in part 1.

But since Adam's curse there is no end to this recurring cycle of birth, procreation, and death (Sweeney's "birth, copulation, and death"). What must be attended to in the endless procession of lives is not the fact that their trips, their hauls, will not bear examination, but rather the quality of their action, which makes each life, however humble, as significant as any other. There is no end to all these agonies, no possible redemption from the cycle, except "the hardly, barely prayable/Prayer of the one Annunciation," the annunciation of the incarnation of the Logos in human flesh—in not only Christ and Krishna, but in all of us.

This poetry of the first six strophes of part 2 is so trenchant and so moving that it may come as a surprise to realize after a number of readings that it is set in the *sestina* form, in which identical rhymes for each of the six-line stanzas are used and in which the final sixth stanza duplicates exactly the rhyme words of the first. But this is not simply a trick, nor a device of virtuosity; whether consciously noted or not, the echoed rhymes etch the meanings more deeply into the consciousness of the reader.

The second half of part 2 alters again, in one long strophe, the significance of the rose-garden experience of *Burnt Norton*. There, everything else seemed "the waste sad time/Stretching before and after," and only the sudden shaft of sunlight seemed worthwhile. In *East Coker*, to this conception was added the lifetime "burning in every moment" as one becomes older; and now the poet emphasizes that again the pattern changes, that the past "ceases to be a mere sequence—/Or even development"; "We had the experience but missed the meaning,/And approach to the meaning restores the

experience/In a different form." "Now, we come to discover that
the moments of agony," as well as the moments of felicity, "are
likewise permanent/With such permanence as time has. We appreciate this better/In the agony of others, nearly experienced, . . .
For our own past is covered by the currents of action."

And it is to communicate such moments of both agony and
felicity that the arts of music, poetry, and painting are properly intended. It is this that justifies the life and the career of the artist.
These moments of agony and felicity, the picture of the whole
pattern, are preserved by time, which destroys each individual life.
Each of them, like Eve's bitter apple, is a symbol comparable to
the Dry Salvages, to

> . . . the ragged rock in the restless waters,
> Waves wash over it, fogs conceal it;
> On a halcyon day it is merely a monument,
> In navigable weather it is always a seamark
> To lay a course by: but in the sombre season
> Or the sudden fury, is what it always was.

In this third part of *The Dry Salvages*, once more the past,
present, future and the way up and way down of *Burnt Norton*
are considered; but now the emphasis is changed from the passive
acceptance of the moment of illumination to the right action of
a whole lifetime, without thought of the consequences: "Not fare
well,/But fare forward, voyagers."

Part 3 relates what has been discussed so far in the quartets
to the scheme of the *Bhagavad-Gita*. This work ("The Song of
God" in the Hindu epic *Mahabharata*) consists chiefly in the
dialogue between Arjuna, one of the Pandava princes, and Krishna,
a god incarnated as his friend and charioteer. Drawn up in battle
against his own relatives, Arjuna has looked around and seen his
kinsmen in both armies; and he questions the purposes and the
rightness of the battle for which they are prepared. Krishna replies
to him by explaining the nature of the Atman, the Godhead within
every being. He explains further that "Action rightly renounced

brings freedom:/Action rightly performed brings freedom:/Both are better/Than mere shunning of action. . . . The wise see knowledge and action as one:/They see truly./Take either path/And tread it to the end:/The end is the same./There the followers of action/Meet the seekers after knowledge/In equal freedom."[11]

In the eighth section of the *Bhagavad-Gita*, "The way to eternal Brahman," from which Eliot takes his quotation of Krishna, are suggested most of the main themes of the *Four Quartets*; and the whole *Bhagavad-Gita* will be found relevant also to *Murder in the Cathedral, Ash-Wednesday, The Family Reunion*, and other of Eliot's works. The tolerance of this religion is echoed in Eliot's use of imagery from several religions. Krishna tells Arjuna that "it does not matter what deity a devotee chooses to worship. If he has faith, I make his faith unwavering. Endowed with the faith I give him, he worships that deity, and gets from it everything he prays for. In reality, I alone am the giver."[12] No serious student of Eliot's poetry can afford to ignore his early and continued interest in the *Bhagavad-Gita*. No work is more relevant except Dante's *Divine Comedy*.

Part 4 is a brief prayer to the Virgin Mary, the Queen of Heaven as invoked in St. Bernard's prayer in *Paradiso* 33. 1, and in *Ash-Wednesday*, 2. Bernard prayed that Mary would bring to Dante the grace to enable him to see God; in part 4 of Eliot's work the prayer of Mary is invoked for all "those concerned with every lawful traffic."

Part 5 enumerates many ways in which "Men's curiosity searches past and future/And clings to that dimension." All that, however, is useless. Only the saint can live constantly at the point of "intersection of the timeless/With time . . . in a lifetime's death in love,/Ardour and selflessness and self-surrender./For most of us, there is only the unattended/Moment, the moment in and out of time,/The distraction fit, lost in a shaft of sunlight." Again the wild thyme, the winter lightning, the waterfall, and "music heard so deeply/That it is not heard at all, but you are the music/While the music lasts" are evoked; but "These are only hints and guesses,/

Hints followed by guesses; and the rest/Is prayer, observance, discipline, thought and action./The hint half guessed, the gift half understood ["I sometimes wonder if that is what Krishna meant"], is Incarnation./ . . . And right action is freedom/From past and future also." But most of us are not saints, and we "are only undefeated/Because we have gone on trying." Between the rose-garden moments and those of agony we are content if we live the proper patterns, if our turning back to the life of time contributes to the making of significant soil, as in *East Coker.*

Little Gidding

Little Gidding was a religious utopian community founded in 1625 in Huntingdonshire. The community, patterned on the Christian family, was founded by Nicholas Ferrar and his family. It was visited by Charles I in 1633 and 1642 and again in 1645 after his defeat at Naseby by Cromwell. Two years later it was attacked and disbanded by Parliament. Its destroyed chapel was later rebuilt, but the community was never reestablished. The chapel, in ruins when Eliot wrote of it, is now restored and in use. Ferrar's community is the setting of J. Henry Shorthouse's *John Inglesant: A Romance,*[13] of which Helen Gardner writes: "It is a book of singular charm and refinement of feeling, and all that is necessary for an understanding of what the name of the poem should suggest can be found in it."[14]

As in each of the other *Quartets,* part 1 of *Little Gidding* gives us a literal picture of the place after which the poem is named and of the approach to it. Literally, the poet approaches in "midwinter spring," the season "when the day is brightest . . . in the dark time of year." Metaphorically, the poet, approaching the condition symbolized by Little Gidding, is suspended in time. His soul's sap quivers between the life of the senses in time and the unimaginable zero summer of the saint's life, burning in every moment.

Putting off sense and notion, he finds as he turns off the road "behind the pig-sty [still visible in 1971, but not in 1979] to the dull facade [of the chapel]/And the tombstone [of Nicholas Ferrar, before the facade]," his conscious purpose in coming there dissolves. He finds himself at the world's end (where love of the world merged into love of the eternal, frequently for Ferrar and now once for himself)—at a place where prayer has been valid, as in all places where the saints and martyrs have stood. To reach such a place and moment, one must achieve humility, an attitude of "Here I am. I can't turn the wheel of life, but it can turn me, as it does the saints. May it happen."

Such a place—whenever, however, and for whatever reason approached—can bring the servant of time in touch with the eternal; the contemplation of the significant lives which contributed to this significant soil can enable him to escape his own enchainment in time (compare "until the chain breaks" in *The Family Reunion* and in the *Bhagavad-Gita*).

Part 2 reevaluates everything that has gone before in the *Quartets*; it accepts the death of air, of earth, of water and fire—those Heraclitean elements associated respectively with the four poems—surrenders the attachment to the fruits of one's accomplishments. It acknowledges that they will be lost and forgotten. Such deaths bring one to the timeless moment of giving oneself to whatever the moment requires. The destruction of the London Blitzkrieg by German fire-bombers makes this surrender necessary and easier, justifying the later comparison of the bombers to the Holy Spirit.

Meeting the ghost compounded of earlier poets (especially his earlier self, Dante, and Yeats), air-raid-warden Eliot ponders the need to comply with the measured rhythms of the human cycle and of life. Such compliance is a refining fire, melting away the dross of self-willed experience. With that revelation, the former self fades as the all-clear siren sounds. In this section of unrhymed terza rima, anyone familiar with Dante will recognize dozens of echoes. This is probably the most successfully Dantesque poetry in English.

Part 3 discusses "three conditions which often look alike/Yet differ completely . . ./Attachment to self and to things and to persons, detachment/From self and from things and from persons;

and, growing between them, indifference." Both action and renunciation, we are told, are better than mere shunning of action,
such as that of Dante's trimmers and Eliot's hollow men. Memory
used properly can lead to detachment, to "expanding of love beyond desire," freeing us from both past and future. Then bad as
well as good—in our own past as well as those of others—can bring
profit; past wrong motives can be purified in present acceptance of
their meaning.

Part 4 sets in parallel the incendiary bombs of the German
bombers and the pentecostal fire of the descending dove, telling us
that acceptance of the purgative flame of detachment—of love for
life's best—is the only viable alternative to the burning love for
self and things and persons. Divine Love, we are told, devised that
choice.

In part 5 the strands of the poem are all drawn together and the
advances of each quartet over the previous ones are consolidated.
The problem in life, as in poetry, is to grasp the whole unity simultaneously and see the relevance of each word or act, each moment,
to the whole pattern. Each part must participate in the rhythms
and meanings of the whole, whether we intend it or not.

The ideal speech of contemporary poetry in any time is memorably described:

> And every phrase
> And sentence that is right (where every word is at home,
> Taking its place to support the others,
> The word neither diffident nor ostentatious,
> An easy commerce of the old and new,
> The common word exact without vulgarity,
> The formal word precise but not pedantic,
> The complete consort dancing together) . . .

The habit of remaining aware of the whole—of complete simplicity, clinging to no illusion—can bring thorough awareness of
our developing natures, ultimately to be crowned with the equiva-
lent of Dante's final vision in Paradise:

> Oh grace abounding, wherein I presumed to fix my
> look on the eternal light so long that I wearied
> my sight thereon!
> Within its depths I saw ingathered, bound by love
> in one volume, the scattered leaves of all the
> universe;
> Substance and accidents and their relations, as
> though together fused, after such fashion that
> what I tell of is one simple flame.

After mirroring in *Little Gidding* this passage of *Paradiso* 33, this "highest point that poetry has ever reached or ever can reach," Eliot turned to the action of drama and wrote no more poetry in such a mode. And, indeed, what more was there to say?

Chapter Thirteen

The Tougher Self

Eliot wrote in 1933, "The ideal medium for poetry, to my mind, and the most direct means of social 'usefulness' for poetry, is the theatre."[1] In *The Cocktail Party*, Eliot entered the popular, competitive commercial theater and his play was a stunning success— one yet unmatched by any other serious verse-play of the twentieth century. According to the *London Daily Express*, 1.5 million people saw the play in Eliot's lifetime and the poet turned down a Hollywood offer of thirty thousand pounds for the film rights because he considered the play "unpicturable."[2] By that time (1949) Eliot, allying his verse to the rhythms of modern English speech, had adopted his flexible three-stress-and-a-caesura line and had brought it to such perfection of control that he could modulate it from the most prosaic-sounding lines to high moments of intense poetry.

The Cocktail Party (1949)

Like Shakespeare's *As You Like It*, *The Cocktail Party* examines a range of kinds of love for others and for self. From Euripides' *Alcestis*, *The Cocktail Party* borrows plot details, symbolic patterns and themes of a husband's self-discovery and a restored marriage. From other Greek classical dramas and the Cambridge anthropologists, it borrows character types, structural patterns, and emotional sequences.

In *The Cocktail Party*, attention is focused not chiefly on the potential saint but on a group of seven characters of varying potentialities. As prefigured in Agatha and Mary of *The Family Reunion*, the characters capable only of humbler choices are here for the first time given as much emphasis as the potential saint, or

178

more. Sparklingly humorous, the play is yet unmistakably a serious comedy, making the audience quite aware of meanings behind those immediately apparent. It explores dramatically such questions as these: Why do marriages and affairs go sour? How and why do we fail in loving? What makes a good marriage? How can a marriage be rejuvenated? How can we find our true selves? How can we help others find themselves? Who can help whom to find themselves?

Clearly these are important questions; just as clearly they are questions for modern psychiatry, and three of the characters are a famous psychiatrist and his two associates: Sir Henry Harcourt-Reilly and his friends Julia Shuttlethwaite and Alexander Mac-Colgie Gibbs. These three (called here "the guardians") resemble the "Clerisy" or charismatic figures of Eliot's *The Idea of a Christian Society* (1939). They are wholly dedicated to helping their clients and those with whom the clients are involved—in this play lawyer Edward Chamberlayne and his wife Lavinia, her novelist protégé and lover Peter Quilpe, and Celia Coplestone, with whom Edward is having an affair. To distinguish between the two groups, these four are here called Reilly's patients (though Peter has probably not consulted Reilly by play's end).

The four patients are each disillusioned and made miserable by the breakdown of their various relationships. The emotional pattern of which their disillusionment is a part is similar for all of them, and, for that matter, all of us. Essentially this picture is set forth: all of us, in our relationships with others, have been crusted over with illusions about ourselves and others, have developed personalities largely false and artificial. Somewhere beneath these facades lie our necessary selves. Before we can achieve meaningful and satisfying lives, we must somehow strip away the illusions and recognize the deeper, tougher selves. Edward says:

> The self that can say 'I want this—or want that'—
> The self that wills—he is a feeble creature;
> He has to come to terms in the end
> With the obstinate, the tougher self; who does not speak,

Who never talks, who cannot argue;
And who in some men may be the *guardian*—
But in men like me, the dull, the implacable,
The indomitable spirit of mediocrity.
The willing self can contrive the disaster
Of this unwilling partnership—but can only flourish
In submission to the rule of the stronger partner.

The pattern of disillusionment is particularized as follows in each close relationship with another person: we each have a dream or aspiration, aimed in general at enabling us to think well of ourselves, and we project onto ourselves and the other person the roles that would fulfill the dream. We intend our decisions and actions to sustain the roles and fulfill the dream. But the actions of the other person fail to match the role we have projected, and we learn that he/she sees us, him/herself, and our relationship differently than we do—is projecting a role onto us to fit his/her desires. We become disillusioned with him/her for not living up to the projected relationship. We alter the role projections to try to maintain the dream, but this only results in repeated mismatch, disillusionment, and blame. "The insuperably, innocently dull," with whom Reilly does not trouble himself, repeat that cycle over and over. "The common cheat" settles on a dream of himself as superior cheater and is also caught in the cycle.

We see Edward, Celia, Lavinia and Peter each go through this cycle one or more times. They, and all of us who experience that cycle, are called by Reilly "self-deceivers." But those never wholly successful in deceiving themselves can escape to another pattern, as Celia, Edward, Lavinia, and to some extent Peter do in the play.

To escape, we must see that our own acts fail to match the roles we have projected onto ourselves—that we have had unrealistic expectations of ourselves, just as the other person has had unrealistic expectations of us. As Eliot wrote in *East Coker*, "to be restored, our sickness must grow worse." This disillusionment is resisted by the drive to think well of ourselves, which is partly dependent on the other person's good opinion. Consequently we become humiliated and have difficulty facing others because we misconceive them. We not only feel alone, but also suffer the deprivation of their approval (which may be illusory, their evaluations being differently based).

If we progress that far, we become aware that we each have an unknown "tougher self" and that these differ from our conceptions of our selves. When we admit the wide discrepancy between the tougher self and the projected personality and see that we were as mistaken about ourselves as the other person was, our sense of humor may operate. (Reilly calls this "the first more hopeful symptom.") We could of course repeat the whole cycle again.

Having accepted that truth about ourselves, we will see that the other person's motives were no less admirable and not much different than our own. We sympathize with their disillusionment and wish them well, recognizing that they have the same right to be themselves as we have to be ourselves. Habitual awareness that we are always strangers to each other and even to ourselves can produce deep respect and, as act 3 shows, deep love for each other—can produce the good life. By avoiding illusion as much as possible, we can grasp "what there is to give and take" and can relate to the real person, not just a projection of our desires.

We are not likely in this life to avoid completely the errors that start the cycle over, but our self-deceptions can become rarer and rarer, and we can, like Edward and Lavinia in act 3, help others (as they do Peter) learn to escape the cycle. The guardians have cultivated the habit of progressing to the end of the cycle—of helping others reach the freedom that enables them to be helpful also.

The nature of one's tougher self is not his responsibility; he may have the potentialities of a saint, like Celia, or his destiny may lie in some other direction, as do those of Edward, Lavinia, Reilly, Julia, and Alex. At any rate, he must discover and come to terms with his basic role—his "destiny." The purpose of Reilly, Julia, and Alex is to help the other characters strip away their illusions and make their decisions. Julia says of Edward and Lavinia, after they have left Reilly's office:

All we could do was to give them the chance.
And now, when they are stripped naked to their souls
And can choose, whether to put on proper costumes
Or huddle quickly into new disguises,
They have, for the first time, somewhere to start from.

Not all people can strip themselves clean of their illusions. Peter Quilpe, for example, does not reach that point in the play but shows promise at the end that he may reach it soon.

The stripping away of illusions is a painful process; the identity one has to face may not fit at all with dearly held notions of oneself. Once our illusions are shed, the lack of them seems at first an intolerable isolation; but Reilly impresses on Edward the fact that we are always and only strangers, and urges him and Lavinia to see their isolation as the bond that could hold them together. Each person can and must make decisions which, once made, set in motion forces in one's own life and the lives of others that cannot be altered. Our freedom is limited by our previous choices, our involvement with others, and our unknown selves.

Since the illusory personality is built up in social relationships, the stripping away of illusion usually results from the breaking-up of those relationships. In Edward's case the awareness follows Lavinia's departure, Peter's reminder of his age, and Edward's recognizing the falsity of his former relation to Celia. Lavinia's enlightenment hinges on the breakdown of her relationships with Peter and Edward. Each of the Chamberlaynes has to be prodded into self-recognitions by Reilly; Celia, on the other hand, is inherently honest with herself, and works out her own salvation with only hints and good will from Reilly—who is, in any case, incapable of understanding her nature and destiny except in vague and second-hand terms. Celia's self-discovery grows out of recognizing her misconceptions of Edward and their affair. She realizes immediately what Edward and Lavinia grasp firmly only at the end of the play: that her pictures of the persons with whom she was involved have been only projected desires, not the real persons. She tells Edward, for example, that she has looked at him now and seen nothing left but a beetle. When Edward says, "Perhaps that is what I am./Tread on me, if you like," Celia replies:

> No, I won't tread on you.
> That is not what you are. It is only what was left
> Of what I had thought you were. I see another person,
> I see you as a person whom I never saw before.
> The man I saw before, he was only a projection—
> I see that now—of something that I wanted—
> No, not *wanted*—something I aspired to. . . .

What follows confrontation of oneself depends on one's moral acumen and the nature of the tougher self that is discovered. Most of the play's critics mistakenly assume the play to state that every person has a choice between Celia's way of sainthood and Edward's making "the best of a bad job." But rather the dilemma facing each person who loses his illusions and confronts his tougher self is that stated by Julia above: "whether to put on proper costumes/Or huddle quickly into new disguises." This is the crucial choice, as Lavinia sensed when she told the disillusioned Edward, ". . . Never mind, you'll soon get over it/And find yourself another little part to play,/With another face, to take people in." And without the proddings of Reilly and his friends, that is just what both Edward and Lavinia would have done.

For almost all persons, Celia's mystic way of sainthood is not even a remote possibility; it is to be thought of not as one of two normally available alternatives, but as a rare extreme on a wide scale of possibilities for those who, like Edward, Lavinia, Celia, Reilly, Julia, and Alex, have chosen "to put on proper costumes." Those who "huddle quickly into new disguises" or who, like Peter Quilpe after the revelations of the first cocktail party, have not yet lost all illusions, can neither become saints nor "make the best of a bad job." But there is hope that they may later, at the low point of another cycle of "the machine" of human interrelations, be stripped clean of illusions and have another chance to choose; Peter seems at the end of the play to be approaching such a time of decision. Further, Reilly says, "When you find, Mr. Chamberlayne,/

The best of a bad job is all any of us make of it—/Except of course, the saints—such as those who go/To the sanatorium—you will forget this phrase./And in forgetting it will alter the condition." The negative view of "the human condition" implicit in the phrase "a bad job" is Edward's, not the author's nor Reilly's. This speech is closely related to Julia's reminder to Reilly that he must accept his limitations.

The Guardians. The relations among the guardians are subtly hinted throughout the play. Each of their actions and speeches in some way fills out the tenuous but tantalizing picture of their interworkings. They do not hesitate to interfere in other people's lives (though Reilly warns that it is a serious thing to do so and that forces are thus set in motion which cannot be altered). They use deception, harassing techniques, and the advantage given by their emotional insights in order to help their "patients." And finally, they emerge as a close-knit trio of enlightened humans who enjoy using their talents and awareness to help others become "similarly" enlightened—though each case is unique. Throughout the play they are surrounded by a considerable air of mystery, resulting in frequent dramatic irony.

The most intriguing of the guardians—indeed, one of the most intriguing characters in modern drama—is Sir Henry Harcourt-Reilly, who is referred to in the play as a doctor but who has been labeled by various critics a psychoanalyst, a priest, God, and an eccentric madman. Interpretations of Reilly as superhuman stem from several causes. His admonitions to his patients to "Go in peace. And work out your salvation with diligence" have been taken by most critics as showing Reilly to be at least an Anglican priest, if not a member of the divine Trinity. And Christ is strikingly suggested in Reilly's words "It is finished," spoken after Celia has left his office. The libation scene in act 2 and the references of the guardians to projected spirits and the process of transhumanization also suggest knowledge of an extra-human sort.

These suggestions, however, may be quickly answered: "Go in peace. And work out your salvation with diligence" is—as more than one critic has shown—the dying statement of Gotama, the Buddha, as translated in a book cited in Eliot's notes to *The Waste Land*. The talk of transhumanization and projected spirits can be explained as Dantean and other Christian or non-Christian mysticism (compare *Little Gidding*), as neoplatonic occultism, or as the ritual of a typical professional or fraternal society. And Reilly's many expressed limitations rob him of credibility as a Christ figure.

To consider the possibilities of Reilly's superhumanity in another direction, Eliot caps a series of plays on the word "devil" by having Celia say, "That's the Devil's method!" when Edward tells her that the Unidentified Guest caused him to realize he wanted Lavinia back while seeming to argue against her return. The humor in this series of remarks has hinged on the popular tendency to link anyone who manipulates the emotions of others with witchcraft or black magic.

Certainly the suggested links between Reilly and God, Buddha, the Devil, and an Anglican priest heighten the curiosity of the audience and suggest, in incommensurable ways, the stature of Reilly; but the suggestions attenuate each other. Their chief use is to demonstrate Eliot's excellent wit and humor. Each of them is, in some particular way, metaphorically potent; but there seems to be no evidence to support a consistent allegorical identification of Reilly, and any reader who takes them too seriously misses some of the play's finest humor.

Certainly at the literal level Eliot takes great care to point out Reilly's humanness and concomitant limitations. In act 2, for example, Reilly expresses misgivings regarding his handling of Edward and Lavinia's problems: "I have taken a great risk." Speaking of Celia, Reilly again unmistakably emphasizes his limitations: "And when I say to one like her,/'Work out your salvation with diligence,' I do not understand/What I myself am saying."

None of these elements seems to imply that Reilly is more or less than human, though assuredly he is an enlightened and dedicated human; his total potentialities are subject to definite limits which Celia, for example, transcends. Alec Guinness, who played the role in the initial Edinburgh, Brighton, and New York runs of the play, said that he considered Reilly simply as a doctor. He pointed out that psychiatry was discussed much less openly in England than in the United States, and this fact probably accounted for the reticence of both Eliot and Guinness to discuss the problem in any detail.

Reilly is an enlightened mid-twentieth-century psychiatrist who recognizes the parallel insights of Eastern mysticism, Christian mysticism, and Jungian psychology and uses them as he is able in his efforts to help his patients. He receives much indispensable aid from Julia and Alex, each of whom has particular and useful abilities for furthering their joint purposes. Reilly's insights into Celia's attitudes, for instance, come via Julia's sneak visit while Celia waits downstairs, not via divine or occult revelation.

The wisdom and abilities of both Reilly and Julia are incomplete—only together are they capable of handling the more difficult problems. This complementarity of Reilly and Julia is seen in the one-eyed and spectacle references and is comically linked, by the ballad which Reilly sings, to their drinking of gin and water, reinforcing the complementarity of the spectacles episode—as does also their ritual of libation and incantation.

Alex, like Julia, serves as an observer, arranger, contacter, and meddler in the lives of the patients. Like Julia again, he indulges in subterfuge, deception, and intrigue—whatever is necessary to monitor and motivate the proper responses in those whom the guardians are trying to help. Seeming at first a somewhat more bland character than either of his associates, he is seen in the third act to have administrative abilities, to be a man of action as well as talk: his references throughout the play to his travels and affairs are not mere inventions. His overtones are those of Eastern religion and of organized social and political influence. He makes something out of nothing (a trick he learned in the East), has connections everywhere, and proves on close examination to be as integral a part of their operations as either Reilly or Julia.

Part of the play's comedy lies in the light irony with which the true qualities of Julia and Alex are stated in act 1 in such ways as to be discounted by the others and the audience. Shortly after the play begins, Celia says that Julia is such a good mimic; Peter adds that she never misses anything, and Alex adds, ". . . unless she wants to." Shortly after, Alex calls Julia "a mine of information," and Celia says "There isn't much that Julia doesn't know." Julia herself says to Edward, "I know what you're thinking!/I know you think I'm a silly old woman/But I'm really very serious. Lavinia takes me seriously./I believe that's the reason why she went away—/So that I could make you talk." In a number of such remarks, Julia alludes to the true state of affairs between Edward and Lavinia, which he has not yet admitted. She repeatedly presses Edward on painful points which threaten to reveal his fabrication regarding Lavinia's sick aunt: "I understand these tough old women—/I'm one myself: I feel as if I knew/All about that aunt in Hampshire."

Such direct hints at the nature of the guardians are robbed of credibility by the manner in which they are given, and also by the guardians' pretense that they do not know each other very well. Julia shows a fine sense of humor, as well as a fine disregard for veracity, when she returns for her umbrella and finds Edward drinking with the Unidentified Guest: "Now what are you two plotting?/ How very lucky it was *my* umbrella,/And not Alexander's—*he's* so inquisitive!/But *I* never poke into other people's business." Julia, of course, does a considerable amount of poking into other people's business, seeming all the while really unlikable.

Alex also makes humorously symbolic statements of the real role of the guardians. Upon returning "to make sure that Edward gets dinner," he says, "I'm rather a famous cook./ . . . that's my special gift—/Concocting a toothsome meal out of nothing./Any scraps you have will do. I learned that in the East." And at another level, the guardians *are* engaged in producing something psychically palatable from the unsatisfactory lives of Edward, Lavinia, and Celia. While Edward and Peter are discussing Celia, the hypotenuse of one of the interlocking love triangles in the play, Alex significantly calls from the kitchen, "Edward, have you a double boiler?"

A few speeches later, Edward explains that there is no curry powder because Lavinia doesn't like it, and Alex suggests the inadequacy of the materials with which the guardians must work (the Chamberlaynes' act-1 condition) when he says, "There goes another surprise, then. I must think./I didn't expect to find any mangoes,/ But I *did* count upon curry powder." (The guardians have already found Lavinia evasive, but had still hoped that Edward would face Lavinia's departure more honestly than he has. Reilly makes it clear in the second act that their lack of honesty has forced him to go to the lengths seen in their confrontation in his office; and earlier Julia has tried hard to provoke Edward to drop his sham.)

Julia admits her subterfuges of the forgotten umbrella and the lost spectacles when she leaves Edward and Lavinia in the third scene of the first act. Edward asks, "Are you sure you haven't left anything, Julia?" and she replies, "Left anything? Oh, you mean my spectacles./No, they're here. Besides they're no use to me./I'm not coming back again *this* evening."

No speech in the play—however inane or comic on the surface— is without demonstrable connections to the central themes. The guardians' series of stories that never get told at the first party may serve as an example. In the opening line of the play, Alex's beginning of a story has been misinterpreted by Julia. "There *were* no tigers," Alex insists (effectively repeated in the last act), as if to answer the critics who would read the play entirely in terms of Christian symbols, ignoring Eliot's precautions to make the lines broader than that. Julia's story of Lady Klootz and the wedding cake leads into speculations on the nationality of Lady Klootz, the family of Delia Verinder with its harmless brother who could hear the cry of bats, and the dead parents of Tony Vincewell—all prefigure the confusion of Lavinia's real aunt, who sent the eggs, with the prefabricated aunt supplied by Edward to explain Lavinia's absence. They also reflect the aborted, tangled relations among the characters of the play. And by prolonging and finally defeating the listeners' expectations of hearing the promised stories, they set the tone of frustration enveloping the four non-guardians. They also parallel the Chamberlaynes' failure to come up with straight stories.

Problems of Act Three. The most stringent and the most repeated criticisms of *The Cocktail Party* have been aimed at its third act, centering around Celia's death, Alex's description of it, and the supposed flatness and lowered interest of that act. Many critcis have protested the "unnecessary violence" of Celia's death.

Without the third act the play's psychic scheme would be incomplete and ambiguous; to omit it robs the audience of the evidence and materials on which must be based any valid estimate of the two previous acts: Are the "guardians" frauds? Only the altered behavior of Edward and Lavinia, as well as of the guardians, can tell us. Have Edward and Lavinia really put on proper costumes? Only the genuine warmth and consideration which they show each other in this so-called near-epilogue can tell us. Does Reilly's "sanatorium" meet Celia's needs? Alex tells us in act 3. And beyond these essential matters, much of the rounding-out of the play's excellent comedy, imagery, and symbolism is accomplished in this final act with its echoes of acts 1 and 2.

Nonetheless, the primary function of the third act is not the communication of reports and information:

ALEX: We have just drawn up an interim report.
EDWARD: Will it be made public?
ALEX: It cannot be, at present:
       There are too many international complications.
       Eventually, there may be an official publication.

So we must presently be satisfied with the allegory of the monkeys who eat crops, Christians who eat monkeys, and heathens who eat Christians who have eaten monkeys.

The important thing in act 3, to repeat, is not ideas, but rather the opportunity for the auditor himself to observe the changed quality of behavior—the changed psychic focus—of the various characters, so that he can leave the theater with a well-grounded and satisfactory estimate of what has been accomplished in the play.

Readers who find the felicity of Edward and Lavinia too tame, their domesticity and goodness unpalatable on the stage, must either have failed to follow the central development of the second act or must simply be uninterested in the matters with which the play deals. Moreover, it seems necessary that Celia's death be as violent and shocking as it is in order that we may see what is truly significant in that death. In Reilly's unshocked and even pleased reaction to the account, which Lavinia makes certain that we shall not overlook, we can see—having now been given the basis for trust in his diagnosis and his comments—that shock is not the proper reaction: that the manner of Celia's death, the realistic and accidental details, do not matter.

What does matter, as Krishna said to Arjuna on the battlefield in the *Bhagavad-Gita*, is the psychic focus at the hour of death— "And the time of death is every moment"; "every moment is a new beginning"; "Oh, I'm glad. It's begun." What mattered was the altered quality of Celia's experience, the essential change in her attitudes, expectations, and concerns. From the fact that all of the characters except Peter Quilpe are capable of humor, of looking at the right side of the coin, even in the context of such topics as Celia's martyrdom, we receive something more than just entertainment and clarification of the dramatic scheme: the play, and the audience, are brought back to the familiar world where we started in act 1. Lavinia's final remark, "Oh, I'm glad. It's begun," brings the auditor back to the concrete sidewalk in front of the theater with the therapeutically right echo in his ears and with a sufficiently non-rational orientation to satisfy the most angry of young men.

Richard Lonkin writes that in *The Cocktail Party*, as in *Four Quartets* and *Notes Toward the Definition of Culture*, Eliot "has used all the resources of his wide and long experience to make simple and understandable for us important things which no other living writer cares or dares to write about."[3] In this play, Eliot made more explicit than might reasonably have been hoped the Aristotelian-Dantean psychic scheme that had been at the center of his prose, his poems, and his plays with surprisingly little change since the days of *Prufrock*. In so doing, he assimilated to drama the chief advances of twentieth-century psychotherapy.

The Confidential Clerk (1954)

Like its predecessors, Eliot's play *The Confidential Clerk* was noticeably influenced by classical drama. But in this case, for the first time, the reader is strongly reminded of heavily plotted Roman comedies which also took many cues from the *Ion* of Euripides. There are clear and detailed parallels between Eliot's and Euripides' plays.[4] In addition to the lost children, the searching parents, and the mistaken identities, the casts of characters and the basic plots are similar. As Ion's father was Apollo, the god of poetry and music, Colby Simpkins's dead father was an organist and his real father turns out to be God, with the confidential clerk Eggerson, called by Eliot "the only *developed* Christian in the play,"[5] standing in as interim father until Colby can find his true vocation.

Briefly, the plot is as follows: Sir Claude and Lady Elizabeth Mulhammer have each had a child born out of wedlock about twenty-five years before the play begins—at least Sir Claude thought he had. But it turns out at the end that the girl who was to bear his child died without giving birth (he was off in Canada for a year or so) and the baby he thought his (Colby) was really the son of her widowed and destitute sister, Mrs. Guzzard. Lady Elizabeth's child had been put out to nurse by her fiance; when its father was killed in Africa by a rhinoceros, his family denied all responsibility for the child, and the embarrassed Elizabeth, unable to press inquiries, failed in her efforts to locate her baby.

As the play opens, Sir Claude has brought Colby, whom he has supported all these years, into his household as a replacement for his retiring confidential clerk, Mr. Eggerson. He hopes that Lady Elizabeth, due home from abroad, will learn to accept Colby as one of the family, after which he may tell her that Colby is his illegitimate son. She accepts Colby immediately and convinces herself that he is her lost baby grown up. Colby, meanwhile, is not sure that he has found his proper vocation as a confidential clerk, not having fully given up his former aspirations to become an organist. Sir Claude has also an acknowledged illegitimate daughter, Lucasta Angel, who is engaged to Mr. Barnabas Kaghan, a promising young businessman. In act 3 Eggerson presides over a meeting of all the principals in which it is learned through Mrs. Guzzard that Colby is her own son, that Sir Claude never had a son, and that Barnabas Kaghan is Lady Elizabeth's son (probably). Learning that his real father was a moderately successful musician, Colby decides to follow his inner promptings to become a church organist. Under the protection of Eggerson, the real confidential clerk, he leaves the household of the Mulhammers for a new life of his own. Lucasta and Barnaby will be married, and Sir Claude and Lady Elizabeth will have their son and daughter. Mrs. Guzzard will have nobody.

The confusions of the plot are compounded in the first two acts, and the third act has a great deal of unraveling to accomplish. I feel in reading it that this play needs to be seen and not just read before it can be criticized confidently. More than any of Eliot's earlier plays, it seems to have verve and vigor realizable only on the stage, though it would place heavy demands on the skills of the director and the players.

Eliot has again dealt with a number of themes found in his earlier works, especially in *The Cocktail Party*: the interrelatedness of lives, the necessity of making decisions and accepting their consequences, the importance of finding one's vocation, the ease and seriousness of self-deception, the dangers of trying to manage other people's lives, and the existence of a tougher self that must be painfully discovered if one is to find fulfillment.

Most of the play's characters echo others in the author's previous plays and poems: Colby is noticeably related to Thomas, Harry, and Celia; and, like them, he can be traced to Prufrock, Gerontion, and the protagonists of *The Waste Land* and *Ash-Wednesday*. Sir Claude Mulhammer, Colby's would-be father, shares with Amy of *The Family Reunion* the shattering of plans and the loss of a son. Eggerson, the confidential clerk, echoes some aspects of Sir Henry

Harcourt-Reilly in *The Cocktail Party*; and of course Sir Claude and Lady Elizabeth must, like Edward and Lavinia, settle for what they have and "make the best of a bad job," which will be altered in the doing (as can already be seen in the new mutual sympathy displayed in act 3 of each play).

Eliot's concern to approach the language and rhythms of speech seems to have been marvelously achieved in this play. In "Poetry and Drama" he explained that when writing *The Cocktail Party* he had "laid down for myself the ascetic rule to avoid poetry which could not stand the test of strict dramatic utility."[6] In reading *The Confidential Clerk* we are even less aware of reading poetry, and yet there is excellent poetry in both of the plays.

If *The Cocktail Party* was distinguished by Eliot's placing great emphasis for the first time on more humble characters not destined to be saints, the same emphasis is even stronger in *The Confidential Clerk*. It is true, as D. E. Jones points out, that B. Kaghan in the play calls Colby the sort of person who might chuck it all and go off to a desert island, but that is the closest we come to a Harry or a Celia in this milder potential-church-organist and perhaps eventual-cleric. In this play, as in *The Cocktail Party*, every character is involved in tracing out his proper identity and inheritance, and several are concerned with resolving the life of two worlds in neither of which they feel at home. All of them, except Colby, are intent on finding satisfactory and close relationships with other characters in the play; only Colby wants to be free of others, and the resolution of act 3 gives all of them what they want, though we may suspect that a stronger relationship will develop between Colby and the Eggersons than he intends.

Throughout the play may be found various echoes of the *Bhagavad-Gita*. Eggerson's almost paradoxical admixture of deference and sure control may prove less puzzling if we remember that Krishna was incarnated as the charioteer and advisor of Arjuna, a parallel already seen in Downing, Harry's chauffeur in *The Family Reunion*, now reinforced by various details in *The Confidential Clerk*. Echoes from the *Bhagavad-Gita* also make Lady Elizabeth's meanderings in mysticism seem less flighty and incoherent, and the theme of playing one's own proper role and not someone else's is central to that religious classic so admired by Eliot and importantly used in a number of his works.

In this respect, Sir Claude raises the question of whether or not one can have a vocation to be a second-class artist; and that is what Colby at the end decides that he has, but the fact that it is his real heritage contents him. And Sir Claude comes to suspect that he was wrong to deny his own real vocation as a second-class potter for his role as a successful but not great financier. As with Celia, it is a larger dose of honesty than any other character in the play possesses that makes Colby unable to accept the sort of compromise that Sir Claude has lived with for many years—that makes Colby refuse both the make-believe of Lady Elizabeth's world and the alternatives offered him by Sir Claude. Only Eggerson sees this and avoids the error of trying to make Colby be what he is not. And thus it is only Eggerson to whom Colby will listen at the end of the play.

Already in *The Cocktail Party* Eliot had felt real compassion and respect for every character. In *The Confidential Clerk* the human dignity of each character is even more marked. Even Mrs. Guzzard is given more compelling claims on our understanding and sympathy than a number of earlier characters in Eliot's plays. (The fairylike wish-granting which seems to stylize her big scene for the sake of farce is not without its poignant symbolic undertones.) Finally, as she points out, each of the characters has been allowed to choose a wish and to have it granted; but, when she and Sir Claude made their choices twenty-five years previously, they had failed to realize that there would be a time limit for them. At the play's end the audience's sympathy with her is reestablished when it is seen that she alone of all the characters has gotten nothing from the climactic recognition scene—she has, in fact, lost what little she had.

There is some question of the accuracy of the "facts" that she reveals.[7] I believe, however, that whether they are authentic or not makes very little difference to the major themes of the play, though our understanding that they are doubtful does add force to the farce.

The Elder Statesman (1958)

Though each of Eliot's plays has been markedly different in one or more ways from its predecessors, a surprising continuity of theme accompanies the innovations of technique. In *The Elder Statesman* may be found most of the main themes already discussed in connection with the earlier plays.[8] However, it deals more fully and warmly with love between persons than any of Eliot's previous works—the poem *Marina* being the only near-exception.

Just as *Little Gidding* marked the ultimate development in directions long integral to Eliot's poems, *The Elder Statesman* is a definitive statement concluding lines of development seen in all of the earlier plays. It seems thus highly appropriate that this play should take as a model *Oedipus at Colonus*, the climactic work of Sophocles' dramatic career.

In act 1 of *The Elder Statesman* we see first the realization of Lord Claverton's daughter Monica and Charles Hemington that they love each other and want to marry as soon as they can without depriving Lord Claverton of the company and care he needs. Next we meet the unsavory Federico Gomez, formerly Fred Culverwell, Lord Claverton's classmate until convicted of forgery. Having made his fortune in Central America, Gomez has come back and intends to force his company on Claverton by threatening to tell the story of a youthful escapade in which their car ran over a man on the road.

Act 2 is set in Badgley Court, a convalescent home where Lord Claverton, accompanied by Monica, hopes to find rest and quiet. Instead, he finds the mistakes of his youth turning up in the persons of Mrs. Carghill, who once sued him for breach of promise, and Gomez. Also his son Michael, repeating his own earlier failings, gives him cause to worry.

Act 3 produces complications and discomforts when Gomez and Mrs. Carghill vent their old resentments against Lord Claverton by getting his son Michael to leave for Central America with Gomez; but it also brings final satisfaction to Claverton. He confesses to Monica and Charles the nature of his ghosts, and discovers the real self behind the sham roles he has played all his life. He also blesses their love and offers the prediction that they will be free of the self-deceptions that have wasted much of his life. In the end, his love for his children and Monica's love for him enable him to die happy.

As throughout Eliot's works, we find in this play many lines echoing and clarifying earlier ones. Colby, for example, told Lucasta in *The Confidential Clerk* that if anyone were to share his private world, "it can't be done by issuing invitations:/They would just have to come. And I should not see them coming./I should not hear the opening of the gate./They would simply . . . be there suddenly,/Unexpectedly. Walking down an alley/I should become aware of someone walking with me." And in *The Elder Statesman* Monica says of the first clearly seen satisfying human love in all of Eliot's plays, "How did this come, Charles? It crept so softly/On silent feet, and stood behind my back/Quietly, a long time, a long long time/Before I felt its presence."

Lord Claverton uses railway imagery similar to that of the *Four Quartets* and ghost imagery suggesting that of *Little Gidding*. He says, "They won't want my ghost/Walking in the City or sitting in the Lords./And I, who recognise myself as a ghost/Shan't want to be seen there." The drink-pouring of Gomez echoes that of Sir Henry Harcourt-Reilly. And Lord Claverton's line "What is this self inside us, this silent observer,/Severe and speechless critic, who can terrorise us/And urge us on to futile activity,/And in the end, judge us still more severely/For the errors into which his own reproaches drove us" suggests the "tougher-self" speech of Edward in *The Cocktail Party*.

Mrs. Carghill's "There were the three of us—Effie, Maudie, and me./That day we spent on the river—I've never forgotten it—/The turning point of all my life!" suggests the three Thames-daughters of *The Waste Land*, and her " 'That man is hollow' " suggests *The Hollow Men*. When Michael says of his father's influence, "And what satisfaction, I wonder, will it give you/In the grave? If you are still conscious after death,/I bet it will be a surprised state of consciousness./Poor ghost! reckoning up its profit and loss/ And wondering why it bothered about such trifles," we are reminded of the surprised soul after death in Dante's *Commedia* and in *Animula*, of Reilly's vision of Celia in *The Cocktail Party*, and of the profit and loss of Phlebas the Phoenician in *Dans le restaurant* and *The Waste Land*. Other echoes too (as in *Burnt Norton*) inhabit this garden.

What is new in this play is the emphasis on love, also paralleled in *Oedipus at Colonus*, in which Oedipus says, "My children, to-day your father leaves you. This is the end of all that was I, and the end of your long task of caring for me. I know how hard it was. Yet it was made lighter by one word—love. I loved you as no one else had ever done. Now you must live on without me."[9] The echoes of *Oedipus at Colonus* are many and detailed, but they are not essential to an understanding of *The Elder Statesman*. The Eumenides of *Oedipus at Colonus* and *The Family Reunion* are replaced here by the live ghosts from Lord Claverton's past, Fred Culverwell and Maisie Montjoy—and by Dick Ferry, his own earlier ghost.

The radiant love of Monica and Charles suggests that of Shakespeare's *Tempest* and, even more, *Romeo and Juliet*—but without the tragic end of the latter.

Like *The Confidential Clerk, The Elder Statesman* is likely to appeal most to mature adults, and especially to parents. It may seem too tame and too happy to the young reader who has deeply empathized with the frustrations of Eliot protagonists more tortured and less loved than Lord Claverton, Monica, and Charles. The play is sure to gain in impressiveness as such a reader gets farther from and understands better some of his own mistakes—and especially after he has become involved in the search for ways of helping his children to avoid repeating them. As in *The Family Reunion* and

The Confidential Clerk, the nature and history of the family curse
is a central concern of this play. It is fitting that Eliot's Greek model
involved Oedipus, a man who, however unwittingly, succumbed to
the curse on his family but salvaged a measure of grace at the end,
even though he did not succeed in ending the curse.

The tone of *The Elder Statesman*, especially when considered in
conjunction with all of Eliot's other works, is one of unexpected and
unearned grace, of liberation and restoration through the healing
power of love—a human love that had seemed inaccessible throughout most of the author's career.

The reader cannot doubt the sincerity and the accuracy of the
dedicatory poem, which points to such a love in the author's second
marriage as is seen in the play. *The Elder Statesman* will command
more and more admiration, and will rival *Murder in the Cathedral*
and *The Cocktail Party* as Eliot's masterpiece of the theater.

Chapter Fourteen

Conclusion

The Nobel Prize, the Dante and Goethe medals, the Order of Merit, the United States Medal of Freedom, the French Legion of Honor, honorary degrees from most of the world's famed universities, and the dubbing of his time as "The Age of Eliot" in standard reference works attest the high reputation Eliot earned as poet, playwright, critic, editor, teacher, lecturer, banker's clerk, citizen, churchman, patron of writers, and publisher.

Much of his fully deserved fame has been accorded on the wrong grounds: his obvious mastery of language and technique and his subtle and assured effects won the praise of many readers who failed to grasp the central intentions of such works as *The Waste Land* and *Ash-Wednesday.* And though his techniques were widely imitated, often the bare detailed effects were borrowed, without any sure sense of the deeper structural logic that made the details appropriate and successful.

When faced squarely, his works deflate the ego of a reader who has to forage through Western (and some Eastern) literature to reach the points from which the poems can be read as poetry—and forage through life to reach the points from which both poems and plays are felt, not just thought. Here, experience proves, is an author one must grow up to. After thirty years of reading him, I find no end to that process in sight. Like Dante, he will bountifully repay all I can give. His works yield more and more as one matures. Approaching sixty, I take joy in *The Elder Statesman*'s promise that as we grow older, we may grow wiser and happier.

Fortunately, we seem launched into a new era of Eliot criticism when much ephemeral and narrowly based earlier speculation can be swept away.

Eliot's adoption of England introduced into his art elements unlikely for either a wholly English or a wholly American poet, expanded his consciousness through mutual qualifyings of two related but divergent social contexts. *American Literature*'s annual bibliography claims Eliot for the United States; *PMLA*'s classifies him as English. In discussing both the differences betwe n English and American poetry and the question of Auden's nationality, Eliot said that whichever Auden was, he himself must be the other.[1] But as one critic put it, Eliot "became more English than the English, while remaining more American than the Americans." The proof of the first half of that quip may be seen in Cyril Connolly's comment:

It has often given me satisfaction just to think that he was somewhere around, as loyal subjects feel when they see the Royal Standard on the Palace, [that] in Russell Square one might run across "his set imperial face" or near his club in Pall Mall or in Gloucester Road or Chelsea.[2]

We may legitimately be concerned with Eliot's biography insofar as it sheds light on his works and on the wholly or partially realized intentions behind them. As more *responsible* biography emerges, the meanings of Eliot's poems and plays are becoming clearer and less controversial. Of irresponsible biography (unfortunately not lacking) the less said, the better.

Eliot's 1927 formal adoption of Anglican orthodoxy (and of British citizenship) was echoed in his poetic works of the same period by the more overtly Christian orientation, themes, and imagery of *Ash-Wednesday, The Rock*, and *Murder in the Cathedral*, but we need not agree with Eliot's theology, any more than with Dante's, to be moved by his poetry. Because his poems express authentic states growing out of belief, we can admire the expression of the state even if we reject the belief; but of course the reader who accepts the belief will derive additional enjoyment from the reading.

Among Eliot's major contributions to our tradition were his labors to reestablish the popularity of verse drama, his revolution in twentieth-century poetic sensibility, his finding of verse forms appropriate to both the speech and the theater of the twentieth-century world, and his leadership in reevaluation of our whole English literary tradition by rubbing it against the whole European tradition, modern and ancient alike. Dame Helen Gardner also emphasizes his revivifying of the dramatic monologue and the poetry of place.[3] Throughout his career Eliot emphasized the responsibility of the poet not only to entertain, but to expand the awareness of his reader and to assist him in man's perpetual struggle to rediscover the best that has been revealed and lost again and again by others before him. The search for the deeper identity, the tougher self, requiring the painful shedding of illusions and the recognition of the falseness of mere projections of what one wants to see, is found in seed as early as *Prufrock* but vastly deepened and broadened in the late plays and the *Quartets*, which go far toward pushing poetry and drama into areas previously reserved to music. It is a great distance from the involved constriction of Prufrock to the free and open simplicity of Lord Claverton's final speeches and of Monica's love for Charles in *The Elder Statesman.*

Surveying the whole body of Eliot's writings from *Prufrock* to *The Elder Statesman*, we are struck by the continual expansion of subject matter and aims no less than by the flexibility and innovation of techniques visible in his works of any decade from 1910 to 1960.

In 1953 Eliot wrote that he did not look forward with joy to literary oblivion or to the time when his works might be read only by several graduate students enrolled in "Middle Anglo-American 42 B."[4] Certainly the pleasures of poetry are various. Not all readers' minds operate in the same ways, nor, as Eliot said, do those of poets. There will always be many readers who want entertainment rather than challenges to their awareness, and Eliot is not for them. There will always be readers who do not object to "the general mess of imprecision of feeling" (*East Coker*), and Eliot is not for them. But for readers who love beautiful language, razor-sharp twentieth-century perceptions both external and internal, and the wide-ranging exploration of the paths and patterns of individual development, of human community, and of the Western cultural tradition, no other poet and playwright can be recommended more highly. No other has done more to expand the possibilities—and the joys—of modern English poetry.

Glancing back to our English—or—American dilemma, we must acknowledge that English-speaking peoples have no monopoly on T. S. Eliot: an admirer in Italy has praised him for revivifying Dante for Italy, even in translation, and in Germany he has been appreciated for revivifying European literature at large. And Dr. K. Hazareesingh of India has claimed him for the whole world, calling him "a mighty spirit who bejewelled humanity at large."[5]

Even should our language be replaced—like those of Sophocles and Lucretius, of Arnaut Daniel and even, to some extent, of Shakespeare—the great works of our time will still be read, loved, and translated; and there seems no danger that Eliot's will not be prominent among them.

Ezra Pound's 1965 dictum deserves the last word in this or any other study of Eliot:

READ HIM!

Notes and References

Note: Abbreviations used here are identified below and in the Selected Bibliography.

Preface

1. *T. S. Eliot: Moments and Patterns* (Minneapolis, 1966), p. 4. This collection of Mr. Unger's Eliot essays is an excellent model for Eliot scholars.

Chapter One

1. Helen Gardner, *The Composition of "Four Quartets"* (hereafter cited as *Quartets*) (New York, 1978), p. 42.
2. F. O. Matthiessen, *The Achievement of T. S. Eliot: An Essay on the Nature of Poetry*, 3rd ed. (New York, 1959), p. xx.
3. Russell Kirk, *Eliot and His Age: T. S. Eliot's Moral Imagination in the Twentieth Century* (New York, 1971), p. 23.
4. Herbert Howarth, *Notes on Some Figures Behind T. S. Eliot* (Boston, 1964), pp. 8–10, 13.
5. R. L. Rusk, *The Letters of Ralph Waldo Emerson*, Vol. 4 (New York, 1939), pp. 338–39. Cited in Lyndall Gordon, *Eliot's Early Years* (New York, 1977), p. 9.
6. *Ezra Pound, Letters, 1907–1941*, ed. D. D. Paige (New York, 1950), p. 30. Hereafter cited as Pound, *Letters*.
7. Howarth, pp. 55, 60, 61, 62.
8. Ibid., p. 22.
9. Ibid., p. 28.
10. Ibid.
11. Ibid., p. 19.
12. "American Literature and the American Language," *To Criticize the Critic and Other Writings* (New York, 1965), p. 44.
13. Letter to Bertrand Russell (June 22, 1927), Russell Archive, McMaster University. Cited in Gordon, *EEY*, p. 12.

14. "The Relationship Between Politics and Metaphysics," a talk to Harvard's Philosophical Society, quoted by John Soldo in "The Tempering of T. S. Eliot" (Harvard dissertation, 1973), p. 166. Cited in Gordon, p. 13.

15. Gordon, p. 3.

16. *TCC*, p. 45.

17. Howarth, p. 114.

18. "The Influence of Landscape upon the Poet," *Daedalus*, Spring 1960, pp. 421–22.

19. T. S. Matthews, *Great Tom: Notes Towards the Definition of T. S. Eliot* (New York, 1973), p. 15.

20. *TCC*, pp. 44–45.

21. Gordon, pp. 3–4, citing as sources H. W. H. Powel, Jr., "Notes on the Life of T. S. Eliot 1888–1910" (M.A. thesis, Brown University, 1954), p. 28, and a St. Louis letter from 'Margery' to Mary von Schrader and Randall Jarrell (n.d.), Berg Coll.

22. *Poems Written in Early Youth* (Stockholm, 1950; London and New York, 1967), p. 33. Hereafter cited as *PWEY*.

23. Valerie Eliot, "note" in *PWEY*, pp. v–vi.

24. *PWEY*, p. 34.

25. Ibid., p. v.

26. Donald Gallup's excellent bibliography must be checked for information on this and all other Eliot writings.

27. *The Use of Poetry and the Use of Criticism* (London, 1933, 1964; Cambridge, 1933), pp. 33–34. Hereafter cited as *UPUC*.

28. "Milton at 150," *Newsweek*, March 8, 1948, p. 79.

29. Matthews, p. 21.

30. "Not All Acclaim Nobel Prize Winner: Are Tom Eliot's Poems 'Music' or just 'Tripe'?" *Boston Globe*, November 7, 1948. (I. A. Richards is quoted as referring to Eliot's "music of ideas"; Amy Lowell as saying, "It's tripe.")

31. Howarth, p. 64. David Ward concisely summarizes some of these influences on Eliot in *T. S. Eliot Between Two Worlds: A Reading of T. S. Eliot's Poetry and Plays* (London and Boston, 1973), pp. 1–12.

32. *Princeton Alumni Weekly*, February 5, 1937, cited in Kristian Smidt, *Poetry and Belief in the Work of T. S. Eliot* (New York, 1949), p. 13.

33. Howarth, p. 133.

34. Gordon, p. 26.

35. *TCC*, p. 126.
36. Donald Gallup, "The Lost Manuscripts of T. S. Eliot," *Bulletin of the New York Public Library* 72:647.
37. Arthur Symons, *The Symbolist Movement in Literature* (New York: E. P. Dutton and Co., 1908, 1919, 1959), p. 59.
38. Gordon, p. 27, note 34; Gordon is discussing "Opera"; I associate her remarks with *Nocturne*.
39. *PWEY*, p. 23.
40. Ibid., pp. 24–25.
41. Grover Smith, Jr., *T. S. Eliot's Poetry and Plays: A Study in Sources and Meanings*, 2nd ed. (Chicago, 1950, 1956, 1974), p. 5.
42. "T. S. Eliot," *Life*, January 15, 1965, pp. 92–93.
43. *Ushant* (New York, 1952), p. 143.
44. Ibid., p. 186.
45. Gordon, p. 26.
46. Ibid., p. 34.
47. Ibid., p. 18.
48. Ibid., pp. 34–35.
49. *La France Libre, Liberté, Egalité, Fraternité* 8 (June 1944): 94.
50. *Criterion*, April 1934, pp. 451–52.
51. Montgomery Belgion, "Irving Babbitt and the Continent," in Richard March and Thurairajah Tambimuttu, comps., *T. S. Eliot: A Symposium* (London, 1948), pp. 51–59.
52. Smidt, p. 41.
53. Trans. by Lawrence Vail, Preface by T. S. Eliot (Paris: Crosby Continental Editions, 1932; New York: Avalon Press, 1945).
54. Gordon, pp. 43–49, 52, 116.
55. Smidt, p. 20.

Chapter Two

1. Donald Gallup, "The 'Lost' Manuscripts of T. S. Eliot," *Times Literary Supplement* (London), November 7, 1968, pp. 1238–40; rpt. ("slightly revised") in *Bulletin of the New York Public Library* 72 (December 1968): 641–52 (plus 3 pages of illustrations).
2. This and all subsequent passages from Dante's *Divine Comedy* are quoted, unless otherwise indicated, from the Temple Classics 3-volume bilingual edition of J. M. Dent & Sons, Ltd. (recommended by Eliot in his "Dante" essay in *SE*) as follows: *The Inferno of Dante*

Alighieri, The Purgatorio of Dante Alighieri, and *The Paradiso of Dante Alighieri,* 14th ed. (London, 1946). Canticle, canto, and lines will be indicated parenthetically in my text. I also recommend the excellent notes and introductory and supplemental materials in Dorothy L. Sayers's Penguin Classics *terza rima* translation in three volumes: *Hell, Purgatory,* and *Paradise* (Harmondsworth, Middlesex, 1949). A superb book on *The Divine Comedy* is Helen Luke's *From Dark Wood to White Rose* (Pecos, New Mexico: Dove Publications, 1975). John Ciardi's Mentor Classics translation (also three volumes) is the most readable English poetry of any translation I know. For teaching, to beginners, I recommend using Ciardi's translation and Sayers's notes.

3. Gordon, p. 37.

4. *Criterion* 13 (April 1934): 452.

5. "Ezra Pound," I-II, *New English Weekly* 30 (October 31 and November 7, 1946): 27–28, 37–39. Paged from 1 each issue. Quoted in Smidt, p. 21.

6. See, for example, Conrad Aiken, "King Bolo and Others," in March and Tambimuttu, p. 22.

7. Letter to Harriet Monroe, September 30, 1914; in Pound, *Letters,* p. 40.

8. Kirk, p. 11.

9. I am grateful to Mr. Michael Slagle for first suggesting to me that Prufrock has parallels for Dante's three beasts, though he identified them somewhat differently than I shall.

10. Gertrude Patterson, *T. S. Eliot: Poems in the Making* (New York, 1971), p. 117.

11. Dante's tercets, beginning "But I, why go?" parallel Prufrock's waverings.

12. "Let us go" thus announces *Prufrock* to be an *Inferno.*

13. *The Rock,* (London and New York, 1934), pp. 47–48. Hereafter cited as *Rock.*

14. Smidt, p. 85.

15. As paraphrased in Jane Worthington, "The Epigraphs to the Poetry of T. S. Eliot," *American Literature* 21 (1949):2.

16. *"The Waste Land,"* in *Eliot in Perspective: A Symposium,* ed. Graham Martin (New York, 1970), p. 107.

17. Balachandra Rajan, *The Overwhelming Question: A Study of the Poetry of T. S. Eliot* (Toronto, 1976), p. 8.

18. Hugh Kenner, *The Invisible Poet: T. S. Eliot* (New York, 1959), p. 12.

19. Roberta Morgan and Albert Wohlstetter, "Observations on Prufrock," *Harvard Advocate* 125 (December 1938):40.

20. Rajan, p. 9.

21. The quotations are respectively from *Ushant,* p. 143; B. C. Southam, *A Guide to the "Selected Poems" of T. S. Eliot* (New York, 1968), p. 35; and Grover Smith, p. 20.

22. David Ward, *T. S. Eliot Between Two Worlds: A Reading of T. S. Eliot's Poetry and Plays* (Boston, 1973), p. 20.

23. Morgan and Wohlstetter, p. 36.

Chapter Three

1. "For T.S.E." in Allen Tate, *T. S. Eliot: The Man and His Work* (London, 1967), p. 89.

2. "What Dante Means to Me," in *TCC,* pp. 125, 130.

3. *Dante* (London, 1929, 1965), pp. 28, 29, and "Dante" in *Selected Essays 1917–1932* (London, 1932, 1951; New York, 1932, 1950), pp. 213–14. Hereafter cited as *SE.*

4. *The Sacred Wood: Essays on Poetry and Criticism* (London, 1920), p. 164. Hereafter cited as *SW; SE,* p. 226.

5. *SE,* pp. 236–37.

6. *Sailing Into the Unknown: Yeats, Pound, and Eliot* (New York, 1978), p. 162.

7. *SE,* p. 247.

8. "Dante," in *SW,* p. 169.

9. *SE,* p. 220.

10. Ibid., pp. 220–21.

11. Guiterriez, "avid of speed and power," might be seen earlier "moving between the legs of tables and chairs"; "Boudin, blown to pieces," might be seen "rising or falling, grasping at kisses and toys,/ Advancing boldly, sudden to take alarm,/Retreating to the corner of arm and knee,/Eager to be reassured." "This one who made a great fortune" may be suggested in "taking pleasure in the fragrant brilliance of the Christmas tree." "That one who went his own way" may have taken "pleasure in the wind, the sunlight and the sea"; and "Floret, by the boarhound slain between the yew trees" for his lust,

may have studied "the sunlit pattern on the floor/And running stags around a silver tray."

12. A. C. Charity, "T. S. Eliot: The Dantean Recognitions," in *The Waste Land in Different Voices,* ed. A. D. Moody (New York, 1974), p. 120.

13. *SE,* pp. 233–34.

14. Grover Smith, p. 336, note 1a; Helen Gardner, *The Composition of Four Quartets* (New York and London, 1978), pp. 35–36; Gordon, pp. 55–57.

15. Gordon, p. 60.

16. Bonamy Dobrée, "T. S. Eliot: A Personal Reminiscence," in Tate, p. 81.

17. *TCC,* pp. 125–35.

18. "Unworthy Poet But . . . ," *Newsweek,* June 8, 1959, p. 52.

Chapter Four

1. Smidt, p. 20.

2. Ibid., p. 21.

3. Pound, *Letters,* p. 40.

4. Ibid., p. 50.

5. These five poems were included: *The Love Song of J. Alfred Prufrock, Portrait of a Lady, The Boston Evening Transcript, Hysteria,* and *Miss Helen Slingsby [Aunt Helen]*.

6. Quoted in Kenner, *Invisible Poet,* p. 96.

7. In 1916–1918, according to W. E. Styler, "T. S. Eliot as an Adult Tutor," *Notes and Queries,* February 1972, pp. 53–54, Eliot gave "at least 121 lectures" at Sydenham, Southall, and perhaps elsewhere under the aegis of Oxford University and of the London Committee.

8. *T. S. Eliot, The Waste Land: A Facsimile and Transcript of the Original Drafts, including the Annotations of Ezra Pound.* Edited by Valerie Eliot (London and New York, 1971), p. xiv. Hereafter cited as *WLF.*

9. Quoted in "T. S. Eliot," *Ezra Pound,* ed. Peter Russell (London: Peter Nevill, Ltd., 1950), p. 33.

10. From T. S. Eliot, *Collected Poems, 1909–1962* (New York: Harcourt Brace and World, Inc. and London: Faber and Faber, 1963), p. 19. Quoted by permission.

Chapter Five

1. William Turner Levy and Victor Scherle, *Affectionately, T. S. Eliot: The Story of a Friendship, 1947–1965* (Philadelphia, 1968), p. 30.
2. "The Three Provincialities," *Tyro*, No. 2 (Spring 1922): 11–13. Cited in Matthiessen, p. 83 and n., p. 94.
3. *Webster's New World Dictionary of the American Language* (1964).
4. *Renascence* 21 (1968): 41–43, 54.
5. "Origen," *Encyclopaedia Britannica* (1968).
6. Ibid. I am grateful to Mr. John Ferguson for sharing this insight with me.
7. Ibid.
8. I am grateful to Mrs. Alice Longsworth for pointing this out to me.
9. Grover Smith, p. 44.
10. Robert P. Tristam Coffin and Alice M. Witherspoon, *Seventeenth Century Prose and Poetry* (New York: Harcourt, Brace and Co., 1946), p. 235.
11. Grover Smith, p. 44.
12. Audrey Fawcett Cahill, *T. S. Eliot and the Human Predicament* (Pietermaritzburg, South Africa, 1967), pp. 34–36.
13. Grover Smith, p. 35.

Chapter Six

1. Eliot criticized Gilbert Murray's translation of Agamemnon's cry in a brief review, *Criterion*, 8 (April 1929):566.
2. Matthiessen, p. 59.
3. This essay (based on Dryden's *Essay of Dramatic Poesy*) is reprinted in *SE*, where it can be readily consulted by readers who want to pursue these varying views, too often indiscriminately quoted as Eliot's own.
4. "A Dialogue on Dramatic Poetry," *SE*, p. 33.
5. *Nation & Athenaeum* 34 (October 6, 1923):11–12.
6. Howarth, pp. 315–16.
7. Printed program—*Homage to T. S. Eliot: A Programme of*

Poetry, Drama, and Music for the London Library at the Globe Theatre, London, June 13, 1965.

8. *The Journals of Arnold Bennett, III, 1921–1928,* ed. Newman Flower (London, 1933), p. 52; cited by Carol H. Smith, *T. S. Eliot's Dramatic Theory and Practice* (Princeton, 1963), p. 51n.

Chapter Seven

1. *WLF,* p. 17.
2. Elizabeth Drew, *T. S. Eliot: The Design of His Poetry* (New York, 1949), pp. 40–41.
3. Gordon, p. 5, citing Charlotte Eliot's "The Master's Welcome."
4. Adrian Stokes, "The Sculptor Agostino di Duccio" (extracted from the third of four essays on the Tempio Maletestino at Rimini; part of a work in progress about the Italian Renaissance), *Criterion* 9 (October 1929):44–60.
5. Mervyn W. Williamson, "T. S. Eliot's 'Gerontion': A Study in Thematic Repetition and Development," *Texas Studies in English* 36 (1957):114.
6. Ibid., pp. 114–15. This lower-case "jew" is in one of three passages that have occasioned charges of anti-Semitism against Eliot by even such astute Eliot critics as Leonard Unger and M. L. Rosenthal. I trust that Mr. Williamson's remarks and mine to follow clear Eliot of the charge here. (It is even arguable that, as in *Ulysses,* anti-Semitism is being criticized.)
7. Both were being written in mid-1919, and both Eliot and Joyce were in close touch with Ezra Pound.
8. Rosenthal, p. 84.
9. Mervyn W. Williamson, pp. 118–19.
10. Matthiessen, p. 63.

Chapter Eight

1. Richard Ellmann, *Golden Codgers: Biographical Speculations* (New York, 1973), p. 155.
2. Donald Gallup's "The Lost Manuscripts of T. S. Eliot," *Times Literary Supplement,* No. 3480 (November 7, 1968), pp. 1238–40, revised in *Bulletin of the New York Public Library* 72 (December

1968):641–52, remains extremely useful, giving precise information on unpublished materials not otherwise available.

3. New York, 1971. The photographic reproductions in this edition are excellent: they are more legible than the originals. And Mrs. Eliot's painstaking care is seconded by her expert critical judgment.

4. "The Histrionic Sensibility: The Mimetic Perception of Action," in *The Idea of a Theatre* (Princeton, 1949), pp. 236–40. This superb book deserves the attention of any reader interested in drama, either read or performed.

5. *WLF,* p. 1.

6. (New York, 1975), pp. 96–107.

7. G. S. Fraser, *The Modern Writer and His World* (London, 1953), p. 209.

8. Jessie L. Weston, *From Ritual to Romance* (Garden City, New York, 1957), p. 126.

9. *Dial* 75 (November 1923):480–83. Repr. in *Dial,* New York 1 (Fall 1959):153–58.

10. "Religion and Literature," *SE,* pp. 343–54.

11. New York, 1942; p. 276.

12. *WLF,* p. 100.

13. *Purgatorio* 26, quoted in "Dante," *SE,* p. 217; the arrangement is mine.

14. Class notes, 1957. Mr. Battenhouse's "Classics of the Christian Tradition" course was one of the best backgrounds to the study of Eliot one could imagine.

15. *WLF,* p. 5 and p. 125n.

16. See *Inferno* III, 58–60; *Ushant,* pp. 164–65; and Aiken's prefatory note to "The Anatomy of Melancholy" in Tate, pp. 194–96.

17. *WLF,* p. 127n.

18. "Buddha's Fire Sermon" is here quoted from *The Sacred Book of the East,* trans. F. Max Muller, XIII (Oxford, 1881), 134–35. (Mahavagga, I, 21, i–iv):

1. And the Blessed One, after having dwelt at Uruvela as long as he thought fit, went forth to Gayasisa, accompanied by a great number of Bhikkhus, by one thousand Bhikkhus who all had been Gatilas before. There near Gaya, at Gayasisa, the Blessed One dwelt together with those thousand Bhikkhus.

2. There the Blessed One thus addressed the Bhikkhus: "Everything, O Bhikkhus, is burning. And how, O Bhikkhus, is everything burning?

"The eye, O Bhikkhus, is burning; visible things are burning; the mental impressions based on the eye are burning; the contact of the eye (with visible things) is burning; the sensation produced by the contact of the eye (with visible things), be it pleasant, be it painful, be it neither pleasant nor painful, that also is burning. With what fire is it burning? I declare unto you that it is burning with the fire of lust, with the fire of anger, with the fire of ignorance; it is burning with (the anxieties of) birth, decay, death, grief, lamentation, suffering, dejection, and despair.

3. "The ear is burning, sounds are burning, &c. . . . The nose is burning, odours are burning, &c. . . . The tongue is burning, tastes are burning, &c. . . . The body is burning, objects of contact are burning, &c. . . . The mind is burning, thoughts are burning, &c. . . . (Author's note: Here the same exposition which has been given relating to the eye, its objects, the sensations produced by its contact with objects, &c., is repeated with reference to the ear and the other organs of sense.)

4. "Considering this, O Bhikkhus, a disciple learned (in the scriptures), walking in the Noble Path, becomes weary of the eye, weary of visible things, weary of the mental impressions based on the eye, weary of the contact of the eye (with visible things), weary also of the sensation produced by the contact of the eye (with visible things), be it pleasant, be it painful, be it neither pleasant nor painful. He becomes weary of the ear (&c. . . . , down to . . . thoughts). Becoming weary of all that, he divests himself of passion; by absence of passion he is made free; when he is free, he becomes aware that he is free; and he realises that re-birth is exhausted; that holiness is completed; that duty is fulfilled; and that there is no further return to this world."

When this exposition was propounded, the minds of those thousand Bhikkhus became free from attachment to the world, and were released from the Asavas.

Here ends the sermon on "The Burning."

End of the third Bhanavara concerning
the Wonders done at Uruvela.

19. *WLF,* p. 27.

20. Ibid., p. 31.

21. Ibid., p. 35.

22. Ibid., p. 117.

23. *Thirteen Upanishads,* trans. Robert Ernest Hume (London: Oxford University Press, 1921), p. 150.

24. See Unger, "Laforgue, Conrad, and Eliot," *The Man in the Name,* pp. 234–37.

25. Thomas Kyd, *The Spanish Tragedy,* in *Elizabethan and Stuart Plays,* ed. Charles Read Baskervill et al. (New York: Henry Holt and Co., 1934), act 4, scene 1. I have used Eliot's spelling of Hieronymo throughout.

26. *WLF,* p. 111, and p. 130n.

27. Ibid., p. 113.

28. John Day, *The Parliament of Bees,* in *Nero and Other Plays,* ed. with intro. by Herbert P. Horne, Havelock Ellis, Arthur Symons, and Arthur Wilson Verity (London: Vizitelli and Co., 1888), p. 226.

29. Stephen Spender, *T. S. Eliot* (New York, 1975). pp. 119–22; this excellent book confirms my warm memories of Mr. Spender from a 1948 Indiana University Writers' Conference in which the procedure was approximately this: one of us would ask him a question. He would seem not to have heard (but we learned to wait eagerly). After some seconds, he would say, "Let me see if I understand . . ." and would rephrase the question, far more precisely saying what we had tried to, and then would give three or four well-organized alternative answers and the conditions each would suit. All of us knew that he understood us much better than we understood either him or ourselves, and both our respect for poets and our humility grew very rapidly.

30. *SE,* p. 342.

Chapter Nine

1. D. E. S. Maxwell, *The Poetry of T. S. Eliot* (London, 1952, and New York, 1961), p. 138.
2. "Dante," *SE*, p. 235.
3. Pound, *Letters*, p. 171.
4. These are reprinted as the appendix in Maxwell.
5. "A Dialogue on Dramatic Poetry," *SE*, pp. 31–45.
6. My translation.
7. An excellent, relevant book on the meaning of Beatrice here is Charles Williams's *The Figure of Beatrice* (New York: Noonday Press, 1961).
8. Suggested by Sister Mary Cleophas in her *"Ash-Wednesday: The Purgatorio in a Modern Mode,"* *Comparative Literature* 11 (Fall 1959):329–39.
9. C. S. Lewis, *The Allegory of Love: A Study in Medieval Tradition* (New York: Oxford University Press, 1958), p. 5.
10. Quoted in Unger, *The Man in the Name*, p. 162.
11. Quoted in Giorgio de Santillana, *The Origins of Scientific Thought: From Anaximander to Proclus, 600 B.C.–500 A.D.* (New York: New American Library, 1961), p. 44. Santillana's "The Logos in the Lightning" chapter echoes much in Eliot's poems.
12. "Lancelot Andrewes," *SE*, p. 307.

Chapter Ten

1. Matthiessen, p. 82.
2. "Homage to T. S. Eliot: A Symposium," *Harvard Advocate* 125 (December 1938):19.
3. Grover Smith, p. 254.
4. Ibid., p. 252; the two *Words for Music* poems were published twice in 1934—in the *Virginia Quarterly Review* and in *Best Poems of 1934;* Ann Brady, *Lyricism in the Poetry of T. S. Eliot* (Port Washington, New York, 1978), p. 24; Gardner, *Quartets,* pp. 33–34.
5. *A Reader's Guide to T. S. Eliot* (London, 1957), p. 201.
6. Gardner, *Quartets,* p. 31.
7. Reproduced in Nancy Duvall Hargrove, *Landscape as Symbol in the Poetry of T. S. Eliot* (Jackson, Mississippi, 1978), following p. 114.

8. The *Landscapes* title is suggested in Mary's "You bring your own landscape . . ." Other *Family Reunion* lines echo the return to childhood memories in *New Hampshire,* the iron thoughts of *Virginia,* the old enchantments of *Usk,* and the long shadow of pride in *Rannoch, by Glencoe.* Harry's hurrying away without explaining much echoes "The palaver is finished" of *Cape Ann* and Sweeney's earlier "I gotta use words when I talk to you."

9. Gardner, *Quartets,* p. 34; Hargrove, p. 120.

10. Hargrove, p. 121.

11. Included in Edd Winfield Parks and Richard Croom Beatty, eds., *The English Drama: An Anthology 900–1642* (New York: W. W. Norton & Co., 1963), pp. 221–45.

12. *After Strange Gods: A Primer of Modern Heresy* (London, 1933; New York, 1934), p. 16.

13. "The Influence of Landscape upon the Poet," *Daedalus,* Spring 1960, p. 422.

Chapter Eleven

1. Cambridge, 1969.

2. David E. Jones, *The Plays of T. S. Eliot* (Toronto, 1960), p. 47.

3. "The Possibility of a Poetic Drama," *SW,* p. 70.

4. Several excellent critiques of this play are available, but none better than that of Francis Fergusson in his *The Idea of a Theatre* (Princeton, 1949), a book whose depth and value are better appreciated each time one returns to it.

5. My class notes, summer 1957.

6. T. S. Eliot and George Hoellering, *The Film of Murder in the Cathedral* (London, 1952).

7. "The Three Voices of Poetry," *On Poetry and Poets* (New York and London, 1957), p. 96. Hereafter cited as *OPP.* For the conditions under which Eliot's early plays were written and the lessons that Eliot drew from them, the reader should also consult "Poetry and Drama" in *OPP* and E. Martin Browne's "The Dramatic Verse of T. S. Eliot" in March and Tambimuttu.

8. Fyodor Dostoyevsky, *Crime and Punishment,* trans. Constance Garnett (New York: Modern Library, 1950), p. 532.

9. C. L. Barber, "Strange Gods at T. S. Eliot's 'The Family Re-

union,' " in Leonard Unger, *T. S. Eliot: A Selected Critique* (New York and Toronto, 1948), p. 415.

Chapter Twelve

1. London and New York, 1978; this volume (*Quartets*) is the single most useful study. Another good recent work is Hargrove (cited above). Some of the better earlier studies are Gardner, *The Art of T. S. Eliot* (New York, 1959); Bernard Bergonzi, ed., *T. S. Eliot, Four Quartets: A Casebook* (London, 1969); Harry Blamires, *Word Unheard: A Guide through Eliot's "Four Quartets"* (London, 1969); Raymond Preston, *"Four Quartets" Rehearsed: A Commentary on T. S. Eliot's Cycle of Poems* (New York, 1946); and especially for exhaustive identification of sources and analyses of their relevance, Grover Smith, Jr.'s, indispensable if still sometimes puzzling book *EPP*. Few analyses are better than Kenner's; an excellent brief reading is found in Smidt.

2. "Dante," *SE*, p. 229.

3. *Quartets*, p. 16.

4. Ibid., p. 26.

5. Ibid., p. 40.

6. Ibid., p. 37.

7. See Unger, "The Rose Garden," in his *T S. Eliot: Moments and Patterns* (Minneapolis, 1966), pp. 69–91.

8. Quoted in H. W. Häusermann, " 'East Coker' by T. S. Eliot," *English Studies* 23 (August 1941):109–10, and cited in Grover Smith, p. 268.

9. Drew, p. 165n.

10. *WLF*, p. 55.

11. *The Song of God: Bhagavad-Gita,* trans. Swami Prabhavananda and Christopher Isherwood (New York, 1954), pp. 56–57. Quoted by permission of the Vedanta Society of Southern California.

12. Ibid., p. 73.

13. London and New York: Macmillan and Co., 1887.

14. Gardner, *The Art of T. S. Eliot*, p. 177.

Chapter Thirteen

1. *UPUC*, p. 153.
2. Peter Grosvenor, "The Shy Genius" (London) *Daily Express,* January 5, 1965.
3. "T. S. Eliot's Recent Work," *Contemporary Review* 184 (July 1952):37.
4. David E. Jones points these out in his excellent chapter "Plays in a Contemporary Setting—III 'The Confidential Clerk' (1953)," *The Plays of T. S. Eliot,* pp. 155–78.
5. Burke Wilkinson, *New York Times,* February 5, 1954, sec. 2, p. 1, col. 7; cited in Jones, p. 167.
6. *OPP,* p. 91.
7. See Grover Smith, p. 242.
8. Jones analyzes *The Elder Statesman* in detail, with great sensitivity toward the relevance of its themes to the whole body of Eliot's works.
9. Sophocles, *The Theban Plays,* trans. E. F. Watling (Harmondsworth, Middlesex: Penguin, 1952), p. 120.

Chapter Fourteen

1. *TCC*, p. 60.
2. *Sunday Times* (London), January 10, 1965.
3. *T. S. Eliot and the English Poetic Tradition,* p. 25.
4. *TCC,* p. 49.
5. G. B. Angioletti, "Encounters with Mr. Eliot," in March and Tambimuttu, p. 139; "Mr. T. S. Eliot," *London Times,* January 12, 1965.

Selected Bibliography

PRIMARY SOURCES

Symbols preceding titles are those used in the notes.

The following titles are listed in the order of their publication as separate works, though many of the poems and essays appeared earlier in periodicals or other people's books, for which consult Donald Gallup's excellent bibliography, listed below.

1. Poems

Prufrock and Other Observations. London: The Egoist, Ltd., 1917.

Poems. Richmond, Surrey: The Hogarth Press, 1919.

Ara Vos Prec. London: The Ovid Press, 1920; New York: Alfred A. Knopf, 1920.

The Waste Land. New York: Boni and Liveright, 1922.

Poems 1909–1925. London: Faber & Gwyer Ltd., 1925.

Journey of the Magi. London: Faber & Gwyer Ltd., 1927.

A Song for Simeon. London: Faber & Gwyer Ltd., 1928.

Animula. London: Faber & Faber Ltd., 1929.

Ash-Wednesday. London: Faber & Faber Ltd., 1930; New York: G. P. Putnam's Sons, 1930.

Marina. London: Faber & Faber Ltd., 1930.

Triumphal March. London: Faber & Faber Ltd., 1931.

Words for Music. Bryn Mawr, Pennsylvania: Bryn Mawr Press, 1935.

Two Poems. Cambridge: Cambridge University Press, 1935.

Collected Poems, 1909–1935. London: Faber & Faber Ltd., 1936; New York: Harcourt, Brace and Co., 1936.

Old Possum's Book of Practical Cats. London: Faber & Faber Ltd., 1939, 1940, 1953; New York: Harcourt, Brace and Co., 1939, 1968.

The Waste Land and Other Poems. London: Faber & Faber Ltd., 1940; New York: Harcourt, Brace and Co., 1955.

East Coker. London: *The New English Weekly,* 1940; 3rd ed. London: Faber & Faber Ltd., 1940.

Burnt Norton. London: Faber & Faber Ltd., 1941.

The Dry Salvages. London: Faber & Faber Ltd., 1941.

Little Gidding. London: Faber & Faber Ltd., 1942.

Four Quartets. New York: Harcourt, Brace and Co., 1943; London: Faber & Faber Ltd., 1944, 1960.

A Practical Possum. Cambridge: Harvard Printing Office and Department of Graphic Arts, 1947.

Selected Poems. Harmondsworth, Middlesex: Penguin Books in association with Faber & Faber Ltd., 1948; New York: Harcourt, Brace & World, Inc., 1967.

The Undergraduate Poems. Cambridge: *Harvard Advocate,* 1949. Unauthorized reprint.

Anabasis: A Poem by St.-J. Perse. London: Faber & Faber Ltd., 1930, 1959; New York: Harcourt, Brace and Co., 1938; 3rd (rev. and corrected) ed., 1949. (Translated from French.)

(*PWEY*) *Poems Written in Early Youth.* Stockholm: Privately printed, 1950; London: Faber & Faber Ltd., 1967; New York: Farrar, Straus & Giroux, 1967.

(*PP50*) *The Complete Poems and Plays, 1909–1950.* New York: Harcourt, Brace and Co., 1952.

The Cultivation of Christmas Trees. London: Faber & Faber Ltd., 1954; New York: Farrar, Straus and Cudahy, 1956.

(*POEMS*) *Collected Poems, 1909–1962.* London: Faber & Faber Ltd., 1963; New York: Harcourt, Brace & World, 1963.

The Complete Poems and Plays of T. S. Eliot. London: Faber & Faber Ltd.. 1969.

(*WLF*) *T. S. Eliot, The Waste Land: A Facsimile and Transcript of the Original Drafts Including the Annotations of Ezra Pound,* Edited by Valerie Eliot. London: Faber & Faber Ltd., 1971; New York: Harcourt, Brace Jovanovich, Inc., 1971.

2. Plays

Sweeney Agonistes: Fragments of an Aristophanic Melodrama. London: Faber & Faber Ltd., 1932.

(*ROCK*) *The Rock.* London: Faber & Faber Ltd., 1934; New York: Harcourt, Brace and Co., 1934.

Murder in the Cathedral. Acting ed., Canterbury: H. J. Goulden Ltd., 1935; first complete ed., London: Faber & Faber Ltd., 1935, 1937, 1938; New York: Harcourt, Brace and Co., 1935, 1936, 1963.

The Family Reunion. London: Faber & Faber Ltd., 1939, 1963; New York: Harcourt, Brace and Co., 1939; Harcourt, Brace & World, Inc., 1964.

The Cocktail Party. London: Faber & Faber Ltd., 1950; New York: Harcourt, Brace and Co., 1950.

(With George Hoellering.) *The Film of* "MURDER IN THE CATHEDRAL." London: Faber & Faber Ltd., 1952; New York: Harcourt, Brace and Co., 1952.

The Confidential Clerk. London: Faber & Faber Ltd., 1954; New York: Harcourt, Brace and Co., 1954.

The Elder Statesman. London: Faber & Faber Ltd., 1959; New York: Farrar Straus and Cudahy, 1959.

(*PLAYS*) *Collected Plays*. London: Faber & Faber Ltd., 1962.

The Complete Poems and Plays of T. S. Eliot. London: Faber & Faber Ltd., 1969.

3. Prose

(*EzP*) *Ezra Pound, His Metric and Poetry*. New York: Alfred A. Knopf, 1917; rpt. in *TCC*.

(*SW*) *The Sacred Wood: Essays on Poetry and Criticism*. London: Methuen & Co. Ltd., 1920.

Homage to John Dryden. London: The Hogarth Press, 1924; rpt. in *SE*.

Shakespeare and the Stoicism of Seneca. London: Oxford University Press, 1927; rpt. in *SE*.

(*FLA*) *For Lancelot Andrewes*. London: Faber & Gwyer Ltd., 1928; Garden City, N.Y.: Doubleday, Doran and Co., 1929; rpt. in *SE*, except for a Crashaw essay.

Dante. London: Faber & Faber Ltd., 1929; rpt. in *SE*.

Thoughts After Lambeth. London: Faber & Faber Ltd., 1931; rpt. in *SE*.

Charles Whibley A Memoir. London: Oxford University Press, 1931; Cambridge: The English Association Pamphlets, No. 80, 1964; rpt. in *SE*.

(*SE*) *Selected Essays 1917–1932*. London: Faber & Faber Ltd., 1932. 3rd ed., 1951; New York: Harcourt, Brace and Co., 1932, new ed., 1950.

John Dryden the Poet the Dramatist the Critic. New York: Terence and Elsa Holliday, 1932.

(UPUC) The Use of Poetry and the Use of Criticism. London: Faber & Faber Ltd., 1933, 1964; Cambridge: Harvard University Press, 1933.

After Strange Gods: A Primer of Modern Heresy. London: Faber & Faber Ltd., 1933; New York: Harcourt, Brace and Co., 1934.

Elizabethan Essays. London: Faber & Faber Ltd., 1934, 1963; New York: Harcourt, Brace and Co., 1956.

Essays Ancient and Modern. London: Faber & Faber Ltd., 1936; New York: Harcourt, Brace and Co., 1936.

(ICS) The Idea of a Christian Society. London: Faber & Faber Ltd., 1939; New York: Harcourt, Brace and Co., 1940. See note to *NTDC*.

Points of View. London: Faber & Faber Ltd., 1941.

The Music of Poetry. Glasgow: Jackson, Son & Co., 1942; rpt. in *OPP*.

The Classics and the Man of Letters. London, New York and Toronto: Oxford University Press, 1942.

Reunion by Destruction. London: The Pax House, 1943.

What Is a Classic? London: Faber & Faber Ltd., 1945; rpt. in *OPP*.

Die Einheit der Europaischen Kultur. Berlin: Carl Habel Verlagsbuch-handlung, 1946.

On Poetry. Richmond, Va.: Whittet & Shepperson [printers], 1947. For Concord Academy, Concord, Mass.

Milton. London: Geoffrey Cumberledge, 1947; rpt. in *OPP*.

A Sermon. Cambridge: University Press, 1948.

(NTDC) Notes Towards the Definition of Culture. London: Faber & Faber Ltd., 1948, 1962; New York: Harcourt, Brace and Co., 1949. Reissued, with *ICS*, in Harvest Books paperback as *Christianity and Culture* (New York, 1960).

From Poe to Valéry. New York: Harcourt, Brace and Co., 1948; Washington: Library of Congress Information and Publication Office, 1949; rpt. in *TCC*.

The Aims of Poetic Drama. London: The Poets' Theatre Guild, 1949.

Poetry and Drama. Cambridge: Harvard University Press, 1951; London: Faber & Faber Ltd., 1951; rpt. in *OPP*.

The Value and Use of Cathedrals in England Today. Chichester: Friends of Chichester Cathedral, 1952.

An Address to Members of the London Library. London: The London Library, 1952; Providence, R.I.: The Providence Athenaeum, 1953.

Selected Prose. London: Penguin Books, 1953.

American Literature and the American Language. St. Louis: Department of English, Washington University, 1953; rpt. in *TCC.*

The Three Voices of Poetry. London: National Book League, 1953; New York: Cambridge University Press, 1954; rpt. in *OPP.*

Religious Drama: Mediaeval and Modern. New York: House of Books, Ltd., 1954.

The Literature of Politics. London: Conservative Political Center, 1955.

The Frontiers of Criticism. Minneapolis: University of Minnesota Press, 1956; rpt. in *OPP.*

(OPP) On Poetry and Poets. London: Faber & Faber Ltd., 1957; New York: Farrar Straus and Cudahy, 1957.

Geoffrey Faber, 1889–1961. London: Faber & Faber Ltd., 1961.

George Herbert. London: The British Council and the National Book League, 1962; Lincoln: University of Nebraska Press, 1964.

(K&E) Knowledge and Experience in the Philosophy of F. H. Bradley. London: Faber & Faber Ltd., 1963, 1964; New York: Farrar, Straus & Co., Inc., 1964.

(TCC) To Criticize the Critic and Other Writings. London: Faber & Faber Ltd., 1965; New York: Farrar, Straus & Giroux, 1965, 1967.

SECONDARY SOURCES

1. Bibliography

For a good brief overview (1969, updated to 1973) of Eliot bibliographies, editions, manuscripts and letters, biographies, and critiques, see:

LUDWIG, RICHARD M. "T. S. Eliot." In *Sixteen Modern American Authors: A Survey of Research and Criticism.* Edited by Jackson R. Bryer. New York: W. W. Norton & Company, Inc., 1973.

A. Of Eliot's writings:

BENTZ, HANS W. *Thomas Stearns Eliot in Übersetzungen.* Frankfurt am Main: Hans W. Bentz Verlag, 1963. Lists 222 translations into nineteen languages.

GALLUP, DONALD. *T. S. Eliot: A Bibliography*. London: Faber & Faber Ltd.; New York: Harcourt, Brace & World, 1969. This superb bibliography, definitive to 1965+, contains much valuable information in its annotations.

————. "The 'Lost' Manuscripts of T. S. Eliot." *Times Literary Supplement* (London), November 7, 1968, pp. 1238–40; reprinted ("slightly revised") in *Bulletin of the New York Public Library* 72 (December 1968):641–52. Indispensable notes on unpublished materials.

GORDON, LYNDALL. *Eliot's Early Years* (below). Good evaluation of biographies.

B: Of Critiques of Eliot's Writings:

FRANK, MECHTHILD; FRANK, ARMIN PAUL; and JOCHUM, K. P. S. "T. S. Eliot Criticism in English, 1916–1965: A Supplementary Bibliography." Special (double) Bibliography Issue of *T. S. Eliot Review* 4, Nos. 1 & 2 (1977).

MARTIN, MILDRED. *A Half-Century of Eliot Criticism: An Annotated Bibliography of Books and Articles in English, 1916–1965*. Lewisburg, Pa.: Bucknell University Press, 1972. This very useful source, monumental but inevitably incomplete, is supplemented by Frank et al.

Invaluable current bibliographies of critiques of Eliot's works are found in *American Literature* (quarterly) and in *PMLA* (annually).

2. Important Sources

ALIGHIERI, DANTE. *The Inferno; The Purgatorio;* and *The Paradiso.* 14th ed. London: J. M. Dent & Sons, Ltd., 1946. Eliot's recommended Dante source.

CORNFORD, FRANCIS M. *The Origin of Attic Comedy.* Edited with Foreword and Additional Notes by Theodore H. Gaster. Garden City, N.Y.: Doubleday & Company, Inc., 1961 (Anchor Books). Heavily influenced Eliot's plays.

Song of God: Bhagavad-Gita. Trans. Swami Prabhavananda and Christopher Isherwood, with intro. by Aldous Huxley. New York: New American Library, 1944, 1951, 1954.

SYMONS, ARTHUR. *The Symbolist Movement in Literature.* New York: E. P. Dutton and Co., Inc., 1919, 1958. A pivotal 1908 influence on Eliot.

WESTON, JESSIE L. *From Ritual to Romance.* Cambridge: Cambridge University Press, 1920; Garden City, N.Y.: Doubleday & Company, Inc., 1957. Influenced *The Waste Land,* as Eliot's notes point out.

3. Critiques

ANDREACH, ROBERT J. *Studies in Structure: The Stages of the Spiritual Life in Four Modern Authors.* New York: Fordham University Press, 1964. Very good on Hopkins, Joyce, Eliot, Crane.

BERGONZI, BERNARD, ed. *T. S. Eliot, Four Quartets: A Casebook.* London and Toronto: Macmillan, 1969. A collection of essays and excerpts.

BLAMIRES, HARRY. *Word Unheard: A Guide through Eliot's "Four Quartets."* London: Methuen & Co., Ltd., 1969. Useful analysis.

BOLGAN, ANNE. *What the Thunder Really Said.* London and Montreal: McGill-Queen's University Press, 1973. Heavy use of Eliot's Bradley thesis, which she edited for publication.

BOWRA, C. M. *The Heritage of Symbolism.* London: Macmillan & Co., Ltd.; New York: St. Martin's Press, 1943, 1954. Good background for readers unfamiliar with symbolist poetry.

BRADY, ANN P. *Lyricism in the Poetry of T. S. Eliot.* London and Port Washington, N.Y.: Kennikat Press, 1978 (National University Publications). Fresh and interesting.

BRAYBROOKE, NEVILLE, ed. *T. S. Eliot: A Symposium for His Seventieth Birthday.* New York: Farrar, Straus and Cudahy, 1958. Valuable reminiscences included.

BROWNE, E. MARTIN. *The Making of T. S. Eliot's Plays.* Cambridge: Cambridge University Press, 1969. Contains important quotations from successive drafts and much new, useful information; by the director of Eliot's plays.

BUCK, PHILO M. *Directions in Contemporary Literature.* New York: Oxford University Press, 1942.

CAHILL, AUDREY FAWCETT. *T. S. Eliot and the Human Predicament.* Pietermaritzburg, South Africa: University of Natal Press, 1967. Often incisive, to the point.

CHARITY, A. C. "T. S. Eliot: The Dantean Recognitions." In A. D. Moody, *"The Waste Land" in Different Voices* (see below). Excellent on Dante and Eliot.

DREW, ELIZABETH. *T. S. Eliot: The Design of His Poetry.* New York: Charles Scribner's Sons, 1949. Jungian interpretations.

ELLMANN, RICHARD. *Eminent Domain: Yeats Among Wilde, Joyce, Pound, Eliot, and Auden.* London and New York: Oxford University Press, 1967, 1970.

————. *Golden Codgers: Biographical Speculations.* New York and London: Oxford University Press, 1973. Excellent and concise on *The Waste Land* materials.

Explicator Encyclopedia, Volume I, Modern Poetry. Chicago: Quadrangle Books, 1966. Brief articles and notes on lines from individual poems.

FERGUSSON, FRANCIS. *The Idea of a Theatre.* Princeton: Princeton University Press, 1949. Excellent on *Murder in the Cathedral.*

FOSTER, GENEVIEVE W. "The Archetypal Imagery of T. S. Eliot," *PMLA* 60 (1945):567–85. Jungian interpretations, some perhaps overdrawn.

FRASER, G. S. *The Modern Writer and His World.* London: Derek Verschoyle, 1953; Harmondsworth and Baltimore: Penguin Books, 1964. A sensible brief overview.

GARDNER, HELEN LOUISE. *The Art of T. S. Eliot.* New York: E. P. Dutton & Co., 1959. Still one of the best studies of *Four Quartets,* relating them to all of Eliot's poetry. Sensitive treatment of metrics and imagery.

————. *The Composition of Four Quartets.* New York: Oxford University Press, 1978. Best available treatment of *Four Quartets.* Quotes successive drafts, gives much new information.

————. *T. S. Eliot and the English Poetic Tradition.* Nottingham: University of Nottingham, 1966.

GORDON, LYNDALL. *Eliot's Early Years.* Oxford and New York: Oxford University Press, 1977. Best biography to date, except for Valerie Eliot's Introduction to *WLF.* Useful note on biographical sources.

GREENE, E. J. H. *T. S. Eliot et la France.* Paris: Boivin, 1951. Good French bibliography.

GREGORY, HORACE, and ZATURENSKA, MARYA. "T. S. Eliot, the Twentieth-century Man of Feeling in American Poetry." *A History of American Poetry, 1900–1940.* New York: Harcourt, Brace and Co., 1942. Interesting early summary including predictions later fulfilled.

HALL, DONALD. *Remembering Poets;. Reminiscences and Opinions: Dylan Thomas, Robert Frost, T. S. Eliot, Ezra Pound.* New York and London: Harper & Row, Publishers, 1978. Includes *Paris Review* interview memories.

HARGROVE, NANCY DUVALL. *Landscape as Symbol in the Poetry of T. S. Eliot.* Jackson: University Press of Mississippi, 1978. Well done and handsomely illustrated.

Harvard Advocate 125, No. 3 (December 1938; Special Issue "For T. S. Eliot"). Unauthorized reprint of *Advocate* poems; interesting commentaries.

HOLROYD, STUART. "T. S. Eliot." In *Emergence from Chaos.* New York: Houghton Mifflin, 1957. Emphasis on spiritual biography.

HOWARTH, HERBERT. *Notes on Some Figures Behind T. S. Eliot.* Boston: Houghton Mifflin Company, 1964; London: Chatto & Windus, 1965. Background and cultural milieu handled sensitively and very intelligently.

JONES, DAVID E. *The Plays of T. S. Eliot.* Toronto: University of Toronto Press, 1960. Better on each play than most studies.

KENNER, HUGH. *The Invisible Poet: T. S. Eliot.* New York: McDowell, Obolensky, 1959. An engaging study.

————. *The Pound Era.* Berkeley and Los Angeles: University of California Press, 1971. Includes significant Eliot material.

————, ed. *T. S. Eliot: A Collection of Critical Essays.* Englewood Cliffs, N.J.: Prentice-Hall, 1962. Varied viewpoints, well selected.

KIRK, RUSSELL. *Eliot and His Age: T. S. Eliot's Moral Imagination in the Twentieth Century.* New York: Random House, 1971.

KLEINSTUCK, JOHANNES. *T. S. Eliot in Selbstzeugnissen und Bilddokumenten.* Reinbeck bei Hamburg: Rowohlt, 1966. Useful photographs and bibliography.

LEAVIS, FRANK R. "T. S. Eliot." In *New Bearings in English Poetry.*

London: Chatto and Windus, 1932. Early favorable criticism; still of interest.

LEVY, WILLIAM TURNER, and SCHERLE, VICTOR. *Affectionately, T. S. Eliot: The Story of a Friendship, 1947–1965.* Philadelphia and New York: J. B. Lippincott Company, 1968.

LITZ, A. WALTON, ed. *Eliot in His Time: Essays on the Occasion of the Fiftieth Anniversary of "The Waste Land."* Princeton: Princeton University Press, 1973.

LUCY, SEÁN. *T. S. Eliot and the Idea of Tradition.* London: Cohen & West, 1960. Oriented toward aesthetics, as one would expect of a good poet in his own right.

MARCH, RICHARD, and TAMBIMUTTU, THURAIRAJAH, comps. *T. S. Eliot: A Symposium for His Sixtieth Birthday.* London: Editions Poetry, 1948; Chicago: Regnery, 1949. Contains delightful reminiscences by friends and acquaintances.

MARGOLIS, JOHN D. *T. S. Eliot's Intellectual Development, 1922–1939.* Chicago and London: University of Chicago Press, 1972. Excellent. Copiously quotes uncollected Eliot writings.

MARTIN, GRAHAM, ed. *Eliot in Perspective: A Symposium.* New York: Humanities Press; London: Macmillan and Co., Ltd., 1970.

MARTIN, JAY, ed. *"The Waste Land": A Collection of Critical Essays.* Englewood Cliffs, N.J.: Prentice-Hall, Inc., 1968 (A Spectrum Book).

MATTHEWS, T. S. *Great Tom: Notes Towards the Definition of T. S. Eliot.* New York and London: Harper & Row, Publishers, 1973.

MATTHIESSEN, FRANCIS O. *The Achievement of T. S. Eliot: An Essay on the Nature of Poetry.* With a chapter on Eliot's later work by C. L. Barber. 3rd ed. New York: Oxford University Press, 1958. A penetrating study; few, if any, better.

MAXWELL, DESMOND E. S. *The Poetry of T. S. Eliot.* London: Routledge & Kegan Paul, 1952; New York: Barnes & Noble, 1961. Reprints *Doris's Dream Songs* in appendix.

MONTGOMERY, MARION. *T. S. Eliot: An Essay on the American Magus.* Athens: University of Georgia Press, 1970.

MOODY, A. D., ed. *"The Waste Land" in Different Voices: The revised versions of lectures given at the University of York in the fiftieth year of "The Waste Land."* London: Edward Arnold, 1974.

MOORMAN, CHARLES. *Arthurian Triptych: Mythic Material in Charles Williams, C. S. Lewis, and T. S. Eliot.* Berkeley: University of California Press, 1960. Points out significant parallels.

NELSON, ARMOUR H. "Critics and *The Waste Land.*" *English Studies* 36 (1955):1–15. Traces in remarkably clear but noninterpretive fashion the range of early reactions to *The Waste Land.*

PATTERSON, GERTRUDE. *T. S. Eliot: Poems in the Making.* Manchester: Manchester University Press; New York: Barnes & Noble Inc., 1971.

PEARCE, T. S. *T. S. Eliot.* London: Evans Bros., 1967; New York: Arco, 1969.

PFEIFFER, CHARLOTTE SMITH. *A Concordance to "The Complete Poems and Plays of T. S. Eliot."* Dissertation Abstracts International 39 (1979): 4921A–22A. (Georgia State University, 1978).

Pound, Ezra, The Letters of, 1907–1941. Edited by D. D. Paige. New York: Harcourt, Brace & World, Inc., 1950.

PRAZ, MARIO. "T. S. Eliot and Dante." In *The Flaming Heart.* Garden City, N.Y.: Doubleday & Co., 1956. Good early study of Dante and Eliot.

PRESTON, RAYMOND. *'Four Quartets' Rehearsed: A Commentary on T. S. Eliot's Cycle of Poems.* London: Sheed & Ward, 1946.

RAJAN, BALACHANDRA. *The Overwhelming Question: A Study of the Poetry of T. S. Eliot.* Toronto and Buffalo: University of Toronto Press, 1976.

———, ed. *T. S. Eliot: A Study of His Writings by Several Hands.* London: Dennis Dobson, 1947.

REID, B. L. *The Man From New York: John Quinn and His Friends.* New York: Oxford University Press, 1968. Fuse to the *Waste Land* manuscripts explosion.

ROSENTHAL, MACHA LOUIS. *Sailing Into the Unknown: Yeats, Pound, and Eliot.* New York: Oxford University Press, 1978. Incisive on Eliot's methods.

SAN JUAN E., JR., ed. *T. S. Eliot: A Casebook on Gerontion.* Columbus, Ohio: Charles E. Merrill Publishing Co., 1970.

SCHNEIDER, ELISABETH *T. S. Eliot: The Pattern in the Carpet.* Berkeley and London: University of California Press, 1975.

SENCOURT, ROBERT. *T. S. Eliot: A Memoir.* Edited by Donald Adamson. New York: Dodd, Mead & Company; London: Garnstone Press, 1971. Includes some useful material.

SMIDT, KRISTIAN. *Poetry and Belief in the Work of T. S. Eliot.* Rev. ed. New York: The Humanities Press, 1961. Excellent; especially good on early background and influences.

SMITH, CAROL H. *T. S. Eliot's Dramatic Theory and Practice.* Princeton: Princeton University Press, 1963. Contains perceptive, well-written studies on each of the plays.

SMITH, GROVER C., JR. *T. S. Eliot's Poetry and Plays: A Study in Sources and Meanings.* 2nd ed. Chicago and London: University of Chicago Press, 1974. Slightly revised, with new chapter on *The Waste Land.* Indispensable. Comprehensive survey of sources and influences, plus interpretations. Often incisive, but sometimes wide of the mark.

SOUTHAM, B. C. *A Guide to the "Selected Poems" of T. S. Eliot.* New York: Harcourt, Brace & World, Inc., 1968, 1970. Interesting snippets.

SPENDER, STEPHEN. *T. S. Eliot.* New York: The Viking Press, 1975. One of better overviews.

TATE, ALLEN, ed. *T. S. Eliot: The Man and His Work.* New York: Delacorte Press, 1966; London: Chatto & Windus, 1967. Contains a number of important essays.

THOMPSON, ERIC. *T. S. Eliot: The Metaphysical Perspective.* Carbondale: Southern Illinois University Press, 1963. Draws heavily on Eliot's Bradley dissertation. Abstract in orientation.

THORMAHLEN, MARIANNE. *The Waste Land: A Fragmentary Wholeness.* Lund: CWK Gleerup, 1978.

UNGER, LEONARD. *The Man in the Name.* Minneapolis: University of Minnesota Press, 1956. Contains "Laforgue, Conrad, and Eliot," a model of appropriate practice in evaluating Eliot's borrowings.

————. *T. S. Eliot.* Minneapolis: University of Minnesota Press, 1961. University of Minnesota Pamphlets on American Writers No. 8. This brief overview would be hard to improve.

————. *T. S. Eliot: Moments and Patterns.* Minneapolis: University of Minnesota Press, 1966. A superb collection of Mr. Unger's essays.

————. *T. S. Eliot: A Selected Critique.* New York and Toronto:

Rinehart & Company, Inc., 1948. Contains many valuable articles
—Mr. Unger's being perhaps the best; also contains an excellent
bibliography of writings on Eliot to 1948.

WARD, DAVID. *T. S. Eliot Between Two Worlds: A Reading of T. S.
Eliot's Poetry and Plays.* London and Boston: Routledge & Kegan
Paul, 1973. Mixed but often penetrating.

WILLIAMSON, GEORGE. *A Reader's Guide to T. S. Eliot: A Poem-by-
Poem Analysis.* New York: Noonday Press, 1953; London:
Thames and Hudson, 1955, 1967. Good basic introductions to the
poems.

WILLIAMSON, HUGH ROSS. *The Poetry of T. S. Eliot.* New York:
Putnam's, 1933. Contains the best early study of *The Waste Land*
that I have read.

WILSON, EDMUND. "T. S. Eliot." In *Axel's Castle.* New York: Scribner's, 1931. Interesting early evaluation.

WILSON, FRANK. *Six Essays on the Development of T. S. Eliot.* London: The Fortune Press, 1948.

WORTHINGTON, JANE. "The Epigraphs to the Poetry of T. S. Eliot."
American Literature 21 (1949):1–17. Still useful.

WRIGHT, G. T. *The Poet in the Poem.* Berkeley: University of California Press, 1960. On Eliot, Yeats, and Pound.

Index